Dress and Morality

Dress
and Morality

Aileen Ribeiro

Holmes & Meier Publishers, Inc.
New York

Frontispiece
Adam and Eve *c. 1514 H. Baldung Grien*

©Aileen Ribeiro 1986
First published in the United States of America in
1986 by Holmes & Meier Publishers Inc.
30 Irving Place, New York, N.Y. 10003
All rights reserved. No part of this publication may
be reproduced, in any form or by any means,
without permission from the publisher

**Library of Congress Cataloging-in-
Publication Data**

Ribeiro, Aileen, 1944–
  Dress and morality'.

  Bibliography: p.
  1. Clothing and dress—Moral and ethical aspects.
2. Costume–Moral and ethical aspects. I. Title.
BJ1697.R53   1986   177'.4   86-14839
ISBN 0–8419–1091–X

Printed in Great Britain

Contents

Acknowledgements	6
List of Illustrations with Acknowledgements	8
Introduction	12
1 Body and Soul	19
2 Vile Bodies	30
3 The World, the Flesh and the Devil	42
4 The Ship of Fools	59
5 Rags of Sin, Robes of Shame and Provocations of Lust	74
6 The Vanity of Human Wishes	95
7 The Great Divide	119
8 Dress and Disorder	146
Notes	172
Select Bibliography	186
Index	187

Acknowledgements

Any book is a kind of hostage to fortune, and I take full responsibility for the way that I have interpreted this wide-ranging subject, although I have had considerable help – both consciously and unconsciously – in the form of ideas and suggestions from friends and colleagues. They are too numerous to name, but I hope they enjoy reading this book as partial recompense for their encouragement.

I owe a considerable debt to the helpful staffs of the British Library, the Courtauld Institute Library, the Costume Research Centre in Bath, the Gallery of English Costume in Manchester, and the library of Liverpool Polytechnic (Liddell Hart Collection). I would like to thank the owners of the illustrations that I have used for permission to use their material, and in many cases for their promptness in providing photographs. For their usual helpfulness and efficiency with regard to photographs, I must thank the staffs of the Witt and Conway Libraries at the Courtauld Institute, as well as the Photographic Department, and the Photographic Survey of Private Collections.

My thanks are, as always, due to Timothy Auger at Batsford for his help and encouragement, and to Richard Reynolds for his work editing this book. I am also grateful to Alice Mackrell for compiling the Index.

For services rendered of one kind or another, I would like to single out Valerie Cumming, Robert Fisher, Celina Fox, Margaret Scott and Tony Skinner. Last, but certainly not least, I would like to thank my husband whose encouragement and patience during the research and the writing of this book made it far less of an arduous task.

'The game's going on rather better now', she said, by way of keeping up the conversation a little.

' 'Tis so', said the Duchess: 'and the moral of that is – Oh, 'tis love, 'tis love, that makes the world go round'.

'Somebody said', Alice whispered, 'that it's done by everybody minding their own business'.

'Ah well! It means much the same thing', said the Duchess, digging her sharp little chin into Alice's shoulder as she added, 'and the moral of that is – Take care of the sense, and the sounds will take care of themselves'.

'How fond she is of finding morals in things!' Alice thought to herself.

Alice in Wonderland

List of Illustrations with Acknowledgements

Frontispiece
Adam and Eve c. 1514.
H. Baldung Grien.
Yale University Art Gallery.

1. *The Muses.*
   Detail from the François Vase by Kleitias.
   Uffizi, Florence.

2. *Choro takes off her fillet at the couch of Pheidiades.*
   Detail from a vase by Smikros.
   Musées Royaux d'Art et d'Histoire, Brussels.

3. *The Emperor Augustus.*
   Capitoline Museum, Rome.

4. *A flute player* c. 410 B.C.
   Detail from a vase by the Karneia Painter.
   Museo Nazionale Archeologico, Taranto.

5. *Head of a woman* c. 110–115 A.D.
   Capitoline Museum, Rome.

6. *Susanna and the elders.*
   Catacomb of SS. Peter and Marcellinus, Rome.

7. *Detail from an ivory diptych of the Life of St Paul.*
   Bargello Museum, Florence.

8. *The figure of Philosophy*
   From *Boethius's De Consolatione Philosophiae.*
   Trinity College MS 0.3.7. fol. 1.
   Trinity College, Cambridge.
   Photo: copyright C. R. Dodwell

9. *The Temptation of Christ* c. 1050.
   Cotton Tiberius C VI fol. 10v.
   The Trustees of the British Library.

10. Title Page of the *Moralia in Job of St Gregory* IIII
    MS 168 fol. 4v.
    Bibl. Publ., Dijon.

11. *Moralia in Job of St Gregory.*
    MS 168 fol. 7r.
    Bibl. Publ., Dijon.
    Photo: copyright C. R. Dodwell

12. *The Temptation of Christ.*
    The Winchester Psalter, Cotton Nero C IV fol. 18r.
    The Trustees of the British Library.

13. St Anne (detail).
    The Bible of Bury St. Edmunds fol. 147v.
    Corpus Christi College MS 2.
    The Master and Fellows of Corpus Christi College, Cambridge.

14. *The Damned Souls from the Last Judgement* c. 1240.
    Tympanum, Bamberg Cathedral.

15. *The Foolish Virgins* c. 1240.
    North Porch, Magdeburg Cathedral.

16. *Lovers' scene on an ivory mirror case.*
    Louvre, Paris.

17. *Weeper from the tomb of Edward III* c. 1377–86.
    J. Orchard (attr.).
    Westminster Abbey, London.

18. *Figure of Vanity* c. 1375–80.
    Detail from the Apocalypse Tapestries.
    Hennequin de Bruges.
    Château d'Angers.

19. *The Great Whore of Babylon* c. 1400.
    Detail from an Apocalypse MS Néerl. 3, fol. 20.
    Bibliothèque Nationale, Paris.

20. *The Dance of the Courtiers* c. 1400.
    Roman de la Rose MS Douce 332 fol. 8v.
    Bodleian Library, Oxford.

21. *Procession of penitents* 1407.
    Hours of the Virgin MS Douce 144, fol. 110.
    Bodleian Library, Oxford.

LIST OF ILLUSTRATIONS

22. *John Foxton's Liber Cosmographiae* 1408.
    Trinity College MS R.15.21.
    Trinity College, Cambridge.
23. *Detail from a Virgil MS, c. 1400.*
    Holkham Hall MS 307.
    The Earl of Leicester.
24. *St Anthony led to the armourer's shop* 1426.
    R. Fournier.
    Valetta MS, Malta Public Library, Valetta.
25. *The Virgin and Child c. 1450–2.*
    J. Fouquet.
    Koninklijk Museum voor Schone Kunsten, Antwerp.
26. *St Jerome and the woman of Bethlehem c. 1456.*
    Jean Miélot's Miracles de Nostre Dame.
    J. le Tavernier.
    MS fr. 9198 fol. 91.
    Bibliothèque Nationale, Paris.
27. *Froissart's Chronicles c. 1470.*
    MS fr. 2646 fol. 164 r.
    Bibliothèque Nationale, Paris.
28. *Lecherye* 1476.
    The Mirroure of the Worlde.
    MS 283 fol. 67v.
    Bodleian Library, Oxford.
29. *Superbia* from a table-top depicting the Seven Deadly Sins.
    H. Bosch.
    Prado, Madrid.
30. *A landsknecht and a woman* 1516.
    U. Graf.
    Museum of Fine Arts, Boston.
31. *Two landsknechte, a woman and Death* 1524.
    U. Graf.
    Kunstmuseum, Basel.
32. *Two views of an unknown English lady c. 1535.*
    H. Holbein.
    The Trustees of the British Museum.
33. *Robert Dudley, Earl of Leicester c. 1575.*
    National Portrait Gallery, London.
34. *Portrait of an unknown man c. 1588.*
    N. Hilliard.
    Victoria and Albert Museum, London.
35. *Caricature c. 1600.*
    Rijksmuseum, Amsterdam.
36. *Caricature of a fashionable couple c. 1615.*
    J. van der Velde.
    Present whereabouts unknown.
37. *Frances Howard, Countess of Somerset c. 1615.*
    W. Larkin (attr.).
    National Portrait Gallery, London.
38. *Robert Devereux, 2nd Earl of Essex.*
    Style of Hilliard.
    Courtesy of the Grimsthorpe and Drummond Castle Trustees.
39. *Queen Anne of Denmark.*
    Anon. engraving.
    Victoria and Albert Museum, London.
40. *Queen Henrietta Maria with her dwarf c. 1633.*
    Sir A. van Dyck.
    National Gallery of Art, Washington. Samuel H. Kress Coll.
41. *Lady Elizabeth Thimbleby and Dorothy, Viscountess Andover.*
    Sir. A. van Dyck.
    National Gallery, London.
42. *'Here be your new Fashions Mistris'.*
    Anon. woodcut.
    British Library.
43. *A cavalier.*
    A. Bosse.
    Victoria and Albert Museum, London.
44. *'The Habit of an English Gentleman'.*
    Anon. engraving.
    British Library.
45. *'Figure à la Mode'.*
    R. de Hooghe.
    Victoria and Albert Museum, London.
46. *'Homme de Qualité'* 1694.
    J. D. de St Jean.
    Victoria and Albert Museum, London.
47. *Nell Gwynn c. 1675.*
    Engraving by G. Valck after Sir P. Lely.
    National Portrait Gallery, London.
48. *Standing woman c. 1700.*
    Anon. French engraving.
    Victoria and Albert Museum, London.
49. *The Garter* (detail) 1724.
    J. F. de Troy.
    Wrightsman Collection, New York.
50. *'Taste A-La-Mode 1745'*
    Engraving by F. Patton after L. P. Boitard.
    Museum of London.
51. *'Pantin a la Mode'* 1748.
    J. June (attr.).
    The Trustees of the British Museum.

LIST OF ILLUSTRATIONS

52. *The Rake's Progress: The Tavern Scene* 1735.
    W. Hogarth.
    Tate Gallery, London.

53. *Pamela rising from her bed* c. 1750.
    P. Mercier.
    Private Collection.

54. *'Miss Chudley in the Actual Dress as she appear'd in the Character of Iphigenia, at the Jubilee Ball or Masquerade at Ranelagh'* 1749.
    Anon. engraving.
    The Trustees of the British Museum.

55. *'La Folie pare la Décrépitude des ajustemens de la Jeunesse'* 1745.
    Engraving by L. Surugue after C. Coypel.
    The Trustees of the British Museum.

56. *'Toilette de la Duchesse des Plumes ou Le Triomphe de la Folie du Siècle'*.
    Anon. French engraving.
    Museum of London.

57. *'Grown Ladies taught to dance by Monsieur Allemande from Paris'* c. 1778.
    Anon. English drawing.
    Private Collection.

58. *'The Beauties of Bagnigge Wells'* 1778.
    Anon. engraving.
    Guildhall Library, London.

59. *'Welladay! is this my son Tom!'*
    Engraving after S. H. Grimm.
    The Trustees of the British Museum.

60. *'Life and Death Contrasted, or – An Essay on Woman'*
    'Death and Life Contrasted, or – An Essay on Man'.
    R. Dighton.
    Sale, Sotheby Parke Bernet, London 23 Feb. 1978, Lot 37.

61. *'A Jessamy'*.
    From *The Follies of Man*, 1790
    Gallery of English Costume, Manchester City Art Galleries.

62. *'Tally Ho'* c. 1788.
    R. Dighton.
    Sale, Sotheby Parke Bernet, London 23 Feb. 1978, Lot 52.

63. *'The Bum Shop'* 1785.
    Engraving after A. Rushworth.
    The Trustees of the British Museum.

64. *'The Fashionable Mamma, – or – The Convenience of Modern Dress'* 1796.
    J. Gillray.
    The Trustees of the British Museum.

65. *'Full Dress' or 'Parisian Ladies in their Winter Dress for 1800',* 1799.
    Anon. English engraving.
    Victoria and Albert Museum, London.

66. *'An Englishman in Paris'* 1807.
    T. Rowlandson.
    The Duke of Wellington.

67. *'The Mirror of Fashion'*.
    T. Rowlandson.
    Sale, Sotheby Parke-Bernet, London 20 July 1978, Lot 4.

68. *'The Dandies Coat of Arms'* 1819.
    G. Cruikshank.
    Sale, Parke-Bernet, New York 3–4 April 1946, Lot 120.

69. *'The Acme of Fashion'*.
    Engraving by McCleary.
    Victoria and Albert Museum, London.

70. *'Fashions for Fast Men'*.
    Punch 13 Nov. 1847.

71. *'The Fashion Behind but not Behind the Fashion'* 1829.
    'P. Pry' i.e. William Heath.
    Andrew Edmunds Gallery, London.

72. *'An Irresistible Arming for Conquest'* c. 1828–30.
    Anon. engraving.
    Victoria and Albert Museum, London.

73. *'Pic nic'* c. 1860.
    Anon. engraving.
    B. T. Batsford Ltd.

74. *'La dame au canapé'*
    C. Guys.
    Sale, Sotheby Parke-Bernet, London 5 July 1985, Lot 401.

75. *'A Quiet Smoke'*.
    Punch, 15 Nov. 1851.

76. *Wigan Pit Brow Girls* c. 1860.
    Photograph by J. Cooper.
    City of Manchester Cultural Services.

77. *Lady with a fan.*
    C. Guys.
    Courtauld Institute of Art.

78. *Nana* 1877.
    E. Manet.
    Kunsthalle, Hamburg.

LIST OF ILLUSTRATIONS

79. *'History repeats itself'*.
    Punch, 18 June 1870.
    'Être et Paraître' 1869.
    Caricature by Hadol.
    Liddell Hart Collection, Liverpool
    Polytechnic.

80. *'The Fast Smoking Girl of the Period'* 1867.
    Anon. engraving from an unidentified periodical.
    Liddell Hart Collection, Liverpool
    Polytechnic.

81. *Form versus Fashion* 1885.
    G. Steell.
    Scottish National Portrait Gallery,
    Edinburgh.

82. *Oscar Wilde* 1882.
    Photograph by N. Sarony.
    National Portrait Gallery, London.

83. *Tea gown*.
    Anon. engraving from a Harrods Catalogue 1895.
    Published in *Victorian Shopping*, ed. A.
    Adburgham, David & Charles, 1972.

84. *Study for Madame X (Madame Pierre Gautreau)* 1884.
    J. S. Sargent.
    Tate Gallery, London.

85. *'The Extinction of Species: or, The Fashionable Lady without Mercy and the Egrets'*.
    Punch, 6 Sept. 1899.

86. *'Rational Costume'*.
    Punch, 13 June 1896.

87. *'Primum vivere, deinde philosophari'*.
    Punch, 25 Jan. 1906.

88. *Evening gown* 1900.
    Fashion plate by Pilotelle in *The Queen*.
    Victoria and Albert Museum, London.

89. *'Resource'*.
    Punch, 2 April 1913.

90. *'Glorinda: A Portrait'*.
    Punch, 23 Aug. 1922.

91. *'The Insurgence of Youth'* 1924.
    Max Beerbohm.
    Victoria and Albert Museum, London.

92. *'Rouge à lèvres'*.
    K. van Dongen.
    Sale, Christie's, London 6 Dec. 1974, Lot 320.

93. *'Manners and Modes: Crossing the Road 1925'*.
    Punch, 1 April 1925.

94. *The Twin Sisters of Castor and Pollux*.
    Drawing by Thomas Lowinsky in Raymond Mortimer's *Modern Nymphs*, 1930.
    Victoria and Albert Museum, London.

95. *'Manners and Modes: The Latest Lines'*.
    Punch, 11 Feb. 1931.

96. *Dior's New Look* 1947.
    Drawing by Sam.
    Harper's Bazaar.

97. *Advertisements for Frederick's of Hollywood* 1968 & 1969.
    Liddell Hart Collection, Liverpool
    Polytechnic.

98. *Cartoon by 'Sprod'*.
    Punch, 27 Aug. 1958.

99. *Cartoon by Emmwood*.
    Daily Mail 2 Feb. 1962.
    Centre for the Study of Cartoons and Caricature, University of Kent at Canterbury.

100. *'Beatnik Flower Power versus the Honey Bee'*.
     Pocket Cartoon by Osbert Lancaster in *The Daily Express*, 9 Aug. 1967.
     Victoria and Albert Museum, London.

101. *'Yes I think I might renew my season ticket after all'*.
     Cartoon by Keith Waite for *The Mirror*.
     30 Jan. 1971
     Centre for the Study of Cartoons and Caricature, University of Kent at Canterbury.

102. *'New Year Revolutions'* (detail).
     Cartoon by Emmwood in *The Daily Mail*,
     31 December 1971.
     Centre for the Study of Cartoons and Caricature, University of Kent at Canterbury.

103. *'Holiday Snaps'* (detail).
     Cartoon by Emmwood in *The Daily Mail*,
     27 Aug. 1973.
     Centre for the Study of Cartoons and Caricature, University of Kent at Canterbury.

104. *'Min and Friend'* 1982.
     Jo Brocklehurst.
     Francis Kyle Gallery, London.

105. *Anti-fur campaign poster* 1985.
     Photograph by David Bailey.
     Greenpeace, London.

106. *Photograph of Katharine Hamnett* 1985.
     Lynne Franks P. R., London.

Introduction

The word 'morality' is derived from the Latin 'mores', the habits and customs of society, and as one recent authority states: 'There can be little doubt that the basis of customary morality is the instinct known as the herd or gregarious instinct, and the innate tendencies of sympathy, imitativeness and suggestibility which are clearly bound up with this instinct'.[1]

All societies have customs and taboos which include clothing, and most historians now discount the theory that clothing was originally devised for mere warmth; in the history of dress, reason and practicality often take second place to traditional, sometimes irrational customs, and even superstition. In many cases, what started out as a functional item of clothing is maintained by force of public opinion and the weight of ritual and habit, long after its original purpose has ceased; official and ceremonial clothing are obvious examples.

As well as being what Nietzsche called 'the herd instinct of the individual', morality serves to assure group solidarity, and with regard to dress, to act as a kind of social lubricant, to ease contacts between people in society. It is thus a conservative force, and the history of dress can be seen as a constant battle against the introduction of new styles, which may be thought of as 'immoral' until their novelty is muted by the passage of time.

This kind of moral indignation is based on what society deems to be acceptable in any given situation. It has been well defined by the art historian Quentin Bell, as 'sartorial conscience'; clothes are not 'immoral' in themselves, but they become so when worn in inappropriate situations. Social disapproval is not codified in law, and the conventions fluctuate as public opinion changes. As the psychologist J. C. Flügel points out, the ease with which we adapt ourselves to change in dress, indicates that

> such conventions do not depend on usefulness, beauty or convenience, but merely social approval and a desire for conformity; but failure to conform to these rules, however trivial ... can produce deep feelings of guilty discomfort similar to those aroused by the infringement of more primitive and permanent taboos.[2]

Each society classifies dress according to sex, age, and status; less easily definable categories are 'proper' and 'improper' with which we will be concerned. As Bell points out, when we talk about dress, we sometimes use words like 'correct' and 'faultless'; we might also add 'impeccable' which literally means without sin. So as well as looking at dress in the light of its relationship to social custom, we will also be trying to define shifting notions of what is 'immoral' by which is invariably meant clothing that is sexually disturbing.

In addition, we will need to glance at the attempts by some reformers to invent an ideal dress – either timeless in order to obviate tiresome and expensive changes in fashion, or practical and hygienic, or aesthetic in periods when the prevailing costume is deemed to be ugly and inartistic. Such attempts are usually doomed to failure, especially those which look at the dress of the past through rose-coloured spectacles, for if the history of dress tells us anything, it is that time does not stand still.

In the past, the propriety of clothing has been pronounced on by authority, in the form of the Church or State. For many hundreds of years, religion was the arbiter of morals, and morality was synonymous with Christianity. The distinguished judge, Lord Devlin, delivering the *Maccabaean Lecture in Jurisprudence* at the British Academy in 1958, found morals to be both a subject for private judgement and for the community; until a century ago, he said, it was virtually impossible to distinguish between religion and morals, a state of affairs which he regretted was no longer the case.[3]

How far society in the west is bound by a religious ethic is not the subject of this book. Lenin, for example, felt that morality was to be subservient to the class struggle, but he knew and would have agreed with Lord Devlin, that 'an established morality is as necessary as good government to the welfare of society'; Soviet society today is presumably no more 'immoral' than western societies which still pay lip service to a code of Christian religious ethics.

From the earliest times, the Christian church handed down a code of morals, which included strictures on clothing. Individualism in this respect was frowned on, and it was not until the Renaissance that the fierce hold of the church on all aspects of morality, including dress, began to slip. Paradoxically, this was also the period when advances in the cut and construction of clothing revealed and enhanced the shape of the body for the first time since the ancient world. Early Christian teachings stress the link between the outward appearance and the state of the soul, and a dislike of individualism in dress which draws attention to the self; this can also be seen in orthodox Judaism, and can lead in some communities to the evolution of what is virtually a uniform bereft of nearly all traces of individuality.[4]

Linked with this notion of a kind of uniform purity is a desire to avoid the giddy wheel of fashion, and even to dispense with it altogether. The Amish inhabitants of Pennsylvania, direct descendants of a seventeenth-century German/Dutch Anabaptist sect (who believe in the complete separation of Church and State), claim to find the whole of late-twentieth-century civilization corrupting; they live in seclusion, farming in traditional ways (the more extreme refuse to use tractors or any machinery), and wearing versions of nineteenth-century costume – homespun dark suits for the men, and cotton print dresses for the women, and with hooks and eyes instead of buttons.

In some communities, fervent religious zeal is linked to a fierce rejection of what is seen as western decadence in manners and clothing.[5] Iran, since 1978, has been ruled by a religious elite determined to create a fully Islamic state completely purged of western influences. Tentative steps under the last Shah to allow women certain rights have now been abandoned, and although there is no specific injunction in the Koran for women to keep in seclusion or to veil their faces, women are forced to hide their bodies in the tent-like *chador*, so that the sight of their charms may not tempt the more excitable opposite sex.[6] As in medieval Europe, in many Islamic countries women are dependent financially and socially on men; a woman's chastity was the important property first of her father, and then of her husband. In order to catch a husband, there must be the correct amount of modesty, and the nicely judged display of physical charms; this can sometimes be a difficult balancing act in societies which are caught between traditional religious values and new western ideas.

It is often in such societies that the religious values, which the west treats lightly, are more enthusiastically enforced with regard to dress. For example, in the west we retain the idea of a white wedding out of traditional sentimentality, for one suspects that a minority of brides are virgins on their wedding day. In Africa, however, where the outward signs of Christianity are as appreciated as its spiritual values, a great deal of importance is placed on a bride's virginity. Pregnant brides in the Roman Catholic diocese of Lagos, reported *The*

Times (13 August 1984), were forbidden to wear white on their wedding day: 'Archbishop Olubunmi Okogie said white was a symbol of purity, and it would be ridiculous for a pastor to proclaim a pregnant woman pure, when her position was obvious to the congregation'. What is acceptable in, say, Los Angeles, in terms of revealing or tight-fitting clothing, may be less acceptable in, for example, a provincial English country town, and positively frowned on in societies where strict traditional moral values are allied to strong religious beliefs. Thus, while young women in New York or London experiment with every new craze in dress without necessarily assigning moral or immoral values to a new garment, greater censorship is imposed in many developing countries; *The Times* (26 January 1984), for example, noted that the women of Swaziland were being urged to show greater modesty in dress, and not to wear slacks, short skirts and see-through clothes. The curious fact is that by the time such authorities decide to crack down on 'immoral' fashions, they are well out of date in the western world which initiated them. We thus have a constantly shifting picture throughout the world of what is currently thought 'immoral' in sartorial terms; it changes due to the extent of western penetration among the young in particular, and the strength of the non-European civilization against which it often collides. It is fair to say, however, that it is generally European fashions which are singled out for criticism, because of their perceived emphasis on the primary sexual areas of the body; while, as Quentin Bell points out, the Chinese find the display of feet improper and a Muslim woman veils her face, the western European draws attention to sexual anatomy – 'Europeans', he claims, 'are far more immodest than the people of any other culture'.[7] In societies which are non-European or which have only a very recent history of cultural links with the west, fashion does not play the part it does in Europe. Europeans, and particularly northern Europeans, have a propensity for restlessness and change which can lead them to push fashion to outrageous and eccentric extremes – fruitful topics for outraged moralists; and for this reason I have chosen to concentrate on Europe, and on England in particular.

The Christian religion (and that of Islam too) derives from a humble founder, and there is a feeling that humility in dress is pleasing in the eyes of God. Dress should reveal not just a humble state of mind, but show by its simplicity that the wearer spends little time on the adornment of the body, and is thus free to devote more – time and money – to the poor. This mixture of religious and personal morality is most evidenced in the habits of religious orders; their ample, loose robes of humble, often coarse fabrics, are both unprovocative and a protection against the temptations of the world. Extreme asceticism can sometimes lead to the wearing of a hair shirt, to mortify the flesh, and to keep the wearer in mind of the body's inevitable decay and corruption. Today's equivalent of such a personal commitment, by way of clothing, to an ideal, is not so much linked with religion (though of course it can still be seen in the dress of religious orders), as with a wider conception of the unity of man with Nature. Alexander Pope's theory in his *Essay on Man* of the interdependence of Man and Nature – 'The Furr that warms a Monarch, warm'd a Bear' – might be the inspiration for those women who refuse to wear fur coats, or even leather shoes, which necessitate the killing of animals. The campaign against fur coats is of fairly recent origin, but it follows in the footsteps of the Edwardian attacks on the 'immorality' of using birds' plumage to decorate the vast hats which were in vogue; such 'murderous millinery' was preached against in pulpits and derided in newspapers, but it was due more to a change in fashion than to a change of heart that women stopped wearing such styles in the second decade of this century.

In western Europe we live in an age only too aware of the finite resources of the world; too much opulence in dress can be thought of as positively immoral, and throughout history has been denounced with varying degrees of severity. Extravagance has often been politically tactless also; one has only to think of the French

Revolution when clothing made of rich silks, and which needed careful manipulation, marked one out as a member of the hated aristocracy.

Outside Europe, the splendour and visible corruption of the lives of dictatorial rulers can also lead to downfall. The incredible expense – the silks, ermine, diamonds and gold – of the 1977 coronation, based on Napoleonic imagery, of the self-styled 'Emperor' Bokassa of the Central African Republic, one of the poorest countries in the world, led to his deposition only two years later.[8]

Fine clothes, being associated with an indolent and aristocratic life, are often proscribed by revolutionary governments, at least to begin with. When, in Orwell's *Animal Farm*, Mollie, the pretty, foolish white mare wonders if after the rebellion she will be allowed to eat sugar and wear ribbons in her mane, she is told sternly that ribbons are 'the badge of slavery'; one of the commandments of the new political creed of 'Animalism' is that 'No animal shall wear clothes'. But Mollie, a classical example of feminine weakness and backsliding, is lured to the opposing side by the promise of ribbons and an easy life.

Orwell's political parable is a minor example of the way in which governments try to control the symbols of political belief as well as the substance of power. This theme is even more pronounced if we look at the past actions of governments determined to curb excessive expenditure on dress. The history of sumptuary legislation is imbued with the belief expressed by Sir Thomas More in his *Utopia* (1516) that 'all classes of society are recklessly extravagant about clothes'; such extravagance is not only evil in itself, but it leads to the sins of pride and envy.

Sumptuary legislation, which in England existed from the fourteenth to the seventeenth centuries had as its avowed aim the protection of native textile industries, but the real purpose was to enforce class distinctions which it was felt were being eroded by dress; in addition, certain styles of dress, notably those which were too tight or revealing, were thought of as wicked and harmful to the morals of the people. Although sumptuary legislation fizzled out in the seventeenth century (in any case it had never been very effective), the ideas which informed it continued to be re-stated in later centuries. Throughout the eighteenth and nineteenth centuries moralists worried both about class struggle, as expressed in the desire of the lower classes to ape the manners and costume of their betters, and about the amount of money spent on sartorial display and emulation. The American economist Thorstein Veblen was a forceful exponent at the end of the nineteenth century of the theory that women's dress in particular was motivated by 'conspicuous expensiveness'; expensive and wasteful clothing was necessary to create the image of the fashionable idle life, and connived at by their husbands as a tribute to their wealth. Like Wilde, Veblen found women's fashion, 'a form of ugliness so intolerable that we have to alter it every six months'. He never seems to have contemplated the fact that women actually liked their clothes, however restrictive, and that they – and presumably men – found them sexually attractive.[9]

The failure of sumptuary legislation indicates the extent to which the state failed to make sartorial morality its concern; if, as we have seen, the common morality of society is a complex and shifting mixture of custom, conviction, experience and prejudice, and if we have to resort to the somewhat baffled description of Lord Devlin, that 'immorality, for the purpose of the law is what every right-minded person is presumed to consider immoral',[10] we might as well give up.

To some degree, however, the state *can* enforce a kind of sartorial morality, and that is by imposing a uniform as a sign of humiliation on its prisoners. This derives from the age-old practice of making criminals wear clothing which distinguishes them from the law-abiding; this can take the form of sack-cloth or generally dishevelled clothing and bedraggled hair, or of wearing just a shirt or chemise as a sign of contrition. A similar feeling informs the clothing of penitents who wished to punish themselves by adopting deliberately humiliating dress.

Prison uniform is obscure in its origins. By the end of the eighteenth century, a number of striped uniforms may indicate that the brightly coloured and often striped dress, motley, of the medieval fool might have been one source of inspiration. Uniforms became necessary when England in the late eighteenth century began to send the first convicts to the penal settlements in Australia; it may well be that the arrow sign (still part of today's shorthand for prisoners, although phased out earlier this century) was introduced at that time while the prisoners were waiting in the hulks (prison ships) for transportation. Prison uniform was both moral and practical. It reminded prisoners of their fall from grace, and it served to identify them if caught; even today, male prisoners who are known security risks have yellow patches sewn on their blue cotton uniforms. Uniform is not compulsory for women; it is not clear how far this is due to a feeling that women should not be regimented in this way. From the earliest days of the penal settlements in Australia, it proved far more difficult to get women to wear uniforms; instead of the stolen finery which many prisoners preferred, magistrates and prison reformers pleaded the cause of 'plain but becoming' uniforms:

> the habit of being obliged to wear the semblance of decency, as is well known to moralists, sometimes produces the virtue of which it was at first only the symbol.[11]

In any question of what makes clothes 'moral' or 'immoral', it is always easier to define the latter, for moralists on the whole have always been quicker to condemn certain styles, than to take a more constructive and positive approach. This book is really a history of the criticisms directed at clothing on the grounds of its 'immorality', a term which is synonymous with clothing which reveals or emphasizes sexual areas of the body. The game of fashion is to some degree an ever-changing confrontation between modesty and sexual display, between desire and disgust, between dress and undress.

One twentieth-century writer finds that men and women in their clothing:

> suggest that what is hidden may be equally or more attractive to the other sex than what is revealed, and so make public what they have nominally agreed to keep private.[12]

Apart from this sexually stimulating disguise, there have been times in the history of dress when the body is openly revealed, and thus clothes perform the function of keeping eroticism alive by constant change. Some authorities have evolved a theory of the 'shifting erogenous zone' (a term first used by Havelock Ellis at the turn of the century, and then taken up by the psychologist Flügel and the dress historian Laver), a system whereby certain parts of the body – sometimes parts with no direct sexual appeal, like the waist or the back – become imbued temporarily with immense sexual attraction. Although acceptable to some extent, this theory has some flaws; certain primary sexual areas such as the breasts and the genitals remain attractive even though – like breasts in the 1920s – they are well hidden. And what Flügel and Laver think of as areas of secondary sexual significance have more to do with the natural development of fashion than any deliberate attempt to reinforce the sexuality of the body by emphasizing a hitherto unrevealed area of anatomy.

As the story of the history of dress unfolds, most of the criticism, certainly in the later periods, will be directed against women. This is to some extent due, as I have implied earlier, to their financial weakness which made them more dependent on their powers of sex attraction, and also to the fact that from the beginning of the nineteenth century, men had lost much of their peacock finery. Flügel found that men's clothes were more moral than women's, for they symbolized duty and self-control:

> in the thickness of material and solidity of structure of their tailored garments, in the heavy and sober blackness of their shoes, in the virgin whiteness and starched stiffness of their collars and of their shirt-fronts, men exhibit to the outer world their would-be strength, steadfastness, and immunity from frivolous distraction...[13]

As a contrast, women's clothes in their expense and variety were indicative of the narcissism of women, a theory clearly at odds with the fact that men in the past were just as decorative in their dress as women.

Flügel was a psychologist and not a dress historian; although his theories are often illuminating and entertaining, they are also overly concerned with Freudian beliefs in the sexual significance of dress. Like Laver after him, Flügel believed certain clothes to be sexual organs – the tie is a phallic symbol, and fur is pubic hair, for example. Also imbued with inter-war ideas of psychoanalysis was C. W. Cunnington, whose popular books on the history of dress include frequent statements on the deep sexual meanings to be found in costume. All these writers believe that men and women give out sexual signals in their clothing, very often unconsciously. But, equally true is the fact that people *deliberately* set out to promote a certain image, which can sometimes be sexual and which they are aware of at the time. And for this reason, the historian should wherever possible look at what contemporaries say about the dress of their time, and not only at what later authorities say, for their preoccupations can affect the evidence before them and distort it; nineteenth-century dress reformers, for example, over-idealized classical Greek dress as the antithesis of what they considered to be their own restrictive costume. And male dress historians, impressed by their own clothes as tools of moral self-gratification, can over-emphasize the follies and frivolities that they see in the history of female costume. Our attitudes to dress are complex and often ambivalent. Our Judaeo-Christian heritage leads us to place little value on the adornment of the body, and makes us ashamed of nakedness; at the same time we have a prurient delight in the sexual implications of the semi-clothed body as it appears, for example, in the pages of tabloid newspapers. In the same way as in the past (perhaps there is still a lingering echo today), female beauty was a satanic temptation to men – women were admired for it and yet denounced for it.

We like to feel that today we are less inclined than in the past to make a direct equation between our dress and our morals. We would perhaps agree to despise, with Carlyle, the fashion-plated dandy 'whose trade, office and existence consists in the wearing of clothes', although we might spend longer than we would admit to on our appearance. Yet the man or woman in the street might link the mini skirts and see-through tops of the 1960s with sexual freedom; and there is firmly ensconced in the public imagination a Hollywood stereotype of the femme fatale, the sexually predatory women with dyed blonde hair, plunging *décolletage* and skin-tight dress. Ask our hypothetical man-in-the-street about the punk clothing of the early 1980s, and he might have strong feelings about the morality of those (of both sexes) who wore that tattered and outrageously dishevelled costume, their hair spiked and crested in lurid colours; such punks are the direct descendants of the early sixteenth-century German *landsknechte* with their slashed outfits and their menacing military air.

Many people today might voice their resentment of the recent trend towards sexual ambiguity in dress, most notably for some men, from the 1960s onwards – admittedly mainly in the fields of entertainment or sexual deviancy – to wear women's clothing. Women, on the other hand, have been pillaging the male wardrobe for many hundreds of years (and have been criticized for it), in their desire for the novelty which is the essence of fashion. It is this desire for change which prompts such thefts – the bloomers, the trousers, the suits and so on, and not, as Cunnington argues, a wish 'to escape from the bondage of sex'.[14]

Today, such borrowings are likely to be interpreted perhaps as the elements of masculinity in the female psyche. In the same way, men too, especially in earlier periods, had much of the 'feminine' in their clothing. Virginia Woolf's eponymous hero/heroine *Orlando* delights in 'the probity of breeches' and 'the seductiveness of petticoats', to be worn with equal ease by either sex. Orlando's (and Woolf's) argument that the kind of clothes we wear affect the way we behave may make us come to terms with the fact that in the second half of the twentieth century we have evolved, for better or for worse, a kind of sexual freedom which is reflected in present day clothing with its often unashamed concentration on the sexual characteristics of the body.

So many questions are raised by the topic of 'Dress and Morality', that it would take a much lengthier book than this to deal with them. Had I but world enough and time, this hypothetical, vast book would cover much more than the England which such exigencies force upon me.

I have chosen to discuss the subject within a chronological framework, for I find thematic books which dart around from century to century rather confusing – it is often, also, an excuse for dress historians who may not be familiar with some of the earlier periods to leave out great chunks of time on the spurious grounds that they are not interesting. With a chronology, however, there are problems, mainly of repetition, for it is inevitable that the same bits of the body will come under fire on frequent occasions. Every moralist, however, attacks 'immorality' in his or her own inimitable way; it is impossible not to agree with Logan Pearsall Smith that 'an improper mind is a perpetual feast'. I have wherever possible used the simplest terms to describe clothing; problems of etymology in any case, especially in the earlier periods, only serve to be confusing. The dress historian should be wary of using terms which may not be clearly defined in terms of present-day knowledge, and which would have been unknown to those he writes about.

He should also be aware of the problems with regard to some of the earlier visual sources, where they might be stylized to conform with the prevailing artistic aesthetic. In any case, there is very little direct visual comment of a 'moral' kind on dress before the fourteenth century. 'Pagan' art celebrates the body and does not condemn it, and Christian art tends to serve God, and not to illustrate sin, unless it be of the wickedness of Eve. Thus, it is often difficult to find examples of the 'immorality' in dress which so exercises the minds of contemporary chroniclers. With the Renaissance, for a host of economic, social and cultural reasons, the proper study of mankind begins to be man, warts and all; both men and women can be seen to glory in the temptations of the world, which include body-enhancing clothing.

This book does not claim to be a history of dress; it is not about why fashion changed – whether due to social forces, technical advances, or the shifting dynamism within fashion itself – but about people's attitudes to certain kinds of dress which they felt, within the prevailing social and cultural framework, to be taboo.

The story is often confused (people had contradictory ideas about what was 'moral' or 'immoral'), and sometimes capricious; it is also amusing and humbling (for nothing is new in the history of denunciation), and it is just one approach to the many-faceted subject of the history of dress.

1
Body and Soul

'Shame isn't spontaneous ... it's artificial, it's acquired ... The Christians invented it, just as the tailors in Savile Row invented the shame of wearing brown boots with a black coat. There was precious little of it before Christian times ...' Spandrell had lifted a long and bony hand, 'I know, I know. Noble and nude and antique. But I believe they're entirely a modern invention, those Swedish-drill pagans of ours. We trot them out whenever we want to bait the Christians. But did they ever exist? I have my doubts.

Aldous Huxley, *Point Counter Point,* 1928

Because so many later attitudes derive from interpretations of classical and Christian attitudes to dress and morality, it is important to see how far they diverge, and what, if anything, they have in common.

The classical world regarded excess in dress – either extravagant dress, or too-revealing dress – not so much as a sin in itself, but as a violation of reason, and against Nature. There was a firm belief, expounded by the philosophers, that man's common sense should be the best guide of his actions.

In contrast, the Christian world tended to regard any minor delight in dress, however trivial, as evidence of irredeemable sin, and as direct disobedience to God's law, which He had handed down to His interpreters on earth.

Attitudes to the naked body are typical of the gulf between the two schools of thought. The Greeks, said the art historian Kenneth Clark, created nudity, and the Christians created nakedness. The Greeks looked at the naked body with pride, although it must be admitted that only the young, idealized male was admired in this way. The Christians regarded the naked body as shameful, indicative of suffering, humiliation and, because of Eve, of betrayal.

Classical Greece is a place which we feel we know well even if we have never been there; we respect it as the fount of our ideas on democracy and thought, we admire the 'purity' of its art which is so much directed towards the representation of perfection. We admire, especially today, its belief that Man was the measure of all things – even Greek gods were imagined in human form – its intelligence, balance and maturity. We like to feel that the Greek idea of 'harmonia' is reflected in the clothes that they wore; taken to extremes, some art historians and some dress reformers wished to believe that the Greeks did not actually wear something as humdrum as clothes, but only beautiful drapery.

The story is much more complicated, and although it is true to say that probably much of Greek dress is dominated by simple rectangular shapes, there are many conflicting theories as to how Greek clothes were made, whether they were merely pinned, or sewn, and a considerable amount of semantic confusion over the names of garments.

Until the great years of classical Greek civilization, that is before the sixth century B.C., we know very little about archaic Greek dress, except that in early vases and wall frescoes the dress depicted is quite fitted and colourfully patterned, reflecting the costume of pre-Hellenic Cretan civilization. Before the sixth century, we find men wearing either a long or short tunic called a *chiton,* and women in a long tunic called a *peplos*; this latter garment is referred to in Homer, and we assume that this early clothing was made of wool.

1 The Muses
Detail from the François Vase, by Kleitias c. 570. These fashionable ladies, wearing the Doric woollen peplos, *show how it might be fastened with a long pin at the shoulder. This is probably the type of dress deplored by Herodotus in his reference to the battle of Aegina, and certainly such pins could inflict severe injury.*

At some point during the sixth century Greek women changed from this, presumably rectangular, fairly narrow woollen dress, into something much more luxurious, the wider (though still possibly rectangular) linen *chiton,* wide enough to be draped in folds, or pleated, and to give the effect of sleeves. This changeover is recorded by the historian Herodotus, talking about the battle of Aegina (568), between the inhabitants of that island, and Athens, after which only one of the Athenians escaped alive:

> when he reached Athens with a report of the disaster, the wives of the other men who had gone with him to Aegina, in grief and anger that he alone should have escaped, crowded round him and thrust the brooches, which they used for fastening their dresses, into his flesh, each one, as she struck, asking him where her husband was. So the poor fellow was killed, and the Athenians were more horrified at his fate than at the defeat of their troops in Aegina. The only way they could punish their women for the dreadful thing they had done was to make them adopt Ionian dress; previously Athenian women had worn Dorian dress ... now they were made to change to linen tunics, to prevent them from wearing brooches.[1]

How far Herodotus is here rationalizing a recent fashion change is hard to say; perhaps he was dramatizing a horrifying event with more concern for theatricality than veracity. One must emphasize that as Greece was a collection of city states, there were bound to be huge differences in the way that the inhabitants lived and dressed. In Sparta, for example, many were startled by the revealing dress of the Spartan women, known as the 'hip-showing ones' (their austere Doric *peplos* was open at the side), and even more so at their love of stripping off for wrestling. Herodotus, along with other Greeks, felt that when a woman put off her tunic in this way, she put off modesty.[2] Although by the seventh century B.C., nude athletics were common in Athens, women did not take part, and thus the Spartan women were regarded as unique; Plato, however, proposed in his *Republic* that Greek women should exercise in the nude.[3]

2 Choro takes off her fillet at the couch of Pheidiades.
Detail of a vase painting by Smikros c. 515–510 B.C. In an intimate setting, the Greeks revelled in the shape of the body enhanced by flowing drapery. Pheidiades is naked except for his himation wrapped round the waist. Choro wears, under her cloak, a chiton *made of byssus which both clings to, and reveals, the shape of the body.*

Herodotus himself was a native of Caria in Asia Minor, close to Ionia, where the Greek cities were famed for their civilization and luxury, and from where, he says, came this more sumptuous dress for women. Generally, we find from the sixth century a movement away from the heroic Homerian styles, to the more easily sculptured and draped linen stuffs, possibly due to a change in trading patterns, and to closer links with the east. From *c.* 560 Greece began regular trading with Egypt which produced the best linen, a very fine, almost transparent and crinkled version known as *byssus* being highly prized.[4]

Wars with Persia, the ordeal which matured Greek civilization, also helped to introduce eastern clothing, tighter-fitting and more complex in cut. Not for the first time in the history of dress, the east was attacked by contemporaries for inspiring decadent, luxurious clothing, which included tailored and fitted garments like trousers and sleeves, and even decorated silk garments[5] all of which was quite unlike the original Greek purity in dress. Even those who wore Ionian dress could be called unpatriotic, as the Ionian Greeks were allied to Persia, and Thucydides in his *History of the Peloponnesian War* tells us that by the middle of the fifth century, some women were returning to 'simple woollen garments in the Dorian style.' Many conservative Greeks regarded wrapping up the limbs in Ionian dress 'as a vile innovation, tending to luxury and lasciviousness'.[6]

The situation is complicated by the fact that surviving works of art do not always show a smooth transition from one style of dress to another; in many cases, it seems, the Doric peplos and the Ionian *chiton* could be worn together, women taking, as they have always done, their styles of dress according to their fancy, and not for political reasons. For this reason, one suspects that although the Greek state passed laws against excessive luxury in dress – the first sumptuary law was passed in 594, limiting women except on festive days to three garments; a *chiton*, a *peplos* and a cloak called a *himation* – and although Plato wished to codify citizens lives including their clothing, such regulation was about as effective as later acts in this vein. Solon's laws, which were meant to curb the luxurious propensities of the Athenian aristocracy, included an important distinction between the dress of good women and whores, insisting that the latter wear thin gauze-like material in saffron or flame-colour.[7]

Although Rome grew up contemporaneously with Greek civilization, its attitudes to life were quite different. Rome was always uneasily aware that the Greeks knew far more about art than they did – Roman strengths lay in a sense of ordered history, administration and law – although they made a habit of despising Greek luxury. The Romans, in fact, are close to the early Christian moralists in their denunciations of finery, looking back in many cases from the corruptions of the Empire, to an imagined time of austere and virtuous simplicity during the Republic.

The Roman satirist, a useful source of information to the dress historian 'represents the old Roman spirit, and draws his ideal from an age of simple habits before Rome was corrupted by the arts of Greece and the luxury of the conquered East. He is apt to forget that luxury is not a synonym for vice'.[8]

The satirical poem was invented by the Romans, and it reached a fine art with Juvenal, the supreme exponent of savage indignation against the decadent courtier, the flatterer and the dissembler. Writing his satires in the early second century A.D., Juvenal (about whom we know very little) harks back to what he considers to be the moral and thrifty past of the early Republic. He attacks philosophers for their homosexuality, and ultra-fashionable lawyers whose dress verges on the effeminate:

> But where will men draw the limit
> When they see a high-born advocate dress in transparent chiffon
> To prosecute loose-living women.[9]

Such men he later describes as 'walking transparencies', the implication being that they are wearing see-through silk garments. Such silks were coming into the west from China in the first century A.D., at which time we find Pliny the Elder deploring the fact that silk, hitherto worn only by women, had in these degenerate days, become popular with men.[10] During the early years of the Empire (Augustus was the first Emperor 27 B.C.–A.D. 14), silks were forbidden to men, but it was difficult to enforce this, especially as the emperors themselves liked such luxury. Suetonius quotes with disapproval the sumptuous costume worn by the unspeakable Emperor Caligula (ruled A.D. 37–41), who:

> paid no attention to traditional or current fashions in his dress, ignoring male conventions and even the human decencies. Often he made public appearances in a cloak covered with embroidery and encrusted with precious stones, a long-sleeved tunic and bracelets; or in silk (which men were forbidden by law to wear), or even in a woman's robe; and came shod sometimes with slippers, sometimes with buskins, sometimes with military boots, sometimes with women's shoes.[11]

Such strong disapproval lay in the fact that the ideal Roman was a man of military bearing, clothed in a simple knee-length tunic (based on the *chiton*), or a long tunic for an older man or official. The Roman Empire legally defined the social classes, and this was reflected in dress, in the stripes on the tunic according to rank, the *augustus clavus* worn by the knights (*equites*) and the *latus clavus*, or wide stripe worn by senators. The dreadful Trimalchio in Petronius's *Satyricon,* a satire on Nero and his circle with its vulgarity and affectations, wears the *latus clavus* on his tunic although he has no right to it.[12]

Although as early as the fourth century B.C., Alexander the Great had introduced long sleeves from Persian dress, they were for many hundreds of years regarded as effeminate. Suetonius delicately hints at Julius Caesar's homosexuality, or at least his over-dandified appearance, as he wore wrist-length sleeves to his tunic. Not until the end of the second century A.D., with the Emperor Commodus (180–193) was the sleeved tunic acceptable.

In the same way, long hair was looked on as oriental and effeminate; most emperors, except for Nero, preferred short and simple styles, and to be clean-shaven was the rule except for philosophers who wore beards. Men in mourning appeared unshaven, as did criminals who also appeared dirty and badly-dressed (*sordidatus*).

One of the tenets of Roman society was the fact that status was reflected in clothing, the most famous garment being the toga, which seemed in its heavy, sculptured woollen folds to incorporate the essence of Roman *gravitas*; symbolic of duty, fidelity, of the power and stability of the Roman Empire. It marked the profound difference between the law-protected Roman citizen who was entitled to wear it, and the non-citizen who was merely subject to the law.

To wear it properly constituted the mark of the Roman gentleman, no easy task, as it was, by the first century A.D. a voluminous garment. Quintilian, head of the most important school of oratory in Rome under Galba (reigned 69) and Vespasian (69–79) devoted a chapter in his *Institutio Oratoria* on the correct wearing of the toga, and the shoes (sandals were improper with the dignity of the toga) which were worn with it, though he does say that it is as reprehensible to be too much a fop in this respect, as to be slovenly.[13]

Symbol of rank though it was, its heavy folds made it cumbersome and difficult to wear; Tertullian (c. 165–c. 220) in his *De Pallio* (in which he advocates the wearing of the pallium or long rectangular cloak) said that the toga had to be laid out in folds with a pincer the night before it was due to be put on, and needed the assistance of a slave to get into. Many writers, like Pliny the Younger (born 61 or 62), describe the relief they felt when they could abandon the toga on leaving Rome, where it had to be worn. Pliny is almost envious of an advocate, a certain Valerius Licinianus, who 'made his entry clad in a Greek cloak – those who have been ritually banished are not allowed to wear the toga'.[14] The exile was due to the fact that he had violated a Vestal Virgin, one of the six priestesses in charge of the cult of the Roman health goddess.

We are not told what she was wearing when this happened, but there would be many moralists who would, as they have always done, attribute her fate to the sexual attraction of her clothing. Seneca, tutor and later minister to the Emperor Nero (reigned 54–68), wistfully looking back to 'the moderation of past ages', attacked 'the folly and vanity of luxury', and particularly the madness of 'garments that will neither defend a woman's body nor her modesty'.[15] Whether this refers to the fine transparent silks already in vogue, or the diaphanous embroidered muslins from India which were being imported, is not clear. What Seneca and others of like mind were sure of, was that women no longer wore the modest, voluminous figure-concealing tunic and cloak of Republican days, but had adopted figure-revealing dress of excessive finery. The *mater familias*, whose family and home formed her whole existence,

3 The Emperor Augustus.
The voluminous imperial toga needed particular care both in the draping and the wearing, otherwise it could easily become careless and undignified.

4 A flute player.
Detail from a vase painting by the Karneia Painter c. 410 B.C.
In what many moralists found to be the decadent and luxurious civilization of the Greek cities of southern Italy, this flute player with her transparent chiton *would have been a common sight at the kind of parties which Petronius was later to depict in the* Satyricon.

had now turned into a bored, pleasure-seeking vain creature whose only interest was in clothes and sexual liberty.

Juvenal's famous satire against women, probably sketched out in the 90s, is particularly savage, not just on the accepted notorieties of the Empress Messalina slipping through the streets at night 'straight for her brothel' in blonde wig and hooded cloak, but on the general female propensity for appalling novelties in fashion. In the old days, he says, poverty and war kept women chaste, but now,

> Luxury, deadlier
> Than any armed invader, lies like an incubus
> Upon us still.

He notes the fact that it has become smart for women to ape Greek fashions and to 'chatter away in Greek', although they should blush for 'their slipshod Latin'.[16]

Much of his wrath is directed at the jewellery worn by fashionable women, their emerald necklaces and vast pearl ear-rings; too much jewellery was a sign of the vulgarity of recent wealth, or of Greek 'decadence'. It is no accident that the *Satyricon* of Petronius is set in the luxurious Greek city of Campania (probably Naples) where the dreadful Trimalchio and his appalling wife Fortunata are covered in jewellery; she is described not only as wearing brightly coloured clothes and gold-embroidered slippers, but a hair net 'of the very finest gold'.[17]

By the end of the first century, a fashionable woman's hair (often eked out with false locks from barbarian women or slaves) was piled high, waved and plaited, and arranged on towering frameworks; it was an easy target in its artificiality for the satirist, and Juvenal makes the most of this opportunity:

> See the tall edifice
> Rise up on her head in serried tiers and storeys.
> See her heroic stature – at least, that is, from in front;
> Her back view's less impressive, you'd think it belonged
> To a different person.[18]

Equally artificial was the fashionable woman's use of cosmetics, the face being whitened with lead or chalk, cheeks and lips reddened with ochre or wine lees, and the eyes outlined with pencils, or antimony, and brightened, according to Ovid, with 'fine ash of saffron which is gathered from the banks of the Cydnus'.

In Ovid's *Art of Love*, a treatise on how to attract members of the opposite sex, women are urged to use art to improve on what Nature has given them, but not to let their lovers be disillusioned by seeing their beauty preparations. In the days of the Republic, only a rustic simplicity was needed, but now (he is writing at about the time of the birth of Christ,

BODY AND SOUL

5 Head of a woman c. *110–115 A.D.*
The elaborate, contrived hairstyles of fashionable Roman women under the Empire were a frequent subject for satirical comment.

in the early years of the Empire), all kinds of beauty aids are necessary for a woman to keep a lover, and 'Rome possesses the immense riches of the world she has conquered'.[19]

With the arrival of Christianity, which began to win followers from the middle of the first century, first in great numbers in the East and then spreading into the *Pax Romana* itself by the second century, a totally new attitude to sin, including the sin of adorning the body, becomes apparent.

Rome had long been a centre for all kinds of cults and semi-secret societies, and many refused to take Christianity seriously, because of its refusal to accept the validity of any other religion. The single-minded intolerance of the early Christians towards any other faith helped it to survive through the days of persecution, until it was recognized in the early fourth century as virtually the official religion of the Empire. The Emperor Constantine, who had shown friendliness to Christianity during his reign, became converted on his deathbed in 337 by dying in the white of Christian purity, having put off the imperial purple. With the coming of Christianity there arrived sin and guilt, and the consequent fierce denunciation of all signs of human depravity, not only as wicked in themselves (the classical world, after all, had denounced sartorial excess), but as anathema to God. While the classical world fixed its mind on how virtue could be achieved, the Christian world fixed attention on sin with an intensifying process of asceticism which led to what Lecky calls 'a vast system of moral discipline ... resting upon religious terrorism'. He continues:

> The Christian notion of the enormity of little sins, the belief that all the details of life will be scrutinized hereafter, (and) ... may be made the grounds of eternal condemnation beyond the grave, was altogether unknown to the ancients.

Early Christian moralists thus singled out every 'new form of luxury or some trivial custom ... for the most extravagant denunciation'.[20]

Christianity being on the whole against individualism in dress, we would not expect to find in the Bible much emphasis on the adornment of the body, except for injunctions to dress modestly. This modesty includes not wearing the clothing of the opposite sex; 'The woman shall not wear that which pertaineth unto a man, neither shall a man put on a woman's garment; for all that do so are abomination unto the Lord thy God' (Deut. XXII, 5). Although the strength of the denunciation is stronger, the feeling that wearing the clothing of the opposite sex is taboo echoes the opinion of the classical moralist.[21]

Most Biblical references are about female modesty and the importance of dressing in a sober manner; 'Favour is deceitful and beauty is vain; but a woman that feareth the Lord, she shall be praised' (Proverbs XXXI), which is echoed by St Paul in his commandment to women to 'adorn themselves in modest apparel, with shamefacedness and sobriety' (I Timothy II, 9).

25

6 Susanna and the elders, detail of a wall-painting from a Roman catacomb.
Susanna, being surprised by the elders with lecherous intent, is shown in the loose-fitting T-shaped dalmatica, *the antithesis of 'immoral', revealing dress. The intentions of the elders are perhaps indicated by the short tunic, although the drapery of the* pallium *or rectangular cloak appears somewhat restricting. In spite of the biblical injunction that men and women should be clearly distinguished by their dress, both sexes wore basically the same costume, consisting of a tunic (short or long) and a rectangular cloak.*

Those women who do not heed God in this respect are like the haughty 'daughters of Zion ... (who) walk with stretched forth necks and wanton eyes, walking and mincing as they go, and making a tinkling with their feet' (Isaiah III, 16). The Lord 'will take away the bravery of their tinkling ornaments about their feet', all their other jewellery and their 'changeable suits of apparel',

And it shall come to pass, that instead of sweet smell there shall be stink; instead of a girdle a rent; and instead of well-set hair baldness; and instead of a stomacher a girding of sackcloth; and burning instead of beauty (Isaiah III, 24).

Although this has been translated in terms of early seventeenth century dress, much of the emphasis lies in denunciation of the most obvious areas of female vanity, the wearing of jewellery and the attention given to the hair – items most frequently picked up by the early Christian moralists.

Women were, admittedly, made in God's image and spiritually His equal, but the nature of women being more animal than that of men, leads them into greater temptations – so the moralists thought. The greatest temptation of all was, of course, that of Eve tempting Adam; unlike the Koran which finds both Adam and Eve responsible together for the expulsion from Eden, the Bible has no doubt of Eve's guilt. As Simone de Beauvoir points out:

In her, the Christian finds incarnated the temptation of the world, the flesh and the devil. All the Fathers of the Church insist on the idea that she led Adam into sin. We must quote Tertullian: 'Woman, you are the gateway of the devil. You persuaded him whom the devil dared not attack directly. Because of you the son of God had to die. You should always go dressed in mourning and in rags'.[22]

The idea of women being the second sex was not new – Aristotle was not alone in his view that women were both morally and intellectually inferior to men – but what *was* new was an extra burden of guilt placed upon them.

Tertullian, the first Latin churchman, quoted above by de Beauvoir, in his *De cultu feminarum* (written in the early third century), made the first detailed foray into female luxury in dress and the perilous temptations offered by silk, jewellery and other finery. At about the same time, Clement of Alexandria in *The Instructor* attacks 'ensnaring garments and unguents (which) should not be admitted into the city of truth'. By 'ensnaring' he means patterned or rich textiles, the worst being dyed with bright colours like purple 'thus inflaming the lusts'. The best quality purple came from the cities of Tyre and Sidon, where there are 'crafty women and effeminate men who blend these deceptive dyes with dainty fabrics'. Dainty fabrics include byssus and other fine linens, but silk, he says, is even worse if it is fine enough to reveal the body. Good Christian women should 'put out of the way fabrics foolishly thin, and of curious texture in the weaving, bidding farewell to embroidery of gold and Indian silks'.[23]

This belief, that women should wear clothing that completely disguises the shape of the body, is to a large extent borne out by surviving visual sources and garments; in catacomb paintings for example, women are depicted in an undertunic of simple, rectangular cut, and a large, ample overtunic with wide sleeves, called a *dalmatica* and usually ungirdled, which when unsewn up the sides and opened out flat, assumed the shape of the cross. Excavations in Egypt show garments in a similar style, usually of linen or wool and very little silk, which was too expensive to be used except for the occasional decorative roundel or square patch. Yet wool could also be richly patterned and woven, and it may be to this that Early Christian Fathers like St Jerome, St Ambrose and St Basil refer when they comment adversely on the rich clothes that people were buried in which could have been used to clothe the living.[24]

If the ideal Christian woman is chaste and modest, even more perfect is the virgin, who is especially close to God and must dress to please Him. 'For those who are white and unstained within, it is most suitable to use white and simple garments', was Clement's view,[25] accepting sorrowfully that when virgins marry, they are more inclined to dress colourfully and in finery to please their husbands. All virgins, however, do not seem to have followed Clement's admonition, for we find St Jerome in the fourth century attacking the so-called 'virgins of the Church' who 'strut about the streets, nodding and leering'.[26] The costume of virgins – white tunic, and black or grey loose mantle – was at about this time to be codified into the dress of the first female religious orders, the – as it were – official virgins of the church.

Other writers on virginity[27] are more informative on what virgins should not wear, than on their ideal costume. One example (out of the many) is Cyprian, Bishop of Carthage (martyred 258) whose *De Habitu Virginum* is one of the first treatises on the place of consecrated virgins in the church. Quoting Isaiah, he states that 'showy adornments and clothing and the allurements of beauty are not becoming in any except prostitutes and shameless women'.

Austerity should extend to the avoidance of public baths (a custom favoured in classical antiquity), for even if virgins dress modestly there, he addresses them: 'you yourself are gazed upon immodestly... in delighting others, you yourself are corrupted'.[28]

Cyprian's greatest venom is reserved for those women who adorn their bodies with jewellery and their faces with cosmetics. Pierced ears are 'wounds inflicted on the ears', and as for face paint:

> the sinful and apostate angels ... taught how to paint the eyes by spreading a black substance around them, and to tinge the cheeks with a counterfeit blush.[29]

Cyprian's denunciations generally owe much in the strength of their invective to Tertullian and to Clement. Clement not only worried about women's use of cosmetics – by so embellishing the face, we find that 'a fornicator and an adulteress has occupied the shrine of the soul'[30] – but about their use of false hair. How might the validity of religious services be affected by the fact that when the priest's hand rests on the head of the person kneeling before him, it might be touching the hair of another? 'Tertullian shuddered at the thought that Christians might have the hair of those who were in hell, upon their head'.[31]

This criticism applies equally to men as to women, for men, it appears, were equally vain about their hair and apt to wear false hair if their own locks were scanty. The early Christians were, however, advised to keep their hair moderately short, and not, as Clement of Alexandria put it, 'gliding into womanish ringlets'; 'if a man have long hair', says the Bible, 'it is a shame unto him' (I Corinthians II, 14). They were also urged never to shave their beards, for not only was the beard a sign which distinguished the Christian from the clean-shaven

---

7 Detail from a fifth-century ivory diptych depicting scenes from the life of St Paul.
This is the kind of dress which many Roman patricians found abhorrent – the long hair, furred mantles, sleeved tunics, and above all, the trousers.

pagan Roman, but it was also the symbol of manhood which it was impious to desecrate; according to Clement, God had counted every hair, and there must be no plucking out.[32] As fine clothes were thought to be a danger to the truly spiritual life, Christians were assumed to wear clothing for decency and warmth and not for show. There was even a deliberate rejection of special garments for the clergy; apart from the various kinds of circular hooded mantles which were part of barbarian wear, ecclesiastical vestments arose mainly out of Roman secular dress.

Clement admired the barbarians who 'love an unencumbered life', not decking themselves in fine clothes and wearing their own hair and beards. Other Church Fathers, however, saw some spiritual danger in equating Christian asceticism with a dishevelled and slovenly appearance, for this, too, was a kind of pride. St Jerome, for example, at the end of the fourth century, found it necessary to attack both the clergy who lived and dressed like nobles, and also the monks who make 'a parade of their bare feet, black cloaks and long, unkempt hair'; even worse was when such monks pretended austerity but practised sensuality, when they 'deceive silly women laden with sins'.[33] By the time that St Jerome was writing, the authority of the Empire was being increasingly undermined by the great barbarian incursions, leading to the fall of Rome in 410, a shock that resounded through the civilized world. Barbarian dress, the dress of the mainly Germanic tribes that had been infiltrating the Empire for many years, consisted of sleeved tunic, trousers, boots and short hooded cloak; it was quite different in style from the basically flowing and unfitted clothing of the Roman establishment. The trousers, symbolic of the barbarian whom the Romans had fought against for many hundreds of years, attracted most censure and there were strenuous but unavailing attempts to forbid them in 397 and 399. Long hair was also banned in 416, the tone of the law leaving no doubt that the rage for German fashions was widespread.[34]

By the middle of the sixth century, all the old Roman ideas of dress as indicative of class and status had begun to fall apart. Procopius in his *Secret History* (550), a story of court intrigue under the Emperor Justinian who had established his court at Ravenna, describes the dress of the upper-class supporters of the rival hippodrome teams in Rome – virtually thugs who robbed people for kicks – as a medley of the old and the new; they wore the *toga praetexta* (the purple-bordered Roman magistrate's toga) to which they had no right, tight-sleeved tunics and 'cloaks, trousers and boots ... (which) were called the Hun style', and their hair also 'hun style', that is shaved at the front and long at the back, and with a long beard.[35]

A conservative Roman of the old school would find this not only grossly inappropriate but also quite offensive and be forced to conclude, sadly, that it was indicative of the disordered state of society, as the old classical world gave way to a violent new one, where Christianity would play a major role.

2
Vile Bodies

> Seek by every means to check the luxury of dress which is excessive and hateful to God ... because these ornaments on clothing – such their wearers think them to be though they are a disgrace in the eyes of others ... are sent by Anti-Christ and prepare for his coming ... These garments, betraying a nakedness of soul, display in themselves signs of arrogance and pride and wantonness and vanity.
>
> Letter from St Boniface to Cuthbert, Archbishop of Canterbury, 747

Almost a century elapsed between the reconnaissance expeditions made by the Romans into Britain in the first century B.C. (of which the most famous were Julius Caesar's in 55 and 54 B.C.), and the conquest of the country by the Emperor Claudius in 43 A.D. Between these dates there seems increasing evidence for a considerable amount of Roman mercantile penetration into southern Britain, and by the end of the first century most of the country was familiar with Roman order, manners and language. By this time, according to Tacitus, 'the sons of the British chieftains began to affect our dress'.[1]

In 212 Roman citizenship was given to every free-born subject in the Empire, thus conferring on them the right to wear the toga; no doubt the vagaries of the British climate meant that most men continued to wear their customary sleeved tunic, trousers, and various forms of the hooded cloak. The scanty information that we have at our disposal tells us that women in Britain seem to have adopted Roman dress in most details; if wealthy, the tunic or *stola* would have been made of fine imported material like silk or a silk and woollen mixture, and the garment was usually made with sleeves. A *palla* or capacious rectangular cloak was the universal female outer covering.

By the time that the Romans left in the early fifth century, a semi-Romanized upper and merchant class was left, but of their life we know very little, nor do we know how they reacted to the waves of Germanic settlers from the mid-fifth century onwards, who founded the early Anglo-Saxon kingdoms. This period is immensely shadowy. Contemporaries in Gaul who might have told something of Britain at this time were preoccupied with their own troubles, and as a great historian of Anglo-Saxon England has pointed out, 'Britain was lost to the Roman Empire, and its fortunes were of little interest to men whose own civilization was at stake'.[2]

Until the conversion of the country to Christianity at the end of the sixth century, England remained cut off from the rest of Europe, a pagan outpost; many, like Procopius, believed that the souls of the dead were conveyed there. What information we have on dress in this period is to be found in visual and documentary evidence from the fairly civilized Gallo-Roman society in Gaul. France at this time was a collection of Celtic and Teutonic tribes, with constantly shifting frontiers; the whole of Gaul had been conquered by the Romans before the birth of Christ, and had been equally subject to Christian influence from the second century A.D., so that there was a well-established convergence of classical and barbarian cultures. Apollinarius Sidonius, for example, born c. 431, of a distinguished Roman family, and later Bishop of Auvergne, reveals in his letters the life of a rich, cultivated and worldly prince of the church, but at the same time shows considerable respect for the power and culture of some of the barbarian tribes, especially the Franks. At Lyons in about 470 he admires the dress worn by the Frankish prince Sigismer, a short white silk tunic ornamented with gold, and a red mantle fastened by a brooch on the right shoulder.[3] He is pleased to note that although the Frankish nobles had moustaches and long hair, they did not wear beards, nor cover their hair in rancid grease and their bodies with tattoos as did some of the more primitive tribes whose clothing had not changed much since Tacitus in his *Germania* (written in 98) had described them in semi-naked state, their open-sided cloaks fastened with a brooch or a thorn, and their fondness for the 'pelts of wild animals'. On the whole, although Tacitus disapproved of some of the habits of the Germanic tribes – their drunkenness and their propensity for warlike behaviour – he was impressed by their sexual morality (the punishment for an adulterous female was to shave the head but it was rarely carried out), and their lack of luxury, all of which he compared, as did many of the early Church Fathers, favourably with the decadence of Roman society.

Although in the more primitive conditions of Britain it is unlikely that much silk would be worn, the styles of costume described by Sidonius would have been similar to those worn here, that is, a mixture of the basic rectangular classical shapes, with barbarian regional elements like trousers and hoods. For women this was a virtual uniform, consisting of a somewhat shapeless undertunic with sleeves to the

8 The figure of Philosophy, *from an illustrated manuscript of Boethius's* De Consolatione Philosophae, *of the late tenth century. The shape of the figure is totally hidden beneath the voluminous draperies of late Anglo-Saxon female dress. The only elements of frivolity in this fashionable costume are the bracelets which hold the long sleeves in at the wrists, and the rather flirtatious frill at the hem of the under-tunic.*

wrist, and an overtunic with wider sleeves which is possibly what is referred to in contemporary accounts as a *kirtle*; covering this was either a mantle based on the rectangular Roman palla, or a semi-circular cloak put on over the head. By the time of the first native school of manuscript illumination in the tenth century, women appear in linen veils, often swathed under the chin and kept in place by jewelled headbands.

For men, dress consisted of a woollen knee-length tunic worn over trousers (*braccae*), and a short square cloak (*sagum*). An alternative to trousers was a kind of sock worn to the knee; both trousers and socks could be kept in place by bands of fabric bound round them from the knee downwards, a kind of cross-gartering. Fur was highly prized – the word *pellitus* had been to the Romans almost synonymous with barbarian – and used for mantles, to decorate dress and to line boots. It seems likely that some body decoration was practised in the form of tattooing; although this was forbidden by a law of 785[4] it seems to have continued until after the Norman conquest, according to the chroniclers. William of Malmesbury, one of the most accurate of such chroniclers, recorded that:

> The English of that time wore short garments reaching to the mid-knee; they had their hair cropped; their beards shaven; their arms laden with golden bracelets; their skin adorned with punctured designs.[5]

Both men and women seem to have worn a considerable amount of jewellery. The epic poem *Beowulf*, composed probably in the eighth century, has not only references to jewelled armour and swords, but also to rings and armlets; such armlets (*armillae*), brooches, necklaces and headbands are listed in Anglo-Saxon wills[6] and have been excavated from early burial sites indicating the continuation of the pagan practice of burying goods with the dead.[7]

By the beginning of the ninth century, after a slow process of cohesion, England consisted of several small kingdoms, although for considerable periods of time those south of the Humber were united under an overlord; only the West Saxon kings were powerful enough to withstand Danish attacks which occurred sporadically from the end of the eighth century for the next two hundred or so years.

It is with the arrival of the Danes that we begin to get some moralistic comment on dress, notably the equation of Viking dress with a lapse in moral standards. One, somewhat later, chronicler found that the Danes were

> effeminately gay in the dress, combed their hair once a day, bathed once a week, and often changed their attire; by these means they pleased the eyes of the women, and frequently seduced the wives and daughters of the nobility.[8]

It is not clear how far the Danes adopted Anglo-Saxon dress, but the implication may be that their standards of personal hygiene were higher.

Some church leaders deplored Danish influence on dress. At the end of the eighth century Alcuin wrote to the King of Northumbria criticizing the clothing of the Northumbrians as too pagan and Viking-like; apart from the general luxury of their dress, he singled out their fondness for long hair and beards.[9]

Most of his remarks were directed at the clergy who not only frequently wore 'pagan' long hair and beards instead of the tonsure (*corona*) which should have distinguished them, but also fashionable and luxurious garments. To a number of clerics like Alcuin, such luxury was not only hateful in itself, but had forced God to send the Viking raids upon the country to show His displeasure at English worldliness.

There was relatively little difference between the dress of the clergy and that of the laity; the secular clergy were often married, and many of the female religious orders were merely societies of ladies of rank who lived a worldly existence. St Aldhelm, writing in the early eighth century to the Abbess Hildalid of Barking, complains about the finery adopted by some nuns:

> satin underclothing, ... scarlet tunics and hoods, sleeves with silk stripes, shoes edged with red fur, hair carefully arranged on forehead and temples with the curling iron – this is the modern habit. Dark veils yield to headdresses white and coloured, sewn with long ribbons and hanging

to the ground; fingernails are sharpened like the talons of hawks or owls seeking their prey.[10]

Aldhelm also complains about their love of jewellery and cosmetics; not only did women rouge their cheeks, but they used *stibium* (antimony) to emphasize their eyes. The problem was that at this period the church laid emphasis on missionary work (large areas of Britain were either still pagan, or clung to the longer-established Celtic branch of the faith which had been officially banished in favour of the usages of Rome), during which both monks and nuns came in contact with the laity and their worldly ways.

In 785 the clergy were ordered 'not to wear the tinctured colours of India, nor precious ornaments'[11] for it seems that earlier injunctions had been disregaded. St Boniface, for example, born in England and sent to Germany as a missionary, urged Cuthbert, Archbishop of Canterbury in 747 to: 'check the luxury of dress which is excessive and hateful to God'.

He singles out for condemnation 'the wide stripes and scarlet borders' which decorate dress, and especially purple garments – all of which can lead to 'lust, unholy intercourse, indifference to reading and prayer, and the ruin of souls'.[12] It is not precisely clear what he means by the stripes; they could either be the continuation of the official Roman stripes on tunics which were adopted as decoration by the early Christians, or the wide decorative borders, often of rich embroidery for which the English were famous, which were used to strengthen the seams of male and female gowns in the Anglo-Saxon period; in either case they were evidence of excessive luxury. One justification made by William of Malmesbury for the Norman invasion in 1066, was not only that the nobility were 'given up to luxury and wantonness', but that the clergy were too.[13]

The Norman conquest produced great changes in dress; the Normans, after all, were originally Vikings, and by the end of the tenth century there was little to distinguish the Anglo-Saxon nobleman from his French counterpart. Edward the Confessor, 'a man

9 The Temptation of Christ c. *1050*.
Jewellery is so prized, and such an obvious form of portable wealth, that the Devil tempts Christ with armlets of twisted gold, a brooch, a jewelled sword, and drinking vessels.

from the simplicity of his manners little calculated to govern'[14] had spent the formative years of youth and manhood in Normandy, and much of the English aristocracy was Normanized; looking at the *Bayeux Tapestry*, a unique record in a period bereft of closely dated visual sources, we can find little difference between the dress of the Normans and that of the English, save that the former have considerably shorter hair.

While not necessarily agreeing with the view held by many eighteenth and nineteenth-century dress historians that Anglo-Saxon dress was in its tasteful 'native simplicity' not subject to a 'restless desire of variety'[15] it does seem that for many hundreds of years it had been relatively stable compared to the fairly rapid changes that coincided both with a new dynasty and the appearance of a somewhat stylized art from to be seen in English manuscript illumination.

To contemporaries used from time immemorial to a kind of bulky Saxon solidity, there appeared towards the end of the eleventh century a new, spiky and elongated style of dress for men, a tightening up of the new long tunic, and long attenuated sleeves which because they were so impractical, could only be worn by the leisured classes. One of the elements of the new feudal system was for a greater consciousness of class to be reflected in dress. It was perhaps unfortunate that this new emphasis on the male figure – a tightening up to be achieved by lacing the tunic at the sides – coincided with the reign of an unpopular king, William Rufus, who was notorious for his homosexual tendencies.

> '... then the model for young men', says William of Malmesbury 'was to rival women in delicacy of person, to mince their gait, to walk with loose gesture, and with their sides naked'.[16]

The naked sides refers probably to side lacing of the tunic, which revealed the shirt or the naked body beneath; Richard I in 1188 had to issue regulations forbidding his crusading army to wear clothes that were slashed or laced, so it was a fashion, exaggerated by art, that endured for almost a hundred years.

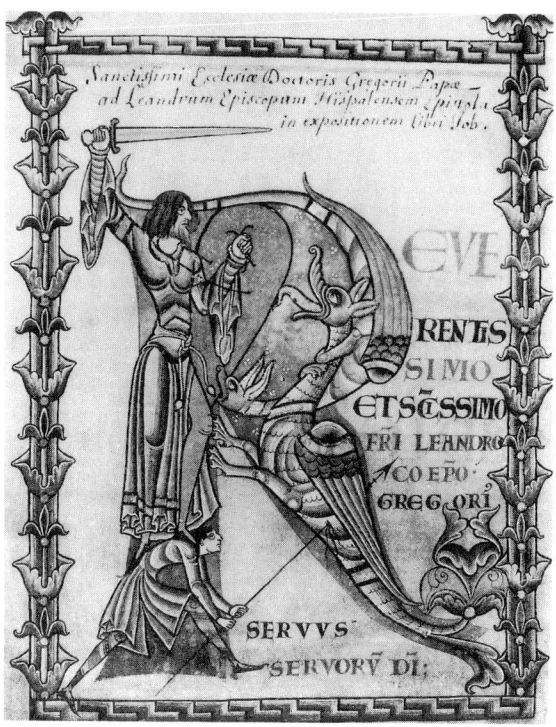

10 *Title Page of the* Moralia in Job *of St Gregory 1111.*
This is masculine fashion at its most elegant and self-conscious, sure to attract the wrath of moralists, as it is fitted extremely tight to the figure, and slit up the side. The long hair, pointed beard, and pointed toes were also commented on adversely.

Not only did the young men at court wear tight tunics, but they also grew their hair long, in deliberate contravention of the martial Norman tradition. Orderic Vitalis in his early twelfth-century *Ecclesiastical History* describes the fashions of the 1090s as a period when men:

> rejected the traditions of honest men, ridiculed the counsel of priests and persisted in their barbarous way of life and style of dress. They parted their hair from the crown of the head to the forehead, grew long and luxuriant locks like women, and loved to deck themselves in long over-tight shirts and tunics.[17]

It was this long hair which brought most condemnation. In 1094 Anselm, Archbishop of

VILE BODIES

Even priests were not immune from this fashion, and synods in 1096 (Rouen) and 1102 (London) urged the clergy to adhere more strictly to clerical dress and to have their heads tonsured. With the establishment of the Cluniac order in England in the eleventh century and even more with the arrival of the Cistercian order in the early twelfth century, church discipline was geatly improved. Admiring the austerity of the Cistercians, Orderic writes in 1135 that he would far rather discuss 'holiness and the miracles performed by the saints than ... the trifles of fools and frivolous extravagances, if only our princes and bishops devoted themselves wholly to lives of spiritual grace'.[20] Right through the Middle Ages there were comments about the propensity of church dignitaries to wear secular dress, an indication, according to the severest monkish chroniclers, of spiritual laxity.

Not only did men wear their hair long and even 'curl their hair with hot irons', but they also popularized the wearing of beards. Orderic says: 'all our fellow countrymen are crazy and wear little beards, openly proclaiming by such a token that they revel in filthy lusts like stinking goats'.[21] Presumably it was the shape of the beard that was at fault, and not the beard itself, for Orderic, as a good monk, would be familiar with the writings of the early Church Fathers on the venerability of honest-to-God unshaped beards. The fashionable male obsession with slenderness and a distortion of the body was equally revealed by the choice of footwear at the end of the eleventh century; shoes with long pointed toes like scorpions. This particular style Orderic attributes to a certain Count Fulk of Anjou 'a man with many, even scandalous habits' who

> had shoes made with very long and pointed toes to hide the shape of his feet and to conceal the growths that are commonly called bunions ... Before then, shoes always used to be made round, fitting the foot and these were adequate to the needs of high and low, both clergy and laity. But now laymen in their pride seize upon a fashion typical of their corrupt morals. What honourable men once thought shameful and utterly rejected

11 Moralia in Job of St Gregory.
MS 168 fol. 7r.
Although Job has the open-sided mantle of official costume, he is otherwise depicted as very fashionable with the long 'womanish' hair, 'goat-like' beard, and the pointed shoes which critics claimed to find sinful.

Canterbury, preached against it at Lent, and his secretary Eadmer wrote in his *Historia Novorum in Anglia*:

> it was the fashion for nearly all the young men of the Court to grow their hair long like girls; then with locks well-combed, glancing about them and winking in ungodly fashion, they would daily walk about with delicate steps and mincing gait.[18]

If this was not bad enough, he continues, 'anyone who is not long-haired is branded with some opprobious name, called "country bumpkin" or "priest".[19]

35

as filth, the men of this age consider 'sweet as honey and flaunt abroad as though it were a special grace'.

Among these 'great evils' of 1089–90, was the fashion for stuffing the toes of the shoes into the shape of a ram's horn, the invention of one Robert, 'a certain worthless fellow at King Rufus's court'.[22]

With the long tunic (trousers were only worn by the working classes) and the growing gulfs between the classes formalized by the feudal system, it became increasingly important to demonstrate status by richness of fabric, which meant fine silk. From antiquity, the east had been the source of the most prized silks, although by the tenth century silk weaving was established in Sicily under Arab rule. Although contemporary records of royal and aristocratic textile purchases show furs and fine woollen fabrics to be the most frequently purchased, reflecting no doubt the draughty conditions in English castles, there was an increased trade in silks as a result of the Crusades. The east was blamed by moralists for such enervating luxuries as fine silks (like damask, which probably originated in Damascus), rich dyes, trailing skirts to tunics and sleeves which were so long they either covered the hands (a Byzantine style) or had to be knotted. Orderic was quick to condemn this evidence of indolence:

> They sweep the dusty ground with the unnecessary trains of their robes and mantles; their long wide sleeves cover their hands whatever they do; impeded by these frivolities they are almost incapable of walking quickly or doing any kind of useful work.[23]

By the end of the twelfth century the extremely etiolated dress for men had given way to a more natural and fluid line more sculptural in effect than the nervous and restless styles typical of the hundred years or so after the Norman Conquest. The items in a fashionable man's wardrobe remain basically the same, a long tunic usually worn with a shorter-sleeved overtunic or a sleeveless surcote and a mantle. The tunic could still be quite tight, for once tailors had discovered aids to fit like lacing and buttons (which by the early thirteenth century appear in works of art), they were determined to experiment with their new skills so that the natural look of the thirteenth century is only a kind of remission before the distortions of the fourteenth century, a period when some authorities think that fashion as we know it begins.

Compared to the alarm manifested by moralists at the disturbing developments in male dress after the Norman Conquest, with regard to female dress there is no such body of public opinion. It is not really until well into the twelfth century that we see any real attempts at fitted garments for women whose costume often appears to be nothing but a bundle of somewhat shapeless draperies. Women were not, however, immune from fashion trends, and from the end of the eleventh century began to elongate their sleeves. They either formed the shape of trumpets, or their ends were so long and thin that they were knotted and twisted round the arm. Veils also, by the twelfth century, follow this tortured line, some of them being knotted on the head, and young girls knotted their hair into plaits often with the addition of false hair. None of this caused as much outcry as did the fashion for tight-lacing of the tunic, both on the torso and on the sleeves. A late twelfth-century poem attacks this kind of lacing on the grounds of health: 'Regard the extent of this folly. They lace up their arms and sides in such a manner as to cause themselves considerable pain'.[24]

It is not clear if both tunics and even the chemise were laced like this; only the most daring and immodest woman would have revealed her flesh in this way.

By the middle of the twelfth century, advances in tailoring techniques with the use of gores, pleated or smocked inserts over the bodice area, and cloth cut on the cross, enabled a more complex garment to be created instead of the simple rectangular T-shaped tunic of earlier periods. Fabrics were more luxurious and refined, accessories more important, and artificial aids to beauty more in evidence. Women generally seem to emerge from seclusion and to play a greater part in society.

This is reflected in the increased attention

12 The Temptation of Christ (*detail*).
The Winchester Psalter c. 1150.
The Devil is dressed in a caricature of female fashionable costume, wearing a tightly laced gown revealing bare flesh and slit up the side. The trailing, knotted train and one sleeve, also knotted, indicates worldly pride and extravagance; the other sleeve, which is possibly unsewn, may be a sign of slovenliness.

given to them by moralists from the twelfth century onwards, a concern felt about the place of women in the feudal system. Such a system of despotic orderliness reinforced class and sex boundaries; the castle was the seat of power which settled relationships between men (women hardly entered into this, for – unless they were great landowners in their own right and this applied in very few cases – they were legally inferior), told men where to live, to fight, to cultivate land and whom to marry.

The other great pillar of the feudal system was the church. Not only were high-ranking clerics great landowners in their own right and thus able to play a part in the community, but the church was the effective supervisor of morals. Soon after the Norman Conquest 'bawdy courts' or church tribunals were set up to exercise jurisdiction over such crimes as adultery and misbehaviour in church; punishments (which were of course limited to the lower classes) included being ordered to appear in public dressed in the white sheet of contrition, or to go bare-legged in shirt or shift in the market place or church.

Church sermons played a major part in attempts to reform manners and dress, part of the general movement of conservative orthodoxy and obedience to authority which was the prevailing rule of the established church in its attempts to combat heresy.[25]

At church women would have heard sermons depicting them as foolish creatures, too prone to follow the desires of the flesh, and subject to pride and vanity. At the same time they might be seen, according to the literary conventions established by the troubadour poets of Provence, as heroines in courtly romances, placed on a pedestal and worshipped. Such '*amour courtois*' – the woman loved could be a virgin, a widow, even another man's wife – was

13 St Anne (*detail*).
The Bury Bible.
In this detail from the Bury Bible (1130s) it is possible to see why some moralists complained of the tightness of women's dress, their open sleeves, and their passion for knotting all trailing draperies, even the veil.

accomplishments should include spinning and weaving, but not reading or writing unless she was destined to become a nun.[26] As soon as possible she should marry: 'Comme le feu de la luxure est surtout allumé en jeunesse, il est sage de se marier tôt pour éviter fornications et adultères'.[27]

Women were in an impossible situation; while they were urged to marry to avoid the sins of fornication and adultery, they were attacked for making themselves attractive to men. And when they did marry, their husbands discouraged too great a display of finery both on the grounds of expense and because it might attract other men. The young woman, married long enough to be getting bored both with marriage and her husband and beginning to cast a roving eye, is a frequent theme in medieval literature.

One of the constant themes in thirteenth-century poetry is the inconstancy of women and their mercenary nature. Finery, say the songs, does not necessarily mean love; a young man should find a girl dressed 'en simples habis',

> Car behours, robe envesie
> Beaus chanters, langue polie,
> Ne souliers agus,
> L'amour pas ne senefie

for revelry, a gay robe, polished speech and pointed toes do not show love.[28]

Other songs have the refrain that a woman feigns love in order to be given presents of clothing. One anonymous thirteenth-century rondeau describes a man giving a girl a tunic and a fur-lined gown, but she is still not satisfied and wants fine woollen hose, shoes with pointed toes, a mantle, and various forms of fashionable headdress – if she could have a slice of your skin 'un tronson de vo pel', she would use it to make a border for her dress.[29]

Vincent of Beauvais' dictum that 'woman ... is the confusion of man, an insatiable beast, a continuous anxiety, an incessant warfare, a daily ruin, a house of tempest, a hindrance to devotion',[30] is borne out in the most famous of all thirteenth-century poems, the *Roman de la*

an essential part of the code of chivalry, but was frowned on by Christian morality which perceived all intimate approaches between the sexes as sinful.

In an age in which virtue was seen to be more important than knowledge or art, the state of virginity was most highly admired. A Lombard crusader Philip of Novara wrote in about 1265 one of the first treatises on manners, called *The Four Ages of Man*, in which he lists a girl's main virtues to be obedience and chastity; her

14 Damned Souls from the Last Judgement c. *1240*. Bamberg Cathedral.
The damned are often shown in very fashionable dress, evidence, presumably, of their too-great fondness for luxury instead of virtue. The King is particularly fashionable with his open-sided surcote decorated with buttons.

Rose, begun in about 1240 by Guillaume de Lorris and continued in about 1280 by Jean de Meun. The earlier part of the poem is courtly in tone, but the later part is totally imbued with the theory that women use their beauty to trap men; it is a cynic's account of the relationship between the sexes.

Marriage, says the *Roman de la Rose*, is an unhappy state especially for the poor husband, for he has to pay for his wife's costly gown which she trails after her in the mud or – even worse – lifts up to show off her tight-fitting hose. On her head she wears a fortune in gold and silver, for she possesses a vast range of headdresses, coifs and golden bands and nets decorated with precious stones. In exasperation, the husband swears that unless she mends her ways, she will be reduced to a gown made of the coarsest fabric, a plain leather belt without a buckle, and shoes made out of his old leather boots.[31] One of many digressions in this very lengthy poem details some of the ways used by women to capture husbands, by emphasizing their sexual attractions. A woman with a fine white neck and breast should make the most of her good fortune by wearing a low-cut dress; if her breast is too large, it can be bound with a handkerchief. If she does not possess the fashionable blonde hair which at this time was coiled and plaited into horns at the side of the head, she should find some false hair, either of blonde silk, or 'cheveus de

VILE BODIES

40

15 The Foolish Virgins c. *1240*.
Magdeburg Cathedral.
Both foolish and wise virgins at this period wear more or less the same fashionable dress; the only distinguishing character of the wise ones is a smugness of expression compared to the misery of the foolish ones seen here.

Gowns are still cut to drape in folds at the waist and to trail on the ground, but there must be lacing at the back to achieve the fan-like pleats under the arm; lacing or sewing also creates a very tight sleeve.

---

quelque fame morte'.[32] It is not clear how much hair from female corpses was used in this way, but for many hundreds of years such accusations were part of the stock-in-trade of moralists.

The way that women deceived men in their use of false hair and cosmetics is a perennial theme in our story. It would be tedious to mention such attacks in detail, so I shall quote from just one at the end of our period which gives some idea of the flavour; it is a diatribe against:

> those women who put upon their head hair that is not their own, or an unnatural colour on their face. For, to put hair on the head or give a new complexion is the special concern of God. They, theefore, who do this kind of thing desire along with Lucifer to be equal to the Almighty.[33]

Turning from some of the more hysterical sermons on dress to the reasoned, temperate tone of Thomas Aquinas, is to see the glimmerings of the more rational world of the Renaissance in his *Summa Theologica* (1267–73).

In the form of question and answer, Aquinas tries to solve the problems long associated with women and their clothing. Does finery constitute a mortal sin? The answer is that if women dress 'from frivolity, or from vanity for the sake of ostentation, it is not always mortal, but venial' – that is, it is a minor, pardonable sin if committed heedlessly; presumably if women dress to provoke lust, this is much more serious – a mortal sin entails spiritual death. Aquinas recognizes that women must dress to please their husbands; they can even use cosmetics if illness or disfigurement require such aids, although otherwise it is a 'lying counterfeit', which, however, 'does not always involve a mortal sin, but only when it is done for the sake of sensuous pleasure or in contempt of God'.[34] Men and women should 'be satisfied with what is suitable', which is dictated by custom:

> Hence Augustine says ... that among the ancient Romans it was scandalous for one to wear a cloak with sleeves and reaching to the ankle, whereas now it is scandalous for anyone hailing from a reputable place to be without them.[35]

While it is important to avoid 'excessive expenditure and parade', it is important to remember that 'dirt and the weeds of mourning may be a subject of ostentation, all the more dangerous as being a decoy under the guise of God's service'.[36]

Such a philosophy of moderation and the happy mean is unique in the Middle Ages; such good advice on the subject of dress was to be virtually ignored when in the next century moralists turned their eyes towards a vision of increasingly rapid changes in dress that we can begin to call Fashion.

3
The World, the Flesh and the Devil

All kinds of raiment are now rather for vain-glory and worldly pomp than for the necessity of nature, diversely decorated... in an infinite variety of ways, and assuredly most of all to excite lust alike in men as in women.

Master Robert Rypon in a sermon,
late fourteenth century.

No one should judge someone else's conscience from dress, for it is God's office alone to judge His creatures.

Christine de Pisan,
The Book of the City of Ladies, 1405

It has been said that real fashion – in the sense that we understand it, in terms of sophisticated cut and construction and frequent changes in style – begins in the fourteenth century. Like all such statements, it must be taken cautiously, for at least from the twelfth century onwards, tailors were learning how to achieve a better fit to clothes with the aid of lacing and, later, buttons.

We tend to assume that there was more going on in the fourteenth-century world, for we enter a period rich in visual and literary sources in England as well as elsewhere in Europe. The twelfth and thirteenth centuries had been periods of consolidation in the feudal system; the relationships of kings spread across Europe and there were in particular close links between the French and English courts. French was the language of poetry, fashion and chivalry, but by the fourteenth century, English increasingly came to be the vehicle for native comment both literary and exhortatory.

It is at this time that we begin to see the bonds of the feudal system beginning to crack a little under the strains brought about both by wide-scale epidemics, and a series of peasant and artisan revolts, leading to economic crises. The great Black Death which swept across Europe in 1348–9 inspired both physical and spiritual fear; such plagues along with famine and financial hardship were picked up by moralists who attributed their existence to God's displeasure at earthly failings which of course included vanity in dress. Wars throughout the century led to heavier taxation and an increased restlessness at the state of serfdom; all these factors contributed to uprisings in Flanders, France and England. The Peasants' Revolt of 1381 showed a new awareness of social distinctions as each class fiercely protected its rights, and there was increasing resentment at the previously unquestioned claim by nobles and clergy to a privileged existence. One of the leading spirits of the 1381 revolt was John Ball (whom Froissart calls 'a crack-brained priest') who preached that although 'we all spring from a single father and mother', the aristocracy 'are clad in velvet and camlet lined with ermine, while we go clad in coarse cloth'.[1] Chaucer's worldly clerics in *The Canterbury Tales* reflect the widespread belief in the easy and luxurious lives led by churchmen at all levels, a feeling which did much to fuel the spirit of anti-clericalism. Many churchmen were aware of this, and John Wyclif attacked not only the prelates' 'precious pellure & ryche clothis', but also the expense of their households, their 'proude & leccherous squyeres'; monks, continues Wyclif, wore clothing so loose that it prevented them working properly when it blew in the wind, and of so much yardage that 'foure or fyve nedy men mygtten welle be clothed with a cope & hood of a monke'.[2]

In a markedly less spiritual century when the Church found it less easy to lay down guidelines about conduct – both from their own apparent inability to live lives of poverty, and from an increasing reluctance by people to accept such guidance – secular authority tried to reinforce class distinctions by a series of sumptuary laws. Like the ancient Greek laws of Solon, legislation not only covered what respectable citizens could *not* wear (such laws were usually negative rather than positive), but tried to enforce a distinctive clothing on the less respectable i.e. prostitutes. Such women had to dress in a way which marked them out from respectable women, either by wearing just their undergown (a virtuous woman would not dream of appearing in public without her upper-gown also), or a distinguishing badge like a striped hood; acts of 1355, 1361 and 1438 ordered such hoods to be worn, and – with a certain air of desperation – the act of 1355 states that prostitutes should wear their clothes inside out. How effective such legislation was in England is not clear; in France in the fifteenth century prostitutes were taken to court a number of times and fined for their adherence to 'respectable' fashions (or rather fashions above their status), such as turned-back collars, silver belts, and fur trimmings on their clothes.[3]

From the fourteenth century onwards, attacks on women gather momentum; it was felt that they were more capable of being tempted into vice through their love of finery, and to tempt men too. By the middle of the century, women's dress was perceptibly more fitted to the body both in the torso and in the sleeves, the latter now being fitted into small rounded armholes at the shoulder. From the beginning of the century women had begun to wear the sleeveless surcote, and gradually the armholes were widened until it became virtually a sideless gown to the waist; as it increasingly revealed the tightened bodice of the gown beneath, it was denounced by some moralists as a dress with 'windows into hell'. Strictly speaking, it was limited to ladies of the nobility, and to saints like St Ursula and St Catherine who came from aristocratic families.

At the beginning of the century however, women still wore voluminous gowns, often with wide sleeves and a long train. Such wide sleeves 'trayleth lowe under the fote', said Robert of Brunne, a canon of the Gilbertine order, in a work of 1303, *Handlyng Synne*, and the skirts of the dress were long enough for devils to sit on[4] – this was to be a recurring comment. It was the headdresses which were the most frequent point of condemnation; the northern European mind had for centuries been conditioned to link virtue with a well-covered head – after the marriage ceremony, a virgin's loose, flowing hair was quickly veiled. Robert of Brunne attacks women who dye their veils with saffron, but by the end of the first decade of the fourteenth century, such layers of linen pinned under the chin were being replaced in the fashionable world by elaborate horned headdresses or jewelled cauls (nets) which contained the plaited hair at the temples. This fashion, which came from France (we have already heard of it in the *Roman de la Rose*), was fairly modest compared to the towering headdresses of the fifteenth century, but to contemporaries it was a startling enough change from the submissive veil which covered both hair and chin. One particularly vituperative lyric attacks the headdresses worn by 'giddy girls':

In hell,
With devils they shall dwell
Because of cauls that clog and cleave to cheeks that swell.[5]

16 Lovers' scene.
*Ivory mirror case, early fourteenth century.
At this period, both male and female dress is modest and loose-fitting. With regard to women, moralists could only complain of their long trains, and headdresses which revealed more of the face and neck than the previous layers of linen veils.*

Friar Waldeby, an Austin friar, and later Archbishop of York, likened women to chimneys, graceful and whitened on the outside but full of smoke and blackness within; finding this parallel pleasing, he says that women 'ornament their head like the chimney top with garlands, crowns and gems set therein; nevertheless nothing comes forth thence but foul smoke and temptation to lechery'.[6]

Towards the middle of the fourteenth century we begin to see a radical change in men's dress, from the ample toga-like long gowns and mantles, to a short and tight tunic which revealed both the shape of the body and the tightly hosed legs. Contemporaries looked on in amazement as the tunic became shorter and tighter in the 1340s, one French chronicler attributing the defeat of his countrymen at the battle of Crécy (1346) to their pride in the latest fashions which God punished. Not only did they wear gowns gathered or pleated at the sides – 'fronciées sur les rains comme femmes', but their tunics were so short that they revealed their genitals, especially when bending down before their lords:

> les uns avoient robes si courtes qu'il ne leur venoient que aux nasches, et quant il se bassoient pour servir un seigneur, il monstroient leur braies et ce qui estoit dedens à ceux qui estoient derrière eux.[7]

Suddenly a host of new extravagant fashions seemed to be around, with an equal number of critics to condemn them. John of Reading, for example, attributed many of the fashions he disliked – long streamers to sleeves, pointed hoods which made people look like demons, and women who emphasized their buttocks by wearing fox-tails under their tight gowns – to Philippa of Hainault and her entourage when she came to England to marry Edward III in 1326. Blaming foreigners for sartorial extravagance was to be a feature of complaints about dress for many hundreds of years.

Echoing the complaints of the French chronicler, John of Reading finds the new short tunics (*vestibus curtissimis*) both foolish and indecorous; they had to be fastened to the hose by points or laces, which, he says, were often called 'harlots'. And the hose were so tight it was impossible to kneel in them.[8]

By the 1360s when these comments were made, the tunic or doublet was very short indeed, leading to its prohibition as 'dissolute' by Pope Urban V; but this was to no avail, the fashion becoming even more extreme by the end of the century. With the new emphasis on the legs, both hose and footwear assumed a new importance. Hose, according to the *Eulogium Historiarum* (1362) were often made of two colours – *mi-parti* or motley – and shoes had long

17 Weeper from the tomb of Edward III c. *1377–1386*.
Westminster Abbey.
There is a considerable time lag between the first scandalized references to the short, tight, male tunic, and its appearance in surviving art. By the late 1370s, the tunic is very short and tight, the body shape being emphasized by the large buttons down the centre front, and on the sleeve, and the elaborate jewelled belt on the hips.

points or curved peaks more than a finger in length, which resembled devils' claws. This fashion was popularly supposed to come from Cracow in Poland (the shoes were sometimes called *cracowes*) and was well established by the time that Richard II married Anne of Bohemia (who ruled Poland), in 1382. Such styles, says the scornful author of the *Eulogium Historiarum*,

45

were only suitable for players or buffoons: 'such young men are lions in the hall, and hares in the field'.[9]

Whether these young men so fashionably dressed were fit only for a comfortable indoor life, and not a martial one, we do not know, but the impressive amount of contemporary comment in existence at least testifies to a widespread belief in increased luxury in dress.

Some moralists equated sensuality with luxurious fabrics. Robert Rypon, for example, in a late-fourteenth-century sermon, describes the history of mankind in terms of the clothing worn; first men were naked and then in skins 'in token that through his sin man was become like the beasts', then woollen garments, and then, 'through the more ample nourishing of carnal delight' garments of linen, and lastly silken clothes made 'from the entrails of worms'.[10] Clothes for *Piers Plowman* signified the state's corruption; the figure of Bribery in Langland's poem of the early 1360s is dressed in scarlet (here it is a very expensive woollen cloth, not necessarily red in colour), and her fingers are covered with rubies, diamonds and sapphires.

Rich and costly fabrics, sumptuous furs, and large amounts of jewellery demonstrated wealth and status; medieval princes underlined their position with a conspicuous display of finery. The registers of the Black Prince, for example, list thousands of pounds spent on jewels; these included buttons, brooches, belt and girdle buckles. Jewels were often scattered over the surface of the clothing; *bezants* were decorative, often sparkling and sometimes jewelled discs which were stitched on in thousands on to gowns, tunics and mantles, as were seed pearls ordered in huge quantities.[11]

In contrast to the finery suitable to a victorious nation – and the English crown was very successful during the early years of the Hundred Years War – lavish displays of wealth were regarded as at least inappropriate if not immoral in times of trouble. When the French king was captured at the battle of Poitiers (1356), it was resolved that during the captivity of the king in England, 'no man or woman was to wear gold or silver, or pearls, or miniver, or gris. Neither must they wear garments or hoods that were decoratively cut about ... nor any other extravagant fashion whatever in their dress'.[12]

It was taken for granted that governments had the right to curb extravagance and luxury which could lead to the corruption of the state. Although there were isolated examples in earlier periods, it was in the fourteenth century that there were the first serious attempts to control and codify dress. Sumptuary laws in England aimed to protect native English textile industries (notably the important woollen trade) – the first act of 1337 states that only the immediate royal family were entitled to wear imported silks – but the main purpose was to enforce class distinctions in dress, which it was felt had, due to an increase in luxury, been eroded.[13]

The 1363 act was much more comprehensive; maybe the attacks by the moralists on dress had had some impact. The preamble to the act deplores 'the outrageous and excessive apparel of divers people against their estate and degree', and lists in detail what people were *not* allowed to wear, and by a process of elimination what they *could* wear. Income and class determined the fabrics worn; ploughmen and agricultural labourers could only wear coarse locally woven woollen cloths, servants and artisans could wear no silk nor jewellery – an especial prohibition was placed on the wearing of buttons which, as fairly recent and fashionable innovations, were reserved for the upper classes. Gentlemen who were not knights (and their wives), if in receipt of rents of more than £200 a year, could wear less expensive silks and furs like miniver; those with a lower income were limited to cloth. Knights on the other hand could wear most silks except cloth of gold, and most furs except ermine which was reserved for royalty.

Grossly simplified, this is the gist of the legislation, except for a mention of the middle classes. The feudal system had not envisaged a merchant class; how far could the fourteenth-century legislators allow such people to dress like their betters? They devised a system whereby merchants/citizens worth £500 per annum could dress like gentlemen worth £100; if they had the munificent income of £1000, they were entitled to dress like gentlemen with £200.[14]

It was immensely cumbersome and very imprecise; it must have been unworkable for it was repealed the following year. The system's importance lies in the philosophy behind this unenforceable ideal, and to indicate the sartorial temptations which those in authority were keen to stamp out in order to establish a clear division between the classes. As one bishop remarked:

> as for pride of dress, so foppish are folk of the present day that it is impossible to distinguish between knight and squire, between cleric and layman, between the wife of an earl and the wife of a burgess.[15]

Pride, and its downfall, is a theme in many of the moral treatises which flourished in the fourteenth and fifteenth centuries; pride was one of the seven deadly sins, and, said Chaucer's Parson 'the general roote of alle harmes', so it was important to prevent it in the young and impressionable. Thus the most famous manual of them all, the *Book of the Knight of La Tour Landry*, was composed by the author, a soldier and a gentleman of letters from Anjou, as advice for his daughters, in the form of moral tales, in 1371–2. It was immensely popular – the English translation was one of Caxton's best-sellers. Like all such works, most of the attacks on women's finery are very generalized and not specific; women, for example, should not be the first to adopt new fashions especially those 'of women of straunge contrey', but once the fashion is established it would be too singular to ignore it.[16] Women should, he says, wear their best clothes not just to impress 'folke of astate', but on holy days; on the other hand he tells the warning story of one woman who kept the congregation waiting while she took so long to dress herself that, when she looked in the mirror, she saw the devil there, which so frightened her that she was never again late for church.

Singled out for specific condemnation were the elaborate headdresses of the later fourteenth century; sometimes these took the form of padded rolls (*bourrelets*) which, La Tour Landry states, the devil so likes as evidence of women's vanity, that he can often be seen sitting between the horns. Some women have even taken to wearing wired headdresses 'with highe, longe pynnes like a iebet (gibbet)'.[17]

The devil also features in a story demonstrating the wickedness of cosmetics, a crime far worse than committing adultery. A knight saw in a dream his deceased wife suffering torments in hell because in life she had plucked her eyebrows, and the hair on the top of her forehead, 'to make her selff the fayrer to the plesinge of the worlde'. For every hair she had plucked out, the devil thrust a burning awl or needle into her brain, while another devil smeared her face with hot pitch, oil and tar because she had 'peinted her visage'.[18]

Unappealing though many of these stories are to the modern ear, this treatise with its emphasis on the weakness of women, their moral delinquency, is typical of the deep misogynist strain in much medieval literature. Women were seen to use their newly-revealed bodily charms, their tight-fitting gowns and sleeves, their décolletage and their face-painting, to ensnare men. The last quarter of the fourteenth century was remarkable for the low-cut necklines to women's dress; the enchantress in *Sir Gawain and the Green Knight* (c. 1370) tries, unsuccessfully, to tempt the hero not just with her best clothes and jewels, but with 'hir brest bare bifore, and bihinde eke',[19] and the French poet Eustache Deschamps in the 1380s believed that such low necklines drove many men to think of rape.[20]

By the end of the century, the short tight tunics worn by men and attacked for many years by the moralists had reached their limits of brevity. Hose with separate legs and tying with laces to the waist gave way to an all-in-one garment like our modern tights. Chaucer's *Parson's Tale* – in its fear of heavenly judgement, so unlike the earlier tales – attacks not only the 'horrible disordinat scantinesse of

THE WORLD, THE FLESH AND THE DEVIL

18 Figure of Vanity.
Apocalypse *tapestries, Angers* c. *1380.*
Vanity at this period is usually depicted as a very fashionable woman combing her hair, and obsessed with her appearance. The artist has given her a skin-tight, low-cut dress, which emphasizes the breast and hips. So tight and immodest is the dress in the 1380s, that in public it is increasingly covered by the voluminous houppelande.

19 The Great Whore of Babylon c. *1400.*
It is particularly apt that the Whore of Babylon – described as richly arrayed 'and decked with gold and precious stones and pearls' – should so often be shown as a Queen, in high fashion of the most seductive kind. Here she wears a tight-fitting gown trimmed with ermine; the neck is cut low, and a jewelled chain draws attention to her hips and legs, as she holds up 'a golden cup ... full of abominations and filthiness of her fornications'.

clothyng', the tunics so short they 'covere nat the shameful membres of man', but the fact that the hose were often coloured red and white, so that it seemed that half the 'shameful privee membres weren flayne'.[21]

By the 1380s both men and women had taken tight clothes as far as they could go, and had begun to wear over their doublet or dress an ample over-gown called a *houppelande*. As a reaction to the skimpiness of doublet and dress, the houppelande was voluminous in cut, with sweeping train and huge sleeves; in addition the edges of the fabric were cut into decorative shapes, and the whole outfit was laden with clinking *bezants* or asymmetrically draped jewelled chains. Chaucer's Parson, who equates outward display with spiritual pride, condemns cutwork or dagging on the gowns which are so long that they trail in the mud, and in William Staunton's *Visions of Purgatory* (c. 1409) he describes 'some there with collars of gold about their necks and some of silver, and some men I

49

THE WORLD, THE FLESH AND THE DEVIL

20 Dance of the courtiers c. *1400*.
Roman de la Rose MS c. *1400*.
The men wear either tunics, or short houppelandes *with wide sleeves; the torso is heavily padded, so that the upper part of the body forms an hour-glass shape Criticism was also levelled at the very tight hose and long pointed shoes, which made vigorous movement impossible.*

Among the women, the queen wears a very cutaway sideless surcote, which reveals the tight-fitting gown beneath it. Gowns generally are very tight-fitting, the bust being further emphasized by a low neckline.

saw with gay girdles of silver and gold ... some with more jagges on their clothes than whole cloth, some had their clothes full of gingles and belles of silver ...'²²

Much moral comment on dress and manners at the end of the fourteenth century is informed by regret for the virtues of a past age, highlighted by the troubles and unrest of the present. During the troubled reign of Richard II (1377–1399), it seemed to contemporaries that extremes in fantastic dress were worn by too many of ignoble rank, symbolic of the fact that the king was unable or unwilling to curb the powers of his over-mighty nobles and their large retinues. Thomas Occleve, in an undated poem (but probably of the 1390s) entitled *Of Pride and wast clothing of Lordis men* laments the fact that lords allow their squires and servants to wear ultra-fashionable clothes – the gowns are grown so huge that tailors will have to cut them up in fields, and the sleeves are so vast that if a lord is attacked, they encumber his men in his defence and make them as useless as women.²³ Contemporary attacks on Richard included the claim that he had allowed such 'lordis' too much power, preoccupied as he was with favourites, fashion and the patronage of art. Although to us this can be seen as somewhat exaggerated,²⁴ there was a definite feeling that excessive concentration on fashion had helped to produce political instability. The poem *Richard the Redeless*, composed just before Richard's deposition in September 1399, states bluntly that fashionable men are evil councillors; it is, says the author, no crime to wear 'comliche clothinge', according to one's estate, but it is a crime to be obsessed by such fads as the sleeves that slide on the ground, and the dagging or 'kervynge' of clothes which costs twenty times as much as the stuff itself.²⁵ Wisdom and morality are rarely to be found at courts – a theme to be often repeated in the future.

Although contemporaries were quick to

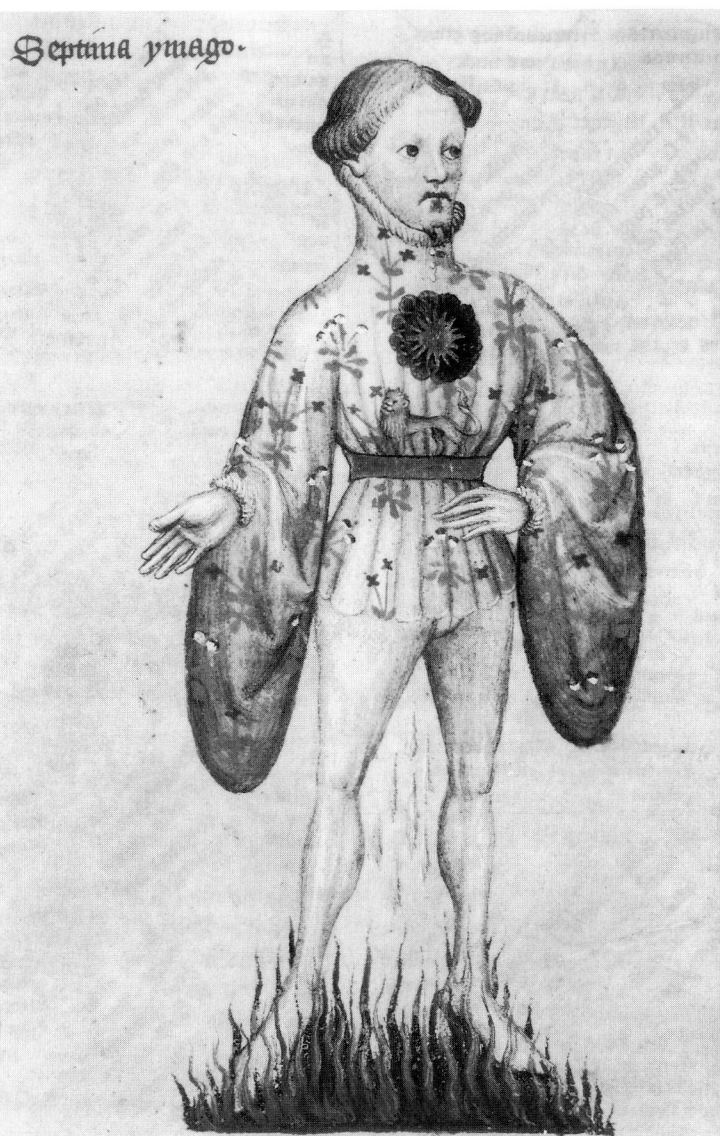

22 John Foxton's Liber Cosmographiae *1408. The short pleated* houppelande *hardly covers what Chaucer describes as 'the shameful privee membres', which are tightly covered by close-fitting hose.*

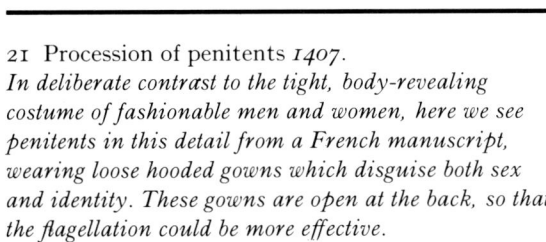

21 Procession of penitents *1407.*
In deliberate contrast to the tight, body-revealing costume of fashionable men and women, here we see penitents in this detail from a French manuscript, wearing loose hooded gowns which disguise both sex and identity. These gowns are open at the back, so that the flagellation could be more effective.

23 Detail from a Virgil MS c. *1400*.
Moralists were quick to condemn the fashion for cutting fabric into decorative scallop shapes; this 'kervynge' can be seen both in the short houppelande, *and in the hood which is twisted into a hat.*

blame innovations in dress on an unpopular and cosmopolitan king, the trends established in the late fourteenth century – the distortion of the body shape by elongated skirts to gowns and huge sleeves, long pointed shoes, and elaborately contrived hoods and headdresses – became even more bizarre in the fifteenth century. Women's gowns became increasingly tight-fitted over the bust, some gowns with front openings even revealing the nipples,[26] and the waist was emphasized by a wide belt with decorative jewelled buckle. The female silhouette for much of the century was elongated and spiky, an obvious way of increasing height being to exaggerate the already high headdresses. *Bourrelets* were often placed on top of jewelled nets, or caps. An equally fashionable alternative was the steeple headdress in the form of a slender cone with yards of floating veil. Monstrelet records in his chronicle that in 1428 a certain Friar Thomas Couette preached in Flanders and Artois against these high headdresses, encouraging children to shout abuse at women wearing them. For a short time for the sake of a quiet life, women wore a cap 'somewhat like those worn by peasants and people of low degree', but as soon as he left the area, they 'began to resume their former colossal headdresses and wore them even higher than before'.[27] It might have been some comfort to these persecuted ladies that the friar was later burnt in Rome for heresy.

Religion was often invoked by those who attacked certain styles in dress. John Lydgate, in an early fifteenth-century ballad on horned headdresses, gave as his firm belief that 'hornes were cast away' at the time of the Virgin Mary who was content to wear merely a 'kovercheef'.[28] By the middle of the century the horns are still being attacked; the author of the poem *Le Miroir aux Dames* describes this fashion as not only contrary to nature but dangerous to souls, for when the Devil was chased from Paradise, he wore such horns. While admitting that the veil is ordained for women as symbolic of their subjection to men, he accuses women of – literally – elevating this sign of penitence from concealment to enticement.[29] Covering the head had, as we have seen, deep religious significance, and to many moralists it seemed particularly scandalous that women treated this frivolously. Fashionable headdresses were not only immoral in themselves, but because they were arranged in such complicated layers involving ribbons, pins and nets, they occupied a large amount of time which could better be spent on good works.

In reply to women who say that they wish to be pleasing in dress to their husbands, *Le Miroir aux Dames* states sternly that while it is necessary for a woman to be obedient to her husband, it is equally important for her not to lose her soul, for extremes in dress result in eternal damnation. Yet by the end of the fourteenth century a more robust and reasoned attitude to the temptations of female finery appears in print. Attacking the usual hypocritical male attitude towards women, Chaucer's Wife of Bath in the *Canterbury Tales* addresses men:

Thou seyst also, that if we make us gay
With clothyng, and with precious array,
That it is peril of oure chastitee

but concludes that 'al the vileynye. That ye of wommen write' is not worth a 'boterflye'.³⁰

But the most famous defence of women was by the authoress Christine de Pisan, the first woman to live by her pen, and not averse to becoming embroiled in controversies, such as her spirited challenge to the view expressed in the *Roman de la Rose* that every woman had her price. In her *Book of the City of Ladies* (1405), an allegory in which Reason, Justice

24 St Anthony led to the armourer's shop *1426*.
A French MS, illuminated by Robin Fournier, of the Life of St Anthony.
St Anthony's trials included temptation by beautiful women. Here a queen and her attendant maidens conduct him through their city to an armourer's shop.

Only queens and virgins were allowed long hair, but otherwise the devilish ladies – notice the horns in their headdresses – wear much the same high-waisted houppelande, *although that of the queen has a long train and huge sleeves which trail on the ground. The artist adds horns to the padded 'horns' (*bourrelets*) of the fashionable headdress, a visual reinforcement of much contemporary literary comment that such headdresses were the work of the devil.*

THE WORLD, THE FLESH AND THE DEVIL

25 The Virgin and Child c. 1450–2.
J. Fouquet.
There seems no reason to doubt that this is a portrait of Agnès Sorel, mistress to Charles VII of France. The role of Madonna gives her a chance to be depicted in unlaced kirtle revealing a startlingly pneumatic bosom. The custom for women to pluck their eyebrows and the hair on their forehead, so denounced by moralists, is clearly in evidence here.

and Rectitude build the City of Ladies away from the threat of male attacks, the author says blame has been unfairly placed on women who enjoy being beautiful and well dressed which they enjoy for itself and not as a means to attract men. It is natural for women (and indeed men) to 'delight in coquettishness or in beautiful and rich clothes', and given the present state of fashion and the customs of the time, 'it would be difficult for them to avoid it, no matter how great their virtues'.[31]

Fifteenth-century dress on the whole is flamboyant in style for both sexes, tending to a distortion of the body: such Gothic extremes derived from the prevailing Burgundian fashions which, due to royal and trading connections, were prominent in England.

The main indoors garment for men was the tight-fitting doublet or *pourpoint*, which by the middle of the century was often padded on shoulders and chest, to give a somewhat top-heavy appearance when worn with long pointed shoes and tight hose. By the early 1460s an early form of the codpiece was in use to protect the genital area.

A ballad against excess in apparel in the middle of the century attacks the 'short stuffede dowblettes' and 'pleytid gowyns' (these were even shamefully worn by priests), the 'long peked shone', the 'hygh cappis' (tall sugarloaf beaver hats and caps were very popular), and the long hair which falls over the face and gets in the eyes.[32] Other anonymous doggerel poems pay particular attention to the immodesty of the leg coverings; the hose were apparently so tight that if the wearer bent his legs too vigorously, they would split at the knee.[33]

Such outrage was caused by these fashions that they are mentioned specifically in the sumptuary legislation of 1463. This stated that those of yeomen status and under were not to have wool or cotton stuffing in their doublets, and those under the rank of a lord were enjoined not to wear 'any gown, jacket or coat unless it be of such length that the same may cover his privy members and buttocks'.[34] This was clearly not effective for the 1483 act re-states this point, implying that some men had tried

26 *Detail from* Jean Miélot's Miracles de Nostre Dame c. 1456.
Illustrated by Jean le Tavernier.
St Jerome points out to a companion the devil sitting on the train of a fashionable bourgeoise of Bethlehem. This apparition is presumably a sign of her immorality in apeing the dress of her betters, notably the wide belt with jewelled clasp and the fur-trimmed train of her over-gown.

to avoid being fined for short gowns by claiming that when seated, their dress was decent. The 1483 act incorporates the words 'he being upright', so there could be no confusion.[35] There were severe financial penalties for tailors (as well as for their customers) if they made such offending garments, as there were for shoemakers if they made shoes with points or 'pikes' longer than two inches, which were forbidden by the 1463 act. In the chronicle of William Gregory we read that the Pope forbad long

27 *Detail from* Froissart's Chronicles *c. 1470. Men's dress at this time causes particular outrage due to the short gowns, tight hose and immensely long 'pikes' to the shoes; the 'hygh cappis' and long hair were also attacked.*

pointed shoes, but to no avail; 'sum men sayd that they wolde wear longe pykys whethyr Pope wylle or nylle, for they sayde the Pope's curse wolde not kylle a flye'.[36]

This kind of attitude ensured virtual non-compliance with any sumptuary legislation, for there was no means of enforcing it, in spite of the often repeated government dismay at the 'excessive and inordinate array and apparel, to the great displeasure of God' which abounded in the land. Both the 1463 and the 1483 acts tried again to limit the most expensive silks to the upper reaches of society, but the considerable increase in a whole range of imported silks from Italy made this impossible. In the same way, the acts had virtually to recognize the fact that people of all classes could and would wear furs if they could afford them – sable and ermine for lords, marten and miniver for all those who were worth £40 a year, and lambskins for those earning only 40 shillings per annum.[37]

Richness and luxury and a general flowering of the arts are often manifested in societies supposedly in a decadent state, and as the Middle Ages waned, the theatre, tournaments, and heraldic entertainments provided a colourful display where allegory and symbolism played a key part. This was also applied to dress, where particular colours linked to certain garments provided a moral commentary on the state of the soul. As white was the colour of purity, it was the obvious colour for the shirt or the chemise, as the heraldic treatise *Le Blason des Couleurs en Armes, Livrées et Devises*, composed by one of the heralds to the king of Aragon, tells us; under the heading 'De l'habit moral d'une femme', we are told that the white linen indicates chastity.[38] Black was not only a good colour for the male doublet – it signified magnanimity – but it was for women a sign of humility; it was thus particularly suitable for their shoes, for black 'dénote simplicité ... qui démonstre aux dames qu'ilz doivent marcher en toute simplicité et non en orgeuil'.[39]

A similar theme is the subject of Olivier de la Marche's *Le Parement et Triumphes des Dames*, composed in about 1493–4, which attributes in verse some moral attribute to each item in a fashionable woman's wardrobe, one of the rather ponderous jokes so popular in the period.[40] The woman first puts on her 'chemise d'honnestete', then a kirtle or 'cotte de chastete', which should also be white; this is followed by a stomacher which should be of red silk because it covers the heart, and laced with blue for this is the colour both of holiness (the Virgin always wears a blue mantle) and of loyalty. After the gown has been put on – Olivier's ideal lady wears cloth of gold, or purple embroidered with gold, and furred with ermine – then the accessories have to be decided upon. These include a purse which has to be of rich material and jewelled to indicate liberality, and a girdle which was, perhaps, the most important element of a woman's dress. The girdle, often richly jewelled and decorated with mottoes and devices, was often a lover's gift,

THE WORLD, THE FLESH AND THE DEVIL

an intimate present from a man to his beloved or his wife. A reproach to an unfaithful lady was to remove her girdle, as happens in the courtly romance of *Le Petit Jehan de Saintré*, where the hero divests his untrue lady of her blue silk girdle tipped with gold, saying:

> 'How have you the heart, Lady, to wear a blue girdle? The colour blue doth signify loyalty, and you are the most unloyal; verily, you shall wear it no more'. With that he took from her her girdle, and folded it, and put it in his bosom.[41]

28 'Lecherye' 1476.
From The Mirroure of the Worlde.
The Mirroure of the Worlde *is a translation of a thirteenth-century moral treatise, in which the Seven Deadly Sins are discussed. These include lechery (although the word is often interchangeable with 'luxury' and 'lust'), shown here riding on a goat, a well-known symbol of lust, and dressed in the most fashionable – and therefore most sinful – costume. This consists of the tight-fitting, somewhat attenuated Burgundian gown (worn all over Northern Europe), and the typically English 'butterfly' headdress.*

29 'Superbia' *from a table-top depicting the Seven Deadly Sins.*
H. Bosch.
Pride is one of the Seven Deadly Sins, and this otherwise modestly dressed Netherlandish housewife demonstrates her excessive love of such finery as jewelled belts, necklaces and fine linen as she gazes into a mirror held up by a devil.

Finally, the fashionable woman, Olivier's paragon, puts on her headdress, which at the time he is writing, would be either a steeple headdress with fine linen veil, or the more subdued French hood faced with velvet which framed the face. While in England, the very unicorn-like steeple headdresses do not appear to have been as popular as they were in the Netherlands, English women had by the middle of the century evolved their own styles, the most fashionable being fine, soaring wings of starched linen stretched over wires and placed on a cap. Such linen and even silk 'couvrechefs' were singled out for attention in the sumptuary law of 1463; the best quality were imported and as they 'do induce great charge and cost' in the realm, their cost was limited to ten shillings.

As we have seen, however, sumptuary legislation in England in the fifteenth century tended to concentrate on the more outrageous aspects of male dress, a theme that was to gather momentum in the early sixteenth century. Compared to the Gothic spikiness of women's dress in the middle of the fifteenth century, by the end of the period, women were fairly modest in their costume, which did not, however mean that they were able to escape from censure. At the end of Olivier's recital of female fashion disguised as moral homily, the last accessory to be picked up is a mirror, to bring to mind the mutability of beauty, and that all the the finery in the world cannot prevent women from the inevitable:

> Le noble corps la mort le met a fin.

Death seemed, as Huizinga points out in his *The Waning of the Middle Ages* (1924), to be very much in the air, a melancholy and sometimes even an absorbing occupation, to be played with by poets and conjured up in the theatre and in the arts. No doubt it was this feeling, along with the horror inspired by frequent war, pestilence and famine, that helped to produce the *Danse Macabre*, the Dance of Death – the visual depiction of the procession of men and women from high to low as they step out to Death's call – which first appears in the 1480s, and then enters the realm of literature. The Dance of Death also appears to have been an actual mimed, dramatic performance, a kind of visual aid to the preacher. Christianity had had no difficulty in finding scape-goats for the economic and political failings of the world; it had found in certain forms of dress the temptations of the world, the flesh and the devil, and had tried to instil fear into those who took fashion seriously by emphasizing the democracy of the common fate of all.

4
The Ship of Fools

But the proude man to the end he may seeme magnificent, doth love ... to have delycat garments and pretious ornaments. And what is a man decked with pretious thinges, but onely a Sepulchre paynted & white lymed without, & full of filthinesse within?

George Gascoigne,
The Droomme of Doomesday, 1576

The garments ar gone that longed to honestye,
And in newe sortes newe fooles ar arrayde,
Despisynge the custom of good antiquyte ...
They dyfforme that figure that God hymselfe hath made
On pryde and abusion thus ar theyr myndes layde.

Alexander Barclay,
The Shyp of Folys of the Worlde, 1508

Sebastian Brant's *Narrenschiff* (1494) – freely translated by Alexander Barclay – uses the idea of a ship of fools to discuss the worldliness and foolish customs of men, who are only too ready to be led astray by Superbia (Pride) which was begotten by Lucifer.

A kind of restlessness was in the air by the end of the fifteenth century, a questioning of accepted values both in the past and in the present. With the Renaissance belatedly arriving in northern Europe in the early sixteenth century, it seemed to contemporaries that they were living through a period of startling changes not only in religion, politics, and society itself, but in one of its most obvious manifestations, dress. The world seemed to be opening out to encompass unbelievable standards of luxury from abroad, as – with the accession of Henry VIII in 1509 – England entered fully into the international spirit of the Renaissance. The sixteenth century is marked not just by this taste for luxury, but by a passion for startling effects in dress which led, by the second half of the period, into a display of conspicuous consumption and a sometimes grotesque distortion of the body which moralists denounced with unparalleled venom.

Determined to be the complete Renaissance monarch, Henry VIII was devoted to every kind of expensive and cosmopolitan innovation, including the masquerade from Italy. Halle's *Chronicle*, describing the early years of his reign, is full of accounts of lavish court masques, at which the king and his court would dress up in elaborate exotic costumes, sometimes as Turks in long robes embroidered with gold and crimson velvet hats, sometimes as Russians in striped caftans and boots, and sometimes as Germans in yellow and white slashed satin.[1]

With regard to men's dress, German fashions had been the dominant influence since the last decade of the fifteenth century; in the 1490s, elegant Burgundian elongation had given way to a kind of squat solidity, expressed especially in wide-lapelled gowns with puffed sleeves, wide

30 A landsknecht and a woman *1516*.
Urs Graf.
The exaggerated virility of early-sixteenth-century dress is clearly depicted in the soldier's tight-fitting doublet and hose. The huge, slashed doublet sleeves deliberately unbalance the proportions of the body, and are the dominant feature of the costume; beside this flamboyant dress, that of the woman is quite insignificant.

flat hats and square-shaped shoes. It is popularly supposed that at the battle of Grandson in 1476, when the last duke of Burgundy was killed, the Swiss mercenary soldiers involved plundered his baggage train, attaching strips of silk to their clothing, and creating a strange tattered look which was quickly copied by young Germans who assimilated it into their costume by slashing the fabric of their doublets and gowns – even, sometimes, their hose – so that a brightly contrasting colour showed beneath.

This fashion arrived in England in the 1480s and was apparently widespread by the following decade. Lamenting the passing of the dress of olden times which was felt to be of a pure simplicity unknown to modern youth, the Poet Laureate John Skelton in his *The Manner of the World Nowadays* equated such 'cutting and jagging', such slashed coats and other 'vain clothing' as evidence of the deterioration of morals and manners.[2] In a similar vein, Alexander Barclay comments that foolish men, 'counterfayt Caytifs'

ar not content
As God hath you made; his warke is despysed.
Ye thinke you more crafty than God omnipotent
Unstable is your mynde; that shewes by your garment.

Honest dress, he continues, is a thing of the past, for all men flock to new fashions; 'despysynge the custom of good antiquyte', they 'go ful wantonly in dissolute aray' with 'moche unmanerly blasinge and garded'.[3]

The last reference is to the custom of slashing fabrics to show bright contrasting colours beneath, and the fashion for adding bands of decorative material either sewn down or left to float free; in many cases there was so much surface decoration that the fabric beneath was hidden. Barclay talks of doublets with sleeves blazing like a crane's wings, for it was customary to have the sleeves of a different colour, often tied into the shoulder with decorative laces similar to those which held the slashed openings on dress together.

To add to the air of artistic disarray and deliberate slovenliness which is such a part of

31 Two landsknechte, a woman and Death *1524*.
Urs Graf.
The exaggerated, asymmetrical, and bizarrely tattered costume worn by these landsknechte, is most clearly shown in the work of Urs Graf, who was one of their number. Death is seated in a tree, reminding the participants of his constant threat, and that they should enjoy themselves while they can. The dress of the camp follower, with her slashed sleeves and jagged, feather-trimmed hat, echoes that of the soldiers.

the new, individualistic Renaissance attitude to clothing, men wore, says Barclay, huge-sleeved shirts (much of which was revealed through undone seams or slashes in the doublet), as big as surplices but cut so low that they left 'theyr neckes naked'. The doublet was often quite abbreviated, allowing much of the shirt – which was often pleated or trimmed with linen cutwork or gold and silver embroidery – to billow through. The fashionable man would wear very tight hose, sometimes striped or *mi-parti*, and the modest codpiece of the late fifteenth century, virtually just a gusset covering the front opening of the hose, now assumed the shape of a permanent erection, sometimes decorated in tassels and embroidery. Sometimes the upper parts of the hose were also slashed, and increasingly trimmed; these were called *upper-stocks* and increasingly detached in construction from the *lower-stocks* which we would call stockings.

The male body appeared unnaturally distorted with tight lower limbs, and a massive torso which was created not only by the bulk of the shirt, and the slashed and layered doublet, but also by a wide-shouldered and often padded or fur-lined coat. It is curious that the Renaissance artists' adulation of classical dress and drapery is not reflected in early-sixteenth-century men's dress in the north of Europe (in Italy there was more reverence for a soft line and a natural body shape); the ideal male image was of a somewhat exaggerated and overwhelming virility.

Although we think of the artistically tattered styles as German, they were almost as quickly adopted in France, and many moralists, like Barclay thus ascribed them; it was from France (along with the pox), he says, that 'variable Garmentes' came, which could dazzle and seduce young women. And in the anonymous poem, *A treatise of a Galaunt* of about 1522, we are told that pride – manifested through shameful copying of foreign and particularly French styles in dress – is the undoing of England. Particularly under attack were the huge collars to men's gowns, their coats shredded into streamers, and their shocking 'newe broched doublettes open at the breste'.[4]

The complaint that men were 'arrayed as women', which the poem makes, is less likely to refer to their long gowns, than to what was seen by contemporaries as an almost feminine delight in colour and in the bizarre fantasy of much of their clothing and its decoration; the low-necked shirts and doublets were also frequently attacked as immodest and unmasculine. At times it seemed to many commentators that, like at the court itself, fashionable men were in perpetual fancy dress. It is perhaps no accident that the carnival, which had its roots in pagan fertility rites, and which was noted for its sexual licence – including cross-dressing – flourished in the sixteenth century although it was later to be increasingly censured by those of Protestant inclination.[5]

It is men who are the dominant visual images of the early sixteenth century; no wonder, as Barclay says, it is men by their clothes who are likely to seduce women, and not vice versa. Compared to the almost fairy-tale Gothic elegance of fifteenth-century women's dress, that of the early sixteenth century has been called by one authority, the 'Flemish hausfrau' look, with its demure hair-concealing hood, and modest square-necked gown, whose only notable feature was the funnel-like sleeves often turned back with a contrasting colour fabric, or fur. Although the styles were not extreme, the fabrics and decoration could be costly; French hoods had a decorative edging (a *habilliment* or *billiment*) which could be made of precious or semi-precious stones, and both overgown and undergown were made of sumptuous and costly fabrics.[6]

The only complaint which moralists could make of female dress, apart from the time and money spent on it, was about the long train of the gown which swept up the dirt with it, causing dust, and annoying passers-by, and making the women themselves filthy, the sight of their begrimed thighs enough

> to stanche the lust
> Of ony man that saw thame naikit.

This was the comment of the courtier and poet

Sir David Lindsay who composed, probably at some time in the 1530s, *Ane Supplicatioun to the kingis Grace in Contempioun of Syde Taillis*. Such 'syde taillis', i.e. long tails or trains, are not only a waste of cloth, but also a cause of envy, for, although strictly speaking they should have been worn only by court ladies, they were being worn by those lower down the social scale in a wicked endeavour to emulate their betters; this, he says, is a sign of pride,

> And Pryde proceidis of the Devil.[7]

It is impossible to know if Lindsay had in mind the actual prohibition of such long trains, although he urges this course of action on the king. Although such legislation was evidently ineffective in previous centuries, the authorities in the sixteenth century made a determined effort to enforce such acts on the people.

They did so for a number of reasons, some protectionist and some hierarchical. The acts passed in the sixteenth century lay great emphasis on the growing taste for luxury which might lead people to impoverish themselves. The 1533 act, for example, attacks 'sumptuous and costly aray and apparel' which contributes to the 'detriment of the common weal', and to 'the utter impoverishment and undoing of many inexpert and light persons inclined to pride, mother of all vices ...'.[8] The first sumptuary law passed by Parliament under Henry VIII in 1510 forbad men under the degree of a lord to wear any cloth of gold or silver, sables, or woollen cloth made out of England, Wales, Ireland or Calais. Those of less than knightly status (with some exceptions) were forbidden to wear silk velvets, satin or damask; a further proclamation of the next year forbad any but lords and knights to wear silk of any sort.[9] The 1533 act went further in its detailed list of luxurious elements in dress which were forbidden to the non-noble; these included prized furs like black genet (the skin of the civet cat), which was limited to royalty, gold chains and ornaments, and richly jewelled *billiments* on women's headdresses. Because men's shirts were increasingly a focus of attention, the 1533 act banned gold, silver and silk embroidery and

32 Two views of an unknown English Lady c. *1535*. H. Holbein.
The all-concealing English hood, and the modest use of slashing on the sleeves of the kirtle, indicates a far more subdued appearance than the deformed, exaggerated styles worn by men at this period. Surprisingly, moralists did not criticize the fairly low-cut neckline to the dress, as much as they complained about the long train, which not only swept up dirt but was a symbol of pride.

silk ribbon to those under the status of a knight; 'ryven shertes' – that is shirts incorporating cutwork (cutting out threads of the linen and securing the exposed threads with needlework) – being highly fashionable, were also limited to those of knightly rank and above.

A new dynasty concerned with propaganda and display, and, in some cases a new aristocracy (replacing those who, during, or as a result of the Wars of the Roses had died or been stripped of their titles) were determined to enforce their status through clothing, against the ever increasing claims of the gentry and the mercantile classes. These latter, along with a growing number of professional people, were able to travel more to the towns, especially London, and attend court. There were thus increased opportunities to find out what the fashions were and help in their dissemination.

Greater social mobility made sumptuary legislation even more difficult to achieve, although the 1510 act offered the inducement of giving half the fine imposed to the informer. Some sporadic attempts were made to put the laws into effect; Cardinal Wolsey in 1515 sent commissions into the shires to enforce the act of 1510, but this only added to his unpopularity and was soon dropped.[10] The act itself almost seemed to recognize the impossibility of the task, for not only were those who had been fined and stripped of their offending garments enabled to sue for their return, but the king was empowered to grant licences of exemption, such dispensations increasing during his reign.

A growing number of thoughtful men during the century found sumptuary legislation both absurd in itself, and prone to make the law look foolish. Montaigne, for example, stated that the best way to prevent too much luxury in dress was 'to beget in men a contempt of gold and silk-weaving, as of vaine and unprofitable things', and furthermore, to limit rich stuffs to 'Enterlude-players, Harlots and Curtizans'.[11]

In this the great French essayist was following in the footsteps of Sir Thomas More whose *Utopia* (1516) was an ideal society where those who committed really shameful crimes were forced to wear gold jewellery and gold fetters, for jewels were seen as worthless toys.[12] In Utopia there were no tailors or dress-makers, for everyone wore the same kind of clothes, which the author does not describe except to say that they are made of wool or linen with no distinctions, for 'as long as the linen is white and the wool is clean, they don't care how fine or coarse the thread is'. Such garments which are 'quite pleasant to look at, they allow free movement of the limbs, they're equally suitable for hot and cold weather', are few in number and last a lifetime, for inhabitants of Utopia believe that those outside their country who are 'recklessly extravagant about clothes' are not necessarily 'any warmer or any better-looking'.[13]

Both More and Montaigne, while strongly disapproving of excessive luxury in dress, use weapons of satire rather than fierce invective to achieve their ends; dress is to be condemned as being ridiculous in itself, rather than as an indication of sin. More, while finding women – even in Utopia – to be rather irrational beings, would perhaps not agree with John Knox's diatribes against them in his *The First Blast of the Trumpet against the Monstrous Regiment of Women* (1558), an argument against the horror of female rulers which is not only 'repugnant to nature' but means the subversion of 'good order'. Women generally are attacked for their 'gorgious apparel' which is 'abominable and odiouse'.[14] For the next hundred or so years Puritan divines were almost to have a monopoly in hysterical invective against the sin of pride in clothing – especially in female dress.

In a land less riven by religious dissension, and more open to the moderating forces of classical reason and enlightenment, clothing was gradually becoming a part of good manners rather than an infallible indication of morals. One of the increasing refinements of the Renaissance, first established in Italy, was the desire to please and to codify standards of dress and behaviour. To the medieval notions of courage, liberality and loyalty, the Renaissance added good manners and charm of demeanour, a more civilized intercourse between the sexes. One book of etiquette, Alexander Piccolimini's *Raffaella* (1540), tries to establish the happy mean between an over-indulgence in fashion and the singularity of its avoidance. There is no medieval dislike of finery here, but a positive enjoyment of the prevailing different fashions in dress, provided they are worn with 'grace', which lies not only in their suitability regarding colours and styles to the wearer, but also in elegance of deportment. To gain the love of a worthy young man, a good complexion is essential, which must be achieved by art if necessary. Women should learn to make the best use of their good points; if she has good hands, a woman should draw attention to them by putting on and drawing off gloves, and if she has a fair breast, she may pretend she is just out of bed and not yet laced, 'so it will be known that her breast is of itself rounded and well-formed, and not shaped by under-proppers and such devices'.[15] Such tricks seem to be rather at variance with the author's injunction to women to be modest, even if he stresses that they should be employed with subtlety. To the understandable comment that surely God will know of such subterfuges, Raffaella replies that 'it is both necessary and profitable to give vent to one's feelings in the days of one's youth, when God can more easily pardon and the world excuse'; it is not so easy in old age when there is greater loss and shame.[16] It is this kind of cynicism, a delight in the frivolity of dress and an acceptance of its importance in society, that so antagonized Puritans like Knox who held to the basically medieval notion of dress as evidence of pride and an incitement to lust. At the same time, with the venom born of fear, Protestants would attack certain styles of dress of which they did not approve, as smelling of 'papery and develyshnes'; with the religious world polarized, invective assumed a grotesque form as opposing religious factions slugged it out in the new printing presses.

By the middle years of the century Puritan moralists found, with regard to men's dress, even more to criticize, as the doublet remained tight, and the cod-piece even larger in size; balloon-like trunk hose covered the upper part of the thigh. Increasingly men could choose styles from around Europe – France, Spain or Germany – to the detriment of the evolution of native English fashions. This was to be a perennial complaint for many hundreds of years. Andrew Borde, described by the Puritan William Harrison as a 'lewd popish hypocrite', and admittedly a not very religious Carthusian monk, wrote in his *First Boke of the Introduction of Knowledge* of 1542, a doggerel account of his travels in Europe, and the perplexity of the Englishman faced with a variety of dress styles and the consequent instability of his fashions:

I am an Englishman, and naked I stand here,
Musyng in my mynde what rayment I shal were;
For now I wyll were thys, and now I wyll were that;
Now I wyl were I cannot tel what.[17]

The complaint that men did not wear their native fashions was a universal one in the sixteenth century; in Castiglione's *Il Cortegiano* (1528), the most famous manual on the education of a gentleman, the Italians are accused of dressing like the French or the Spanish – even like the Turks. Most books of etiquette lay stress on the fact that when in Rome, a gentleman should dress like the Romans, in short that travellers should wear the dress of the country they find themselves in. Contemporaries would easily have been able to distinguish the clothing of one country from another by what might appear to us fairly slight differences in colour range and cut; in just the same way, although men today on the whole dress in a more or less uniform way, we are able to pick out, say, the American tourist from the German businessman.

The sixteenth-century gentleman was meant to beware of taking up changes in fashion too quickly. Such a tendency, stated Thomas Elyot's *The Governor* of 1531 (the first English humanist treatise which dealt with political theory, education and moral philosophy), gives men the reputation of being 'noted dissolute of manners'. In an age when dress was equated with the person wearing it, it was very important to avoid excess and exaggeration; if the apparel oft proclaims the man, moderation was the keynote in a period when fashions could easily assume a kind of bizarre fantasy. Too much glitter and bright colour, says the author of *Il Cortegiano,* makes a man look like a jester, and consequently he will be taken lightly. This is echoed in Giovanni della Casa's courtesy book, the *Galateo,* composed in the early 1550s, and translated into English in 1576:

Thou must weare no garment that shall be too light, or overmuche daubde with garding; that

33 Robert Dudley, Earl of Leicester c. *1575*.
A sense of opulence and an exaggerated line dominate male dress of the 1570s. Jewels decorate his cap and short gown, over which he wears the Garter collar with the Great George. Although such a great noble was above criticism with regard to his clothes, moralists generally attacked the stuffed (bombasted) and paned trunk hose, which give an almost feminine, skirted appearance to the costume.

---

men may not say, thou hast Ganymede's hosen or wearest Cupides doublet.[18]

Other tendencies to be avoided, especially by those of 'meane or rather base condition' who go 'proudly prying about them like Peacockes', include an excessive amount of jewellery – 'their neckes be laden with chaines, their fingers full of rings, ... and every other parte bespangled'[19] – and too much reliance on cosmetics. Some men have in recent years, says Robert Peterson in his translation of *Galateo*, taken to wearing 'their heads & their beards curled with bodkins, and have their face, and their necks, & their hands, so starchte and painted, that it were to muche for a girle, nay harlot, that makes a merchandize of it, and sets herselfe to the sale'.[20] Such effeminate customs were widely supposed to derive from France, an idea not without foundation if we look at the prominence given to beautiful young men at the court of Henri III (1574–89); the elaborate toilette of such *mignons* – their face masks, scented Cyprus hair powder and their cosmetics – is described in detail in a contemporary work, *Description de l'Isle des Hermaphrodites*.[21]

There was certainly an almost feminine air about male fashions in the middle years of the century, with their pointed doublets emphasizing a small waist, and the round, padded trunk hose echoing the curves of female hips. By the early 1560s, trunk hose were so large and globe-like, that proclamations were passed in an attempt to reduce their size. In 1562 specific instructions were issued to tailors to limit the amount of lining and stuffing in hose; to prevent the 'monstrous and outrageous greatness of hosen'; tailors were urged to make them of modest proportions, not 'to be bolstered, but to lye juste unto their legges, as in ancient tyme was accustomed'.[22]

Considerations of class never being far from sumptuary legislation, it was ordered that no one under the degree of a baron could wear in his hose velvet or satin, but just the cheaper and lighter silks like sarcenet or taffeta. The new queen Elizabeth I was fond of order and outward uniformity, and was determined to make sumptuary legislation work; using magistrates to carry out her Acts of Apparel, resulted, unusually, in a number of prosecutions for infringements. One unfortunate man, arrested in the Ward of Blackfriars in 1565 'in a very monsterous and outraygeous greate payre of hose' had them displayed 'in some open place ... where they maye aptly be seen and consideryd of the people as an example of extreme folye'. Ridicule was also part of the punishment of one would-be fashionable tailor in 1570 who was ordered to be led through the streets, with one leg of his hose's stuffing and lining 'cutt and pulled out', and the other left alone.[23]

A further proclamation (1566), which again had tried to limit the girth of fashionable hose, ordered potential offenders to be inspected as they entered the City of London.[24] It seems unlikely that many cases came to court, for the law could be open to a variety of interpretations; those who were prosecuted and humiliated tended to be those of lowly status like servants and apprentices, whose clothing, by an act of 1559, their masters had to examine to see that it was simple and modest according to their station. Although a number of English etiquette books urged masters to 'apparell not your ... Servantes in sumptuous apparell, for it increaseth pryde and obstinacye, and many other evils',[25] it seems that such exhortations were often ignored. 'Outrage in apparell' would, according to Roger Ascham in *The Scholemaster* (1570), only be reformed if an example was made at the top of society, at court.[26]

The upper ranks of society, and especially the court, were widely believed in the last decades of the sixteenth century to be both frivolous and vain; there was the paradox of a deeply corrupt court and yet an admired queen. John Donne's satires of the 1590s attack the fops and the buffoons at court, 'the fine silken painted fooles' who rate their own importance by the richness of their attire; and at the same time John Marston's satire *The Scourge of Villainy* laughs at the swaggering gallant, full of 'cannon-oaths', who assumes martial poses though he is basically a coward. Late-sixteenth-century prose and poetry is deeply concerned with artificiality, dissembling and the pretensions of those who ape their betters. Marston's bombasted 'hero' who claims to have seen active service, is really just a clothes-horse covered in 'ribands, plumy-crested', 'drawn and quartered with lace'; he is 'naught but clothes and scenting sweet perfume', not really a man but

>an incarnate devil
>That struts in vice and glorieth in evil.[27]

As religion increasingly came to determine one's viewpoint regarding dress (a gulf which was to be exacerbated during the seventeenth century), certain garments and fabrics assumed moral qualities of their own. Francis Thynne's tract *Debate between Pride and Lowliness* (c. 1570) purports to be a discussion between velvet trunk hose with gold lace embroidery and lowerstocks of 'pure Granado silke', and humble cloth breeches with only one lining; for velvet French trunk hose read pride, and for the plain cloth breeches (which covered the body from the waist to the knee) read lowliness.[28] Trunk hose with a codpiece were worn into the 1580s, though they had shrunk considerably in size from the girth of the 1560s, thus making them even more immodest. Described by Montaigne as 'filthy breeches, that so openly shew our secret parts'[29] they were totally disapproved of by sober men. Some young men, of course, did go round looking like etiolated Hilliard gallants in bombasted doublets, tiny frill-like trunk hose, and with long, slender imitation-nude legs, but those of a Puritan cast of mind who tended to find 'Romish' pomp in such dress, preferred dark, usually black attire which did not show off the body shape. It is easy to exaggerate the dress divide in relation to religion; Catholic moralists disliked the exposed body as much as the Protestants did, but it was the extreme wing of Protestantism which, paradoxically, adopted Spanish sobriety of attire (black suit and plain linen ruff or collar) and made it into Puritan dress – perhaps the first real anti-fashion for men.

By the 1580s a man of fashion, however elegant, looked quite unbalanced and top heavy, due to the large amount of padding on his doublet; the front of the doublet had curved into an exaggerated belly point, and the top of the sleeves were often built out to an enormous size. It was this doublet style – which made a man look positively pregnant – that attracted the wrath of the Puritan Philip Stubbes in the flag-ship of all moral diatribes, *The Anatomie of Abuses* of 1583. These monstrous doublets, he says, 'hang doune to the middle of their theighes or at least to their private members, being so hard quilted, stuffed, bombasted and sewed, as thei can neither woorke nor yet well plaie in them through the excessive heate thereof'. Such a style is not only impractical, but 'shows the disposition of the wearer, how he is inclined, namely to gluttonie, gourmandice, riotte and excesse'; such doublets were stuffed with up to six pounds of bombast, and on top 'slashed, jagged, cut, carved, pincked, and laced with all kinde of costly lace of divers and sundrie colours'.[30] Even the humble jacket which was sometimes worn over the top of the doublet for warmth, can come, he says in a variety of sinful guises:

> ... some bee made with collors, some without, some close to the bodie, some loose coveryng the whole bodie downe to the thigh like bagges or sackes that were drawne over them ... some are buttened doune the breast, some under the arme, and some doune the backe ... some with greate sleeves, some with small, and some with none at all, some pleated and crested behinde, and curiously gathered ...[31]

Pride in dress is, to Stubbes, the greatest sin of all; he is sure that it offends God more than 'pride of the harte' or 'pride of the mouthe'; it

34 Unknown man c. *1588*.
N. Hilliard.
This elegant young man would be likely to incur the wrath of a moralist like Stubbes, for wearing such a doublet with a pronounced peascod-belly shape, a 'great and monsterous' ruff, and very short trunk hose which allow his legs to be seen, almost as though naked.

is impossible to wear rich clothes, 'the devilles nettes, to intangle poore soules in', and not to be infected with this sin.[32]

Not only are the wearers of such clothes to be blamed, but just as blameworthy are the tailors who tempt 'poore soules' to styles which 'tende to vice'. As, in the second half of the century, a far greater variety of fashions was available to a much wider section of society, tailors were increasingly condemned by moralists for exploiting the gullible. William Harrison in his *Description of England* (1577) berates the 'fickle-headed tailors, who covet to have severall trickes in cutting, thereby to draw fond customers to more expense of monie'; they will tempt men with 'the Spanish guise ... the French toies ... the Morisco gowns ... the short French breeches' and so on.[33]

With greater urbanization and consequently greater social emulation, attempts at keeping dress within bounds were hopeless; the proclamations of the later years of Elizabeth's reign including the last one of 1597, which listed in detail what silk stuffs, gold and silver lace, and embroidery, could or could not be worn, were impossible to enforce – hardly any prosecutions exist – and although there was still a widely held belief that sumptuary regulations were a good idea, they were repealed in 1604.[34]

It was the immense variety of dress, the 'confuse mingle mangle of apparell' which appalled Stubbes as an indication of how much more time and money was spent on the body at the expense of the soul. He notes a variety of high-crowned hats 'like battlements', and some with bunches of feathers like 'cockescombes ... ensignes of vanitie', high-heeled shoes and even jewellery. Harrison too is horrified at the fact that 'some lustie courtiers and gentlemen of courage 'wore earrings of gold, pearls and other precious stones 'whereby they imagine the workmanship of God not to be a little amended'.[35]

Worst of all, to Stubbes, are the 'great and monsterous Ruffes', some of which were starched. He describes the setting of ruffs with heated sticks put into damp linen in great detail, on the principle, presumably, of being conversant with every aspect of this evil to better refute those who defended such iniquity. Starching-houses, where these operations took place, are described as 'consecrate to Belzebub and Cerberus, archdivels of great ruffes'.[36]

Starch was introduced in the 1560s, and enabled ruffs of huge size to be worn; there were constant proclamations against 'outragious' double ruffs (1562) and 'ruffes of excessive length & depth' (1577 and 1580). Not content with the large size alone, some people, said Stubbes, wear ruffs 'wrought all over with silke woorke and peradventure laced with golde, and silver, or other costly lace of no small price'. It was impossible to win in this situation with one who disliked ruffs so greatly; even unstarched ruffs were dismissed as unsightly – they 'goeth flip flap in the wind like ragges that flew abroade, lying upon their shoulders like the dishcloute of a slut'.[37]

With regard to women, who have played a modest role so far in the story of sixteenth-century dress, all this was soon to change. By the middle of the century the relative simplicity of female dress gave way to more complex styles; there were separate bodices and skirts, elaborate underskirts, and a wide variety of over-gowns. As with men there was an increasing pre-occupation with surface decoration and patterning of all kinds – embroidery, lace, braid, sequins and spangles.

What strikes us most about women's dress in the second half of the century, is its stiffness and rigidity, which is created partly by tight-lacing, and partly by a boned understructure to the skirt. A firm and straight torso was the creation of either a buckram-stiffened stomacher front to the bodice, or a separate laced corset beneath the bodice. It is unlikely that such artificial stiffening of the bodice was in use before the sixteenth century, but by the middle of our period a variety of methods achieved the long, flat, pointed front which was in fashion. In Robert Crowley's *Epigrammes* (1550), women are accused of buying 'wastes of wyre'[38] for tight-fitting stays. A more usual method to produce the totally rigid look so admired by fashionable women was to place a busk – a long pointed piece of bone, metal or whalebone – in the centre front of the corset. These busks were an intimate part of a woman's dress and often given to her as love-tokens; with their somewhat phallic shape and the fact that they pointed towards the genitals, they were often the source of much ribald comment. It was even suggested that, as they were so constricting as to produce miscarriages, they were worn by women of easy virtue precisely for that purpose:

> The baudie buske ... keepes downe flat
> The bed wherein the babe should breed

was the comment of an Essex parson, Stephen Gosson in his *Pleasant Quippes for Upstart New fangled Gentlewomen,* of 1595.[39]

Another deforming feature of the new body shape, and one which attracted much moral censure, was the farthingale or hooped petticoat. In its early form, a series of hoops widening from the waist to the hem, it appeared in Spain at the end of the fifteenth century, from where it spread to the rest of Europe; it seems to have been worn, says the contemporary historian Edward Halle, at court masques in England as early as 1519 (perhaps as part of Spanish fancy dress) and it is listed in the royal wardrobe accounts in the mid 1540s. Crowley, as part of his attacks on women's dress in his thirty-one epigrams mentioned above, makes a specific reference to the woman who has,

> A bumbe lyke a barrell,
> Wyth whoopes at the skyrte.[40]

At about the same time, a treatise attributed to Charles Bansley, *Shewing and Declaring the Pryde and Abuse of Women Now a dayes* pours scorn on the rounded protuberance of the hooped underskirt, which, like the medieval train, forms a comfortable seat for the devil:

Downe for shame wyth these bottell arste bummes,
And theyr trappynge trinkets so vayne
A bounsinge packsadel for the devyll to ryde on
To spurre them to sorowe and payne.[41]

Such sinful fashions, as they come from Rome, says the author, are especially to be avoided for their 'papery and develyshnes'. But denouncing the farthingale was not an exclusively Protestant occupation; the anonymous author of *Le Blason des Basquines et Vertugalles* (published in Lyons in 1563) finds that farthingales not only serve to deform the body, but hide the

35 Caricature c. *1600*.
Inspired by the sin of pride, these ladies dress up in their finery, having chosen to wear the padded 'bum roll' (rather than the farthingale) to create the wide bulk which fashion demands. The anonymous artist finds that pride inspires women to wear false hair and false faces; i.e. vizard masks.

---

results of carnal knowledge. Wearing such a garment can thus lead to a loss of reputation:

> Que vous servent ces vertugalles,
> Sinon engendrer des scandalles?

Modest women, we are told, should leave off farthingales, tight stays, jewellery and face painting, and

> Montrez, montrez par le dehors
> Que Dieu habite dans vos corps.[42]

By the last years of the sixteenth century, the fairly modest bell-shaped Spanish farthingale had given way to the huge French drum-shaped style. Gosson describes them as:

> These hoopes, that hippes and haunch do hide,
> And heave aloft the gay hoyst traine...[43]

He firmly avers that farthingales were first adopted by prostitutes, who, when they had got the pox, found such hooped skirts served to hold out their fine dresses from the – presumably infected – smock beneath.[44]

Why, he laments, do women wear such clothes for the sake of pride? Pride continues to be the main reason ascribed by moralists to the otherwise unreasonable extremes in clothing which women wear; Pride, personified in Marlowe's *Dr Faustus*, 'can creep into every corner of a wench; sometimes like a periwig, I sit upon her brow; next, like a necklace I hang about her neck, or like a fan of feathers I kiss her lips; and then, turning myself to a wrought smock, do what I list'.

So various and complicated was female costume by the end of the sixteenth century, that a moralist like Stubbes grew quite dizzy describing all the styles he hated. He lists in detail the types of overgown which a fashionable lady would wear, 'some with sleeves hangyng doune to their skirtes trailing on the ground, and cast over their shoulders like cowe tailes', and some with short sleeves 'cut up the arme and poincted with silke Ribons';[45] he discusses the elaborate trimmings to silk petticoats, and laments women's fondness for stockings 'of all kinde of chaungable colours ... wanton light colours ... cunningly knit & curiously indented in every point, with quirkes, clockes, open seame ...'. He finds parents must take some blame for this state of affairs, that their daughters dress like 'proude Harlottes', like 'artificiall woman-puppits'. Stubbes certainly had a point when he states that too much finery led women to 'babishnesse'; how could women even claim to be on a footing with men, when they were obsessed by their appearance? Women not only wore endless complicated layers of clothing, so many kinds of 'pelfe and trash', according to Gosson, that they were unable to walk even and had to dash around in coaches, but every element in their dress was richly trimmed, plainness being despised. There was, for example, such a passion for embroidering even their underwear, that young men could get entangled in the cut-work of their mistresses' smocks.[46]

Never was there such a period when the bright, distorted and glittering dress of the fashionable woman was thought to reflect the shallowness of her soul, her essential immorality. This is how the satirist Marston describes her:

Her mask, her vizard, her loose-hanging gown
For her loose-lying body, her bright spangled crown,
Her long slit sleeve, stiff busk, puff farthingale,
Is all that makes her thus angelical.
Alas, her soul struts round about her neck,
Her seat of sense is her rebato set,
Her intellectual is a feigned niceness,
Nothing but clothes and simpering preciseness.[47]

The *rebato* referred to is a high laced collar, an alternative to the huge ruffs which women, like men, wore over supports. Stubbes in his *Anatomie of Abuses* deplores the 'greate ruffes and neckerchers of Hollande, Lawne, Camericke' which are starched and propped up with 'supportasses ... the stately arches of Pride'; some women wear more than one ruff, 'pleted and crested full curiously ... clogged with gold, silver, or silke lace ... wrought all over with needle worke, speckeled and sparkeled here and there with the Sunne, the Moone, the starres, and many other antiques strange to behold.'[48]

Fine lace (which had arrived in England by the middle of the century) came from Flanders and Italy to add a spiky gossamer splendour to collars, ruffs and caps. To complement the elaborate layers of clothing, women wore headdresses of great complexity – linen and lace caps, some built up on wires, netted gold cauls, various kinds of hoods and hats, and (worst of all, according to Stubbes) a biretta-like cap 'like the forked cappes of Popishe Priestes' – results of 'the variable fantasies of their serpentine minds'.[49]

The rage for novelty and bizarre experimentation in dress which is such a feature of the late sixteenth century, led women for the first time to adopt some of the features of male dress. Earlier in the century there had been isolated references to women dressing like men, but these were not specified, and throughout the period there were comments that the clothing of the opposite sex was adopted during the Christmas and New Year celebrations.[50] By the 1580s women were not only wearing men's beaver hats, and ruffs, but also doublet-like bodices with shoulder wings and decorative ribbon-trimmed *aglets* or *points* (for men these were practical too, for they served to tie the breeches to the doublet). Such a doublet, said Stubbes, was 'a wanton, lewde kind of attire, proper onely to manne' and those women who wore it were guilty of 'stinkyng before the face of God, & offensive to man'.[51]

It is impossible to say how far carnival practices had inspired women to don elements of male dress; we may be on much safer ground to assume that the custom of masking the face came from the masquerade. Alexander Barclay in the early sixteenth century had noted the custom during the carnival of people wearing black masks to:

> Defyle theyr faces: so that playne trouth to tell,
> They ar more fowle than the blacke Devyll of hell.[52]

By the second half of the century, women were wearing black velvet masks out of doors to protect their complexions; Stubbes found that they made women look like devils, and Gosson believed that they indicated a need to hide from the world, a disguise suitable only for wantons.

Any attempts to enhance the complexion were frowned upon by Puritans such as Stubbes and Gosson; not for them the acceptance of cosmetics in moderation as seen in Italian courtesy books.[53] By the end of the sixteenth century, dress was so startling and exaggerated, that the face and hair would fade into insignificance unless they too were artificially enhanced. Both face and breast were whitened in a number of ways, the most dangerous being preparations made from white lead; borax was also used to give whiteness to the skin, and the whole was glazed over with egg white. To complete the rather crude and painted appearance, the cheeks were daubed with red (made from madder, or ochre, or cochineal, or red crystalline mercuric sulphide); to redden the lips women used cloth or paper impregnated with the red dye from the East Indian brasil tree.[54] Then the face might be decorated with beauty spots, and brightly coloured false hair added to the high-piled coiffure of the period, which was often placed over wired under-structures. It was all a gift to the moralists:

> These flaming heads with staring haire,
> These wyers turnde like hornes of ram,
> These painted faces which they weare,
> Can any tell from whence they cam?
> Don Satan, Lord of fayned lyes,
> All these new fangeles did devise.[55]

The widespread use of false hair was a symbol to many critics of the falseness and corruption of the times; they claimed that not only was its use immoral and an 'Ornament of Pride' (Stubbes) but it was derived in many cases from dubious sources. Stubbes averred that fashionable women enticed fair-haired children 'into a secrete place, and for a penie or two, thei will cut of their haire', and Shakespeare in *The Merchant of Venice* was only repeating a common belief when he has Bassanio refer to false hair – 'those crisped snaky golden locks' – as

> the dowry of a second head
> The skull that bred them in the sepulchre.

William Averell's dialogue between the different parts of the body, *A Mervailous combat of contrarities* (1588) includes the statement that women who have 'their heads set out with strange hayre ... like the head of Gorgon, saving that they want the crawling snakes of Medusa' can turn their admirers into stone, for they lose their reason while gazing on such 'painted pride'.[56]

Attacks by moralists on late-sixteenth-century dress should not really surprise us, for in the whole of the history of dress there has probably never been such a period noted for such extravagance and distortion, such display of decoration and invention. It is perhaps possible to make a link here between the English becoming self-consciously nationalistic in politics, society and culture, and the fact that from at this time onwards, the English fondness for exaggeration and imagination in dress becomes a perceptible feature of national character.

5
Rags of Sin, Robes of Shame and Provocations of Lust

> The English, I say, are more sumptuous then the Persians because, despising the golden meane, they affect all extreamities.
>
> Fynes Moryson, *An Itinerary*, 1617

> The greatest provocations of lust are from our apparrell.
>
> Robert Burton, *The Anatomy of Melancholy*, 1621

Marked changes in style are hardly ever linked to a new century or dynasty, and in a sense the sixteenth century in dress with its colour, distortion and flamboyance, ends in the mid-1620s, when a more classical and restrained 'baroque' feeling enters all the arts, including those of costume and textiles. It is thus inevitable that this *folie de grandeur*, coupled with a growth in Puritanism, should lead to a concentration of moral attacks on dress under James I. The early years of the seventeenth century saw a general growth in trade (including luxury goods like imported silks and lace) and a considerable increase in capitalism made possible by the expansion of the money market. A new climate of peace (although the end of the war against Spain was not popular in all quarters) helped to encourage all the arts, and in spite of deep religious and growing political divisions, England was fairly socially and economically stable, prosperous and cultivated.

The ending of sumptuary legislation in 1604 was a formal recognition of a society in a state of flux, that the classes were no longer as clear-cut as moralists fondly imagined they had been in the past. Merchant families with money could marry into the aristocracy, and there was no prohibition – except that of moral censure – on those who emulated their betters in dress and luxury. An anonymous account of *Some Abuses which are Committed against the Common-wealth* is typical of the many accusations that men were impoverishing themselves through expense in dress, and that the lure of fashion was so strong that 'every poore gentlewoman ... or curates wife' wears 'jingle-jangles and trinketts like so many ladies, a thing so undecent, that I cannot overpasse it with silence'.[1] At the highest levels of society, also, relative upstarts could succeed if they caught the King's eye. Queen Elizabeth had been mainly successful in keeping her court on a tight rein, but James's court, described by the Puritan Lucy Hutchinson as 'a nursery of lust and intemperance', was riddled with scandal and full of disorder. The appearance of the King himself, with his 'rowling' eyes in pursuit of favoured young men, his padded clothes 'for steletto proofe' (this was, however, just as much a contemporary tailoring device, as evidence of a fear of assassination), his skin as soft as silk due to lack of washing, and his 'fingers ever ... fidling about his cod-piece' – although exaggerated by political opponents[2] – was rather unsavoury.

To many contemporaries, it seemed that native simplicity was being swept away on a tide of imported luxury; 'there is suche a madness in England as that we cannot endure our home-made clothe, but must needes be clothed in silke' was the comment of Lord Carew.³ Rich silks, sumptuous embroideries, and a wide variety of fashions from all over the world, were available for those who had the money. When Fynes Moryson contemplated the fashions, 'I might seeme to number the starres of Heaven and sands of the Sea'⁴; according to Thomas Dekker in *The Seven deadly Sinnes of London* (1606) the modish young gallant has:

> his codpeece ... in Denmarke, the collor of his Dublet and the belly in France; the wing and narrow sleeve in Italy; the short waste hangs over a Dutch Botchers stall in Utrich; his huge sloppes speakes Spanish; Polonia gives him the Bootes...⁵

The theme that sin 'may be committed either in French, Dutch, Italian, or Spanish, and all after the English fashion', as Lucifer explains in the prologue to Middleton's play *The Black Book* (1604), is a recurring one in the literature of the period. Such a gallimaufry of clothing would be worn particularly by tasteless would-be gallants coming to London in search of vice and entertainment; such a man, dubbed a 'gull' (a slang word for a young man of fashionable pretensions who was often taken for a ride by unscrupulous tradesmen, and led astray by rakish companions) would spend all his time at St Paul's showing off his clothes. He would, according to Dekker's mock etiquette book *The Gull's Hornbook* (1609), be sure that his cloak slipped from his shoulders, so that the costly lining could be seen, he would take off his hat to none 'unless his hatband be of a newer fashion than yours', and – this was especially infuriating to a playwright like Dekker – sit on the stage at the theatre, like 'a feathered ostrich', laughing in all the wrong places and criticizing the acting and the costumes.⁶

Not only were the fabrics of fashionable clothing luxurious in themselves, but they were covered in embroidery and applied trimmings; even the finest silks were cut and pinked with decorative jagged holes. The Puritan parson of St Martin's church in Ludgate, Samuel Purchas, found:

> The Christian, that knowes Apparell to be sinnes Liverie, as if he gloried in Sinne, doth as much swagger himselfe out of Civill and Christian decencie, as much emulates the old Serpents deformitie, as much strives to cut, race, pinke, print, jagge and fashion himself out of humane Feature, to put off a Man, and put on a Monster, in a humour of Gallantrie.⁷

Such a 'monster' would wear his doublet tight-fitting, the rigid torso achieved by buckram stiffening or padding; he would probably, in the first two decades of the century, wear the fashionable 'slop' breeches, padded, pleated and gathered under the knee, so that they looked rather like a stiffened skirt. At this period, male dress achieved an effect of three-dimensional richness, pattern piled on pattern; doublet, breeches and cloak were embroidered, or decoratively cut, or trimmed with lace, braid and spangles. At a formal function, such 'court caterpillars' (as Lucy Hutchinson called them) would be startling in their 'prodigal glistenings' and 'spangled damnations'.⁸

To add to the effect of rich distortion, men would wear either a ruff, or (and this was more fashionable) a lace collar supported on a frame; the most popular lace was *reticella*, a fine spiky, snowflake-like lace from Italy, a collar of which could cost the equivalent of a year's wages for a working man.⁹

Such ruffs and collars came in a variety of colours; Purchas found them, 'marching under more colours then Tamerlane's Tents, some Livid and Blew, some Red, some Dunne, Dusky, Ash-coloured, Pale, Greenish, Yellow, Muddy, and all the colours of the Moon'.¹⁰

Of these colours, yellow was the most popular, in spite of – or because of – a notorious reputation gained during the trial in 1616 of Frances Howard, Countess of Somerset, accused of poisoning her impotent ex-husband with the aid of a Mrs Turner, a famous yellow starcher, who was eventually hanged in her yellow ruff.¹¹ Consequently yellow starch was forbidden by the King – even the cart-drivers,

36 Caricature of a fashionable couple c. *1615*.
J. van der Velde.
The gallant on the left, with his hair 'like a forest or some wilderness', also follows the example of Dekker's gull by wearing his cloak over one shoulder; he follows the latest fashion by adopting the voluminous slop breeches.

The artist pokes fun at the deformity in female dress, notably the sugar-loaf hairstyle, and the drum-shaped farthingale, on which the fur muff can rest as on a shelf.

---

according to Ben Jonson's play *The Devil is an Ass* (1616), were wearing it – and he ordered the clergy to preach against it in church.

Not only did men spend a fortune on their ruffs or collars, but they copied women in their attention to curled, perfumed, and sometimes false hair. Barnaby Rich disapproved of such gallants who:

> are so perfumed, bespiced, and bepoudered, that a man may well vent them the breadth of a streete. And from whence cometh this wearing, & this imbrodering of long lockes, this curiositie that is used amongst men, in freziling and curling of their hayre, this gentlewoman-like starcht bands, so be-edged and be-laced, fitter for Mayd Marion in a Moris dance, then for him that hath either that spirit or courage that should be in a gentleman.[12]

Hair that was once 'cut round and plaine', complained Purchas, is 'now with hot Irons crisped, with staring Fore-tops frighted with Womanish nicetie'; the hair was often combed high or eked out with false hair to look, according to *The Gull's Hornbook*, 'like a forest or some wilderness'.

A style which attracted enormous criticism was the fashion for growing one lock of hair longer than the rest; such lovelocks first appeared in the 1590s and remained in fashion for the next thirty or so years. The most celebrated attack was that of the Puritan, William Prynne, in his book *The Unlovelinesse of Love-Lockes* (1628), who declared such 'unnaturall, shamefull' styles to be derived from the Red Indians, 'the Heathenish and Idolatrous Virginians', but inspired by the Devil who used

37 Frances Howard, Countess of Somerset c. *1615*.
Attributed to W. Larkin.
Frances Howard, court beauty and centre of a scandal involving adultery and murder, was no doubt aware of the erotic contrast between her imprisoning lace cartwheel ruff, and what the moralist Brathwait called 'those rising mounts, your displayed breasts'.

them to pull their wearers into hell. Those who wore such lovelocks were 'Ruffians, Rovers, Fantastiques, Humourists, Fashion-mongers ... Effeminate, Lascivious, Voluptuous, Singular, or Vaine-glorious persons'.[13]

In torrents of words and with a certainty of moral judgement, critics like Prynne pronounced on the follies of their day. If the reader of Prynne's book were to wonder at this concentration of effort on something as insignificant as a hair style, the author has his answer ready; if 'we once begin to play, and dandle, with small and pettie Vices, yea, though it bee but with Vanities, Toyes and Idle Fashions, they will quickly draw us on to

38 Robert Devereux, Earl of Essex.
Style of Hilliard.
Fuel to inflame the wrath of Puritan moralists, in this portrait of the late 1590s of Queen Elizabeth's favourite, (executed for treason, 1601) lies particularly in the earring, and the love-lock which falls over the fine reticella lace collar.

scandalous great and hainous sinnes at last.'[14]

In spite of such diatribes, it proved impossible to make men shorten their hair, which by the 1620s was quite long, curling over the shoulders. Attempts were made at the universities to forbid students wearing their hair longer than the tips of their ears, but these were as fruitless as attempts to curb the same styles, and other finery, among some Anglican divines; with all other men, it was accepted that only moral censure might work.

Moral censure was even more brought to bear on women's dress in the early seventeenth century, for its complexity, variety and artificiality. We have already seen in the late sixteenth century how moralists singled out for attack tight-lacing, hooped petticoats and the lavish use of cosmetics, and as these styles were still in fashion in the first two decades of the century, so they continued to be criticized. Joseph Hall in *The Righteous Mammon* (1618) asked his readers to imagine what their ancestors would think if they could return to earth and see modern ladies:

> Here is nothing to be seene but a verdingale, yellow ruffe, and a periwig ... a poudered frizle, a painted hide ... breasts displayed ... Is this ... flesh and blood? is this ... hayre? is this the shape of woman? or hath nature repented her work since my dayes, and begunne a new frame?[15]

The basic elements in women's dress remained much the same as in the late Elizabethan period – a boned, pointed bodice with a richly trimmed stomacher piece was worn with a skirt, and then an overgown with elaborately cut hanging sleeves – but with a multiplicity of accessories. Thomas Tomkis in his *Lingua, or The Combat of the Tongue* (1607) mocks, without too much exaggeration, the incredible preparations for the day to be made by a woman of fashion:

> ... there is such doing with their looking-glasses, pinning, unpinning, setting, unsetting, formings and conformings, painting blew veins and cheeks; such stir with sticks and combs, ... busks, bodies, scarfs, necklaces ... rebatoes, borders, tires, fans ... puffs, ruffs, cuffs, muffs.... that yet she is scarce dressed to the girdle; and now there's such a calling for fardingales, kirtles, busk-points, shoe ties, etc, that seven peddlers' shops – nay all Stourbridge fair – will scarce furnish her: A ship is sooner rigged by far, than a gentlewoman made ready.[16]

The large farthingales which had caused so much outrage (and merriment) to satirists, were out of fashion by the second decade of the century. James had tried to forbid them in 1613 and 1616 (they took up too much space, and had on the latter occasion caused an accident when a number of guests became wedged in the entrance to the masquing hall). However, such

39 Queen Anne of Denmark.
This anonymous engraving, published after the Queen's death, shows fossilized court dress c. 1613. Although, by the second decade of the seventeenth century, the huge tip-tilted farthingale was out of fashion, the Queen insisted that it be worn at court. Moralists attacked the very low neckline, and the widespread use of artificial aids to beauty, such as the dyed blonde hair which the sitter made fashionable.

edicts were ignored until the death of Queen Anne, who was fond of the farthingale for court wear, in 1619.

Not only did Anne of Denmark like vast farthingales, but she was inordinately proud of her white bosom which was revealed in the low-cut gowns worn at court. The Venetian ambassador, in a famous dispatch in 1617, described the queen as wearing a farthingale four feet in width under a dress which displayed her bosom 'bare down to the pit of the stomach'; it was the fashion, he says, generally for 'the plump and buxom (to) display their bosoms very liberally', and it may be a reference to this propensity that is meant when he states that English women dress 'so well and lasciviously as to defy exaggeration'.[17]

Thomas Tuke in his *A Treatise against Painting* (1616) denounces women for their breasts 'layd forth to mens view', and for their use of cosmetics; cochineal reddens the nipples and blue veins are painted to emphasize the white skin of the bosom. The burden of his tract is that women spend more time 'in powdring, pranking and painting, than praying.'[18]

Dramatists like Ben Jonson had great fun with the battery of cosmetic aids deemed necessary for women of all ages, but especially with the vulgar and recently rich who aped the fashions. In *Epicene, or The Silent Woman* (1609), Mrs Otter, a citizen's wife, spends £40 a year on mercury and hogs' bones which were boiled to make a wash for the face; in addition:

> All her teeth were made i' the Blackfriars, both her eyebrows i' the Strand, and her hair in Silver Street. She takes herself asunder ... when she goes to bed, into some twenty boxes, and about next day noon is put together again, like a great German clock.[19]

Beauty was thought to be only worthy if accompanied by virtue. The royalist poet Francis Quarles, in talking of beauty, declared: 'If Virtue accompany it, it is the Heart's Paradice; if Vice associate it, it is the Soul's Purgatory'.[20]

The idea that beauty implied sexual voracity in women, and that it was a snare laid out for unwary men, took a long time to disappear; most men would have agreed with Francis Bacon that 'virtue is like a rich stone, best plaine set'. In a book published in 1615, with a title that aptly sums up the gist of the work, *The Arraignment of Lewd, Idle, Froward and unconstant women: Or the vanitie of them, choose you whether*, the author, Joseph Swetnam, urged men to beware of woman, for: 'she has a thousand waies to entice thee, and ten thousand waies to deceive thee ... (and) to suck away thy wealth, but in the winter of thy misery, shee will flie from thee'.

He implored men to remember that 'many women are in shape Angels, but in qualities Devils, painted coffins with rotten bones'.[21]

This very popular work, which over the next twenty years went through ten editions, did not go unchallenged; a number of replies[22] asserted that only evil men could be led astray by women's dress, and some even accused Swetnam of contributing to delinquency in women by suggesting lewd fashions that they might not have thought of for themselves.

Another topic which exercised the minds of the moralists of the period, was women's increasing fondness for wearing masculine doublets (a fashion which Stubbes in his *Anatomie of Abuses* of 1583 had already remarked on), men's hats and even short hair. In 1620 James I called in the Bishop of London to tell his clergy 'to inveigh vehemently and bitterly in theyre sermons against the insolencie of our women, and theyre wearing of brode brimd hats, pointed dublets, theyre haire cut short or shorne';[23] this was the comment of John Chamberlain, an indefatigable retailer of gossip both political and social, who agreed with the sentiments expressed by the king, but who also realized the futility of any attempts to carry out such orders.

Women, it would appear, were now to be censured for their short hair, instead of the dyed and false hair which had been the main complaint in the earlier period; by short hair, was probably meant, in any case, hair shorter than had been previously worn – because it would not have had to be much shorter to be the same length as that worn by men, already well over their shoulders. Prynne in *The Unlovelinesse of Love-Lockes*, when he turned his attention to female sartorial sins (it 'would require a large and ample volume to batter and confound them'), picked out 'the mannish Viragoes, or audacious Men-Women (who) doe unnaturally clip and cut their Haire'.[24]

By 1620, the long pointed line of the bodice and the doublet was beginning to give way to a more relaxed, less stiffened construction, with the waist at the natural level. The greater freedom in movement given by this new style was also cause for attention. The anonymous author of *Hic-Mulier: or, The Man-Woman* urged women to stop prostituting themselves for dubious finery; a woman will give 'kisses to have her hayre shorne', and 'will give her honestie to have her upper parts put into a French doublet'. Such doublets, with their 'loose, lascivious, civill embracement', were 'all unbutton'd to entice, ... and extreme short wasted to give a most easie way to every luxurious action.'[25]

The trend towards a looser-fitting and more negligent dress gathered momentum in the reign of Charles I. Under the aegis of a stylish young French queen, women's fashions assumed a soft, gently rounded look, a modest indolence; lavish trimming and a superabundance of patterned stuffs and embroidery gave way to plain silks, especially the lustrous taffetas and satins seen in the portraits by van Dyck. The fluid lines of the new fashions were particularly appealing to baroque artists who disliked the minutiae of fussy layers of dress and patterned textiles.

A particular style that they liked was for a fairly loose-fitting or unstructured gown. Such gowns were worn informally in the early seventeenth century; in Webster's play *The Duchess of Malfi* (c. 1614) the villain Bosola finds the duchess in a 'loose-bodied gown' so that he cannot tell if she is pregnant. The equation between a loose gown and a looseness of morals was quickly made; Richard Brathwait in his etiquette book *The English Gentlewoman* (1631) says that such loose gowns do not only serve to

40 Queen Henrietta Maria with her dwarf c. *1633*. Sir A. van Dyck.
When John Chamberlain deplored 'the insolencie of our women, and theyre wearing of brode brimd hats, (and) pointed dublets', this is the kind of costume he would have had in mind, although he would not have ventured to criticize the Queen in this way. The fashion for women to adopt versions of male attire for hunting or outdoor exercise is a theme of seventeenth- and eighteenth-century dress, but to begin with it was attacked for its audacious, mannish novelty.

hide bodily deformities, but they 'sort best with these adulterate beauties'.[26] These *déshabillé* gowns might suit a court masque, or an intimate breakfast, or the artist's studio, but they were quite out of place in a more mundane setting. Sir William Brereton, later a Parliamentary general, travelled round the British Isles in the 1630s, and reaching Shrewsbury he found a smith's wife 'in a loose-bodied gown, gentlewoman-like', who was being jeered at in the streets for her pretension. Brereton was quite unsympathetic to her plight, and is pleased to note that her 'pride and arrogance was most justly rewarded with shame, reproach, and scorn'.[27]

All clothes, says Brathwait, are 'ragges of sinne ... robes of shame' which can easily turn into 'light-flaming fuell of licentious liberty'. It is particularly important for women to avoid light-coloured and impractical fabrics, 'cobweb attires which can neither preserve heat, nor repell cold'. His belief is that 'soft Cloathes introduce soft Mindes. Delicacy in the habit begets an effeminacy in the heart'.[28] Like most moralists, he was conservative in matters of dress, preferring the old styles to the new, the former being invested with the charm of familiarity and the virtue of sobriety. It is true to say that the stiff boning and long busks of Jacobean styles made women assume a formal, upright posture, whereas the loose gowns allowed a languor which, to many critics, positively reeked of sexuality, allied as it was to a passion for a contrived negligence. To the poet Herrick in his poem *Delight in Disorder* (written probably in the 1630s), the untied stomacher lace and the loose scarf thrown over the shoulders indicate that

> A sweet disorder in the dress
> Kindles in clothes a wantonnesse.

Herrick also delighted in women's bare arms, which were beginning to be revealed as the sleeves shortened. There is an early reference to this fashion in Taylor's *A Glasse for Gentlewomen to dresse themselves by* (1624) where he attacks women for baring 'their armes beyond that which is fit for every one to behold'.[29] This

41 Lady Elizabeth Thimbleby and Dorothy, Viscountess Andover.
Sir A. van Dyck.
Herrick's 'delight in disorder' is conjured up in the looser, unboned gowns of the 1630s, over which are draped silk scarves. As well as the display of the softly rounded breasts (which the artist has emphasized by reducing the amount of visible chemise), moralists found time to complain about the sight of the naked arm to the elbow.

---

seems a surprising and unwarranted attack until it is realized that, although women had often worn very tight sleeves, their arms had not been revealed, in public at least, since classical antiquity; the bare arm was to the 1630s what the ankle was to the Victorians.

Other ways in which women could tempt men, were by revealing as much of their breasts as possible, a fashion which remained popular throughout the seventeenth century, even during the Interregnum. The breast was either pushed up by boned stays, or revealed in *déshabillé*. Brathwait exhorted women to 'eye those rising mounts, your displayed breasts, with what shamelesse art they wooe the shamefaste passenger....'[30] This had obviously no effect, for a number of tracts published during Puritan rule continued to denounce low necklines which revealed the bosom. 'This laying out of naked Breasts, is a temptation to sinne, both in the Actor and the vaine Spectator', stated one author in 1654;' those who have their garments made on such a fashion, that their necks and breasts are in great part left naked' ... 'invite customers, by setting open their shop windows.'[31]

The treatise quoted from, *Divers Reasons and Arguments Against Painting, Spots, naked Backs, Breasts, Arms &c*, was in the main an attack on beauty spots, tiny black velvet spots in the shapes of stars, hearts, etc. which fashionable women placed on their faces and breasts; the author says they are erroneously called 'beauty' spots, for 'the Devil loves to put fine names on foule things', which are in reality

'base and Beastly-Spots, the spots of the proud, wanton, idle Droans of the World'.[32]

Such a patently frivolous custom was to be linked with the defeated aristocracy, although it seems to have been widely adopted; a bill was proposed in 1650 'against the vice of painting, wearing of black patches, and immodest dress of women', but it got no further.[33]

The Civil War and the ensuing Commonwealth had little effect on women's dress. To the reproach of the extreme Puritan wing of the new government, who had of course been denouncing excesses in dress for years, no sumptuary legislation ever got beyond the proposal stage. This may have been due to the influence of John Milton (the intellectual mentor of the republican movement) whose *Areopagitica* (1644) had scoffed at the idea of such laws, and to the fact that all men in power – even revolutionaries – are constrained by the realities of what they can enforce. So they contented themselves, as in the 1650 proposal, with vague denunciations of 'immodest' dress, which could either mean the loose-bodied gowns, and the low necks which we have referred to, or to the adoption of men's dress. As well as the

42 'Here be your new Fashions Mistris'.
Anonymous engraving to the frontispiece of a penny book.
During the Interregnum, a number of tracts were published attacking the excesses of female fashions, such as the patches depicted here. This jack-in-the-box pedlar shows off the variety of patches for sale, as well as a face mask, a feathered fan, and ribbons.

occasional borrowing from the male wardrobe which has been noted, many women – camp-followers and others – had adopted men's clothing for security and ease; Charles I had in 1643 to issue a proclamation stating, 'Let no Woman presume to Counterfeit her Sex by wearing mans apparell'.[34]

Charles I had, on coming to power in 1625, already been noted for the sobriety of his clothing, in contrast to the excesses of his father's court. The kind of restrained elegance which we associate with Charles was not just the creation of van Dyck, but part of a trend towards greater subtlety in colours, and a more natural and undistorted body shape; men should, according to Henry Peacham's etiquette book for young gentlemen, *The Compleat Gentleman* (1622) aim for the 'moderate and middle garbe' for too much display in dress was an undoubted sign of vanity and vulgarity.

It was, however, impossible to stop gallants showing off in this way. In a later work by Peacham, *The Truth of Our Times* (1638) he describes a 'proud cox-combe in the fashion, wearing Taffata and an ill-favoured locke on his shoulder', who 'thinkes that all that weare cloth and are out of fashion, to be clownes, base and unworthie his acquaintance'.[35] By the 1630s, the French influence in dress – doublets slashed on breast and sleeves, and long tubular breeches – was paramount; some, like Peacham, lamented the fact that the English 'so doat upon new fashions' from France, from where 'came your slashed doublets (as if the wearers were cut out to be carbonado'd upon the coales) ... your long breeches, narrow towards the knees, like a payre of smith's bellowes'.[36]

'Young men of the Court ... drowne halfe their stature in great boots, sometimes they plunge themselves from the armepits to the heeles in their breeches, and sometimes they drowne all the fashion of their faces in the brimmes of their hats, being as broad as the Parasolo of Italy', was the comment of Edward Grimston in *The Honest Man: or, The Art to please in Court* (1632).[37]

Large-brimmed hats, trimmed with feathers, and worn tilted to one side of the head, doublets either slashed or half-unbuttoned allowing the shirt to billow forth, breeches unbuttoned at the knee, and floppy leather boots – all these were part of the casually dishevelled look of the 1630s, which many moralists found deliberately slovenly, a calculated affront. Such a style is well described in James Shirley's play *The Lady of Pleasure* (1637):

> ... your doublet must
> Be more unbutton'd hereabouts ...
> Your doublet and your breeches must be allow'd
> No private meeting place here ...

The only cloak to pass muster in fashionable circles is a short cape; a coat 'may be allowed a covering for one elbow'.

This kind of disdainful aristocratic asymmetry in dress was on the whole, as we might expect, anathema to the Puritans, although there were some Parliamentary supporters who dressed as richly as their Cavalier opponents – the civil war cut right across class frontiers.

There was also a growing movement towards darker colours, and a greater sobriety in dress in the later 1630s, with plain linen replacing lace for collars and cuffs. Such sobriety was not necessarily cheap; Puritans could dress richly in expensive black woven silks, and the crispest of starched linen from Holland. They could even be guilty of the sin of placing too much importance on their appearance; 'one may be as proud of plaine apparel as well as of costly. And some are as proude of their falling bandes and little sets, as others are of their great ruffes.'[38]

Those who were genuinely indifferent to their clothes, wore, like the Quakers, plain drab suits of home-woven cloth without any trimming or even any buttons and allowed their hair to grow plain and straight. It could be pointed out, however, that as this was deliberate singularity, it was in itself a kind of moral arrogance, which contemporaries were not slow to comment on.

For the word 'Puritan' encompasses many different shades of religious opinion, from the extreme 'anarchist' wing, to those moderate members of the middle classes who had political sympathies with the Dutch Republic. As Lucy Hutchinson pointed out, the word 'Puritan' was a term very loosely applied to anyone who opposed the views of the court party, and thus included a wide range of political and religious beliefs. Only the extreme Puritans cut their hair short, to be jibed at as 'roundheads', and Lucy Hutchinson was scathing about the appearance of those whose hair was cropped 'close round with so many little peaks as was ridiculous to behold'. Colonel Hutchinson, a famous Parliamentary soldier, had 'a fine thicksett head of haire ... although the godly of those days, when he embrac'd their party, would not allow him to be religious because his hayre was not in their cutt.'[39]

Although short hair was worn by the righteous, it did not catch on in fashionable circles,

43 A cavalier.
A. Bosse.
A casual unbuttoned elegance, both of doublet and breeches, is characteristic of the French fashions which arrived in England in the second quarter of the century, and which were adversely commented on by some critics as calculated slovenliness.

where hair in the 1640s and 1650s grew even longer and more luxuriant. William Prynne again sallied forth to attack long hair, this time in verse, with *A Gagge for Long-Hair'd Rattle-Heads who revile all civill Round-heads* (1646). He urges the 'rattle-heads with more haire than

44 'The Habit of an English Gentleman'.
This satire of the late 1640s mocks the long hair, the patched complexion, and the be-ribboned suit of the fashionable gallant. It was fashionable to look as though your clothes had been thrown on, and the accompanying rubric tells us that he wears 'a long wasted dubblet unbuttoned half way ... his sleeves unbuttoned ... his breeches unhooked ready to drop off, his shirt hanging out, (and) his codpeece open tied at the top with a great bunch of riband'.

wit' to stop scoffing at the roundheads, or else they will not be admitted into heaven; in any case, those who jeer are roundheads themselves at night, when 'Their Peri-wigs at Bed-time are laid by'.[40]

By the time that this pamphlet was written, many men, if their own hair was not long or thick enough, were beginning to wear wigs. Thomas Hall, a Puritan clergyman, published in 1653 a tract on *The Loathsomnesse of Long Haire* in which he avers that even clergymen wear long hair 'appearing like Ruffians in the Pulpit', and sometimes wigs, 'these Periwigs of false-coloured haire which begin to be rife.... and are condemned by Christ himself'. Such long and false hair he attributes to the general licentiousness of the times which is caused by 'the want of the golden reines of government'.[41]

Not all critics of dress and the disturbed state of the times took such an extreme view of long hair. John Bulwer, for example, stated that men should not wear their hair long just because St Paul forbad it, but because it is unclean; on the other hand, as Nature has given us 'a fruitful grove of hair', men should exercise moderation and not cut it too short. His famous book, *Anthropometamorphosis: Man Transform'd; or The Artificial Changeling* (1650) is a plea against the deformation of the body by whatever means, an attack on:

> the mad and cruel Gallantry, Foolish Bravery, ridiculous Beauty, Filthy Finenesse, and loathsome Lovelinesse of most Nations, Fashioning and altering their Bodies from the Mould intended by Nature.

Although this book is mainly about the barbarous deformities practised, in the name of ritual and custom, on the face and body in non-European countries, he includes (due to popular demand, he says) some reference to his native land. As his thesis is that any deformity is unnatural, he attacks 'the frizled and over-powdered Gallants of our times' who make a habit of dyeing their hair with 'depraved Tinctures', and who shave their beards which are 'the natural Ensigne of Manhood'. Turning to clothing, he finds that: 'The slashing, pinking and cutting of our Doublets is but the same phansie and affectation with those barbarous Gallants who slash and carbonade their Bodies'. Men distort their feet with long-toed shoes so that 'we can hardly kneel in God's house', and they hang around their waists huge bunches of ribbons – 'these Ribben-Bushes that our modern Gallants hang at their Cod-piece' (he means the opening of the breeches).

He longs for sumptuary laws to 'represse the Apish Fantasticalnesse of Apparel'. In place of current finery, he rather impractically proposes clothes cut 'according to the natural shape and proportion of the Body, as we may probably imagine the Skin-garments were, wherewith the Lord God ... first cloathed the Nakednesse of our first Parent'.[42]

Any sumptuary legislation was, however, a dead letter. Charles I had in 1643 issued a proclamation 'against waste and excess in Apparell', which was particularly directed against the wearing of gold and silver lace, fringe and ribbon[43] but during the war this was ignored; attempts to reform dress during the Commonwealth were, as we have seen, equally useless. However the idea, in principle, of some kind of sumptuary legislation remained in many people's minds. One was the diarist John Evelyn, who in his book *Tyrannus or the Mode, in a Discourse of Sumptuary Lawes* (1661), finding that inconstancy in dress contributed to inconstancy of mind, urged the king to limit changes in fashion to the four seasons of the year, and to encourage the wearing of native woollen cloth for both summer and winter.

Like Bulwer, Evelyn picked out as particularly absurd the fashion for men to wear yardages of looped silk ribbon at their waists; one such man he describes as: 'a fine silken thing ... that had as much Ribbon on him as would have plundered six shops, and set up twenty Country Pedlers: All his Body was dres'd like a May-Pole ...'[44]

By the time that he was writing, the doublet had gradually shrunk in size until it was no more than a short-sleeved bolero, ending at mid-chest, and revealing both the shirt, and the bunches of ribbon at the waist. The outfit was completed by wide, open-ended breeches, which had been introduced in the 1640s, also trimmed with ribbon, and which had vastly increased in size during the 1650s. It was possible, according to Samuel Pepys, to put both legs into one compartment of such breeches and walk around all day without knowing it – this had happened to a friend of his in 1661. The width of these breeches and the amount of fabric they contained contributed to their name of 'petticoat' breeches; Evelyn disliked them for he thought they were effeminate and turned men into 'a kind of Hermaphrodite'.

Such styles which Evelyn attributed to 'la Mode de France', were part of that sartorial and cultural imperialism of Louis XIV which was to dominate society for the rest of the seventeenth century; 'when a Nation is able to impose, and give laws to the habit of another.... it has (like that of Language) prov'd a Fore-runner of their Conquests there'.[45]

It is a debatable point whether the new style in dress of the later 1660s – a loose-fitting knee-length 'vest' (the ancestor of our waistcoat) and a coat – should be ascribed to France or to England. From the early 1660s it appears that a short-sleeved vest was worn at the French court, at the same time that a similar garment, possibly inspired by theatrical interpretations of the Orient,[46] was introduced into England; an alternative style was for a wide-sleeved coat to be worn over the top of such a vest. Throughout the 1660s coats of various types were worn over the vestigial doublet and the petticoat breeches; by about 1670, however, the amount of material in the petticoat breeches being too inconvenient when worn with a long coat, narrower breeches fastening below the knee became the mode, and the doublet was replaced with a waistcoat. This three-piece suit was to remain the basis of male attire for the foreseeable future; for the next hundred years there was relatively little change in its essential cut apart from fairly minor elements like pocket flaps and cuffs, and a gradual shortening of the waistcoat.

From the casual, rather sloppy and unstruc-

RAGS OF SIN, ROBES OF SHAME AND PROVOCATIONS OF LUST

45 'Figure à la Mode'.
R. de Hooghe.
By the later 1660s, the short doublet had totally parted company from the vast petticoat breeches, but both were lavishly trimmed with bunches of ribbon. Evelyn complained that the breeches made men look effeminate, and that the tout ensemble *made them look like may-poles.*

tured lines of male dress in the middle years of the seventeenth century, by the 1660s, men were beginning to assume a more dignified formality in their clothing. The coat became increasingly fitted to the body, emphasized by its curving seams trimmed with gold or silver braid, and the skirts, stiffened with horse-hair or buckram, flared out in side pleats, rather like a woman's dress. When worn with a powdered and curled wig, this figure-hugging and skirted costume, with its trimmings of lace and light-coloured ribbons, could easily be described as somewhat feminine. The Oxford antiquary Anthony Wood writing in 1663, found it: '... a strange effeminate age when men strive to imitate women in their aparell, viz. long periwigs, patches in their faces, painting, short wide breeches like petticotes, muffs, and their clothes highly scented, bedecked with ribbons of all colours.' Even the king's soldiers, he insisted, wore muffs, and in dirty weather they protected their shoes with wooden pattens.[47]

The anonymous author – he describes himself as a 'Compassionate Conformist' – of *Englands Vanity or the Voice of God Against the Monstrous Sin of Pride in Dress and Apparel* (1683) sneered at those 'pretty' men who 'have gotten the Boddice on, to make us look slender and pretty; And the Epicene Sleeves do very well fit both the Hee and the Shee'.[48]

By this time the new name for the gallants of an earlier age was a 'fop', popularly supposed to be rather effeminate in dress although at the same time searching for a rich heiress to rescue him from the financial predicament caused by a London life devoted to the theatre, to gambling and other kinds of dissipation, and above all to the passionate pursuit of the latest fashions.

46 Homme de Qualité 1694.
J. D. de St Jean.
This type of fashionable fop, taking snuff, was the butt of many satirists for his somewhat 'effeminate' appearance, especially in his use of patches, and his large fur muff.

Such fops are the stock characters of Restoration drama, epitomized, perhaps by Sir Fopling Flutter in Etherege's play *The Man of the Mode* (1676). Sir Fopling, with his devotion to the latest modes, his fashionable mouthing of French phrases – he even affects a lisp 'in imitation of the people of quality of France' – and his pose of indolence, is typical of the genre. When Dorimant admires his loose gown (such gowns were increasingly worn as relaxation from the formal, fitted suit), Sir Fopling avers that 'it serves to wrap me up after the fatigue of a ball ... We should not always be in a set dress; 'tis more "en cavalier" to appear now and then in a "déshabillé".'

Formal, heavy, baroque costume demanded an equally ponderous form of hairstyle in the form of a large wig. Various kinds of false hair had been worn since the beginning of the century, but from the middle of the period, whole wigs called periwigs, were increasingly worn; made of human hair (the most prized) or animal hair, they were by the 1660s, quite full and arranged in elaborate curls. By the end of the century they were huge and heavy affairs, full-bottomed and built up on top of the head in peaks, then sprayed with scented powder. The fashion was universal and even the clergy wore them; the author of a contemporary history of wigs wondered how they dared rebuke their congregations for luxury and excess in dress, when they themselves wore wigs of such immoderate size that they hid half their face.[49]

The size of such wigs was a gift to the authors of comedies of manners. In Vanbrugh's *The Relapse* (1696), the periwig-maker Mr Foretop tells his client that he has made him 'a periwig so long, and so full of hair, it will serve you for hat and cloak in all weathers'. Lord Foppington then complains that it is still not big enough, as 'a periwig to a man should be like a mask to a woman: nothing should be seen but his eyes'.

The wig was the crowning glory of a man's appearance; hours were spent in arranging the curls and powdering it, so that the fop could make a spectacular entrance in public. *The Ladies Dictionary* of 1694 wonders why there are so many complaints about the time spent by women on their dress, when some men, too, can think it such an important pastime; the fop, for example, after: 'trifling with the Curls in his Wig, tying and untying his Cravat, writhing himself into as many Postures ... sallies forth of his Chamber like a Peacock, beseeching the Winds to favour his delicate Friz, and not to put a Lock or a Curl out of Joynt'.[50]

After Puritan rule, when there had been some success in stamping out swearing, drunkenness and gambling, and enforcing Sunday observance, it was inevitable that society should become less strait-laced, and the new post-Restoration climate was marked by licence and debauchery at every level; there was a crime wave in London and a considerable increase in prostitution.

Puritanism had, however, entrenched itself in middle-class lives, and it turned from an interest in politics, to a desire, motivated by the corruption at court and in society, to reforming vice. In the 1690s, inspired by a revival of religious militance, Societies for the Reformation of Manners were set up in London and the provinces; they replaced the bawdy courts which had been abolished during the Interregnum, and they concerned themselves with prostitution, homosexuality, and all kinds of indecency. Prostitutes were particularly singled out for attack; 'Impudent Harlots, their Antick Dresses, Painted Faces and Whorish Insinuations, allure and tempt our Sons and Servants to Debauchery', complained the Tower Hamlets Society for the Reformation of Manners.[51] What were the harlots actually wearing? 'Antick' dresses could either be the loose *déshabillé* of the mid-century which had, suitably enough, become a kind of whorish uniform, or, odd though it sounds, be a stage costume based on loose 'classical' drapery. For we learn in Bernard de Mandeville's *The Fable of the Bees* of a few years later, that in the municipal

---

47 Nell Gwynn c. *1675*.
Engraving by G. Valck after Sir P. Lely.
Nell Gwynn, actress and mistress to Charles II, was aptly described by Pepys as a 'bold, merry slut'. In spite of the lamb (the usual accessory of St Agnes, Christian saint and virgin martyr), the sitter in her dress shows a far from innocent appreciation of her own charms, depicted as she is in a loose shift which almost falls off her shoulders.

P. Lely Pinxit. *The Sculpters part is done the features tell / of Ma:am Gwin No Arte can shew her Will,* G. Valck sculp.

brothels in Amsterdam, there were prostitutes in loose gowns 'like the Roman Dresses of stroling Actresses'.[52] Given the reputation of actresses on the English stage, the link between harlotry and the theatre was easily made.

In such an atmosphere, women of fashion were encouraged to be interested solely in entertainment and dress – even their education, which had declined in quality since the Restoration, was mainly directed towards domestic pursuits and the attainments which might attract a husband; in the plays of the period, they are caricatured as incurably indolent and frivolous.

While a kind of cynical hedonism was the rule in society, there is an increasingly old-fashioned air about the intemperance of tirades against women's dress; the author of *Englands Vanity* (1683), for example, sounds positively Jacobean in his attack on 'the Loosness, the Staring and Gaping, the Idle and Dissolute Carriage of the very Virgins and Young Ladies who set themselves out on purpose to be pick't up and Gaz'd on'.[53]

As always, the display of the breast was looked upon with particular disapproval. It merited a whole treatise by the Abbé Boileau in 1675 (*De l'Abus des nuditez de gorge*), translated into English and amplified in 1678 by Edward Cooke, under the title of *A Just and Seasonable Reprehension of naked Breasts and Shoulders*. Even after the 'recent dreadful Judgements' of 'Plague and Flames', Cooke is sorrowful to find that there is no diminution of 'general gawdry in London', but there is more 'vanity of Fashion' than before. Women show their breasts not just at dances, but even at church; 'they come thither to wound the eyes of the most innocent and just, and to give death to those who are yet but weak and staggering in virtue'. Such women 'are the true Amazons of the Devil'.[54]

From the 1660s onwards, the bodice of the dress tightened so much that it virtually became a corset; with the wide décolletage in fashion, the breasts bulged out. They were, without doubt the most prominent part of a fashionable woman's appearance, and emphasized, said Cooke by 'overlacing their Gown-bodies and so thrusting up their Breasts'.[55]

Cooke's translation of Boileau is quoted in a most useful, if occasionally confusing, compilation called *The Ladies Dictionary* of 1694; amplifying the quotation above, the dictionary tells us that women can lace too straightly, 'as if they were angry with Nature.... but as for their looser parts, them they let loose ... Their breasts they lay open like two fair apples'.[56]

Balanced editorial comment is evident in the *Ladies Dictionary*, which does not defend the 'prostituting of naked Necks or Breasts', but takes the moralists to task for their uncritical attacks on women's dress; if they 'spy any thing in the Dress, Cloaths or Garb of Women beyond what they approve, or have been us'd to', all those who wear such fashions, or make them, are 'condemned as Antichristian, and only fit to attend on the Whore of Babylon'. Furthermore, such moralists 'would make weak people believe, that every touch of Colouring added to the Cheeks is a semblance of Hell fire; and their curled hair ... an Emblem of the Never dying Worm'.[57]

Even on the subject of cosmetics, the *Ladies Dictionary,* while disapproving of too many 'Artificial adornments and Embellishments', believes that in moderation, 'Art and Ingenuity study to help and repair the defects of deformity'. This progressive attitude was out of step with the more usual comments, both serious and satirical, of the time, which condemned the use of paint and of any cosmetic aids, as vain and immoral in themselves, and misleading to men. The anonymous author of a *Satyr against Painting* (1697) accuses made-up women 'in gawdy Dresses' of luring 'Foplings ... to thy Caresses'; he comforts himself, however, with the belief that wiser men,

> ... know thy Glories quickly tarnish,
> Of fading Colours made, and Varnish.[58]

In a similar vein, the poem *The Folly of Love* (1691) pokes fun at the 'old Madam' who tries to cheat time by the use of such devices as false hair, a glass eye, ivory false teeth, 'stiff Steel-Bodies' which hide her hunch-back, and even 'artificial Buttocks'.[59] We recall in Congreve's *The Way of the World* (1700) the maid Foible's admonition to old Lady Wishfort who has been too generous with her paint: 'Your ladyship has frowned a little too rashly, madam. There are some cracks discernible in the white varnish'.

To many contemporaries, it seemed as if they were living through a period of unparalleled luxury and foreign vices; in the same way (I am repeating a theme that the reader has heard before and will hear again), there was a regret for the days of 'ancient simplicity' which were contrasted to the present degenerate times. This was the view of the author (possibly John Evelyn's daughter Mary) of *Mundus Muliebris* of 1690. Sub-titled *The Ladies Dressing-Room unlock'd,* it begins with a lament for the good old days when women used their needles in preference to reading romances or seeing 'smutty Farces', and then lists in detail the vast wardrobe of dresses and accessories required by a fashionable lady. The dresses include formal gowns with back drapery, and elaborately trimmed petticoats with rows of lace and 'Fringe to sweep the Mall,' and a whole range of undress or informal gowns; a battery of 'Washes, Unguents, and Cosmeticks' includes 'Plumpers' to fill hollow cheek cavities, and 'Spanish Paper' to redden the cheeks.[60] Among the manifold accessories – the perfumed gloves, muffs, jewellery and so on – are the towering lace headdresses of the period, trimmed with ribbons, and so tall that they had to be arranged on a frame. Such headdresses were often likened to the steeple of a church ('Like Steeple Bow', or Grantham Spire', said *Mundus Muliebris*) or to the sails of a ship. In *The Parable of the Top-Knots* (1691) a woman wearing such 'a speaking Gallimaufry of Ribbons, Laces, Silks and Jewels . . . sails forth . . . like a new-launch'd Vessel, with Pendants and Streamers flying . . .'[61]

According to the satirists, woman in the late seventeenth century was a mass of artifice, disguised from top to toe. Partly replacing the black velvet face masks which were worn to protect the reputation at the theatre (where no decent woman should be seen), and which were frowned on by the moralists, some women took

48 Standing woman c. *1700.*
Anon. French engraving.
Moralists at the end of the seventeenth century deplored the time and money spent in constructing the fashionable woman, from her towering 'top-knot', artificial complexion and elaborately trimmed gown. The petticoat worn with this mantua has, in Mary Evelyn's phrase, enough 'fringe to sweep the Mall'.

to gilding the lily of their complexions by wearing patches. There are isolated references to this custom from the middle of the century, but it became much more fashionable, as part of the 'foreign manners' which Mary Evelyn so deplored, in the last decades of the period. The *Ladies Dictionary*, in a piece of special pleading defending their use, says, that after all, the very shapes of such patches can inculcate moral lessons; the stars remind us of heaven, flies indicate the vanity of the things of this world, and little worms make woman think 'upon meditations of Death and the Grave, where those Insects are to be her Companions'.[62]

It is easy, when reading some of the more critical, usually Puritan, comments on dress, to be carried away by the torrents of words into thinking that all men denounced women for their love of dress. 'It is certain', says one commentator on the subject, 'that, let women dress how they will, they cannot please everyone; either the old or the young will find somewhat to carp at, and it is impossible to escape the laughter of the one, or the censure of the other'.[63] He goes on to say that it is as absurd to say that the dress of the past is always the best, as it is to chase after the latest fashions.

The *Ladies Dictionary* echoes this theme, stressing the foolishness of assuming that the past was noted for its frugality, for Fashion has always been an ever-changing kaleidoscope: 'Fashion brought in Silks and Velvets at one time ... the Tunick and Vest at another. Fashion brought in deep Ruffs and shallow Ruffs, thick Ruffs and thin Ruffs ... Fashion brought in the Vardingale, and carried out the Vardingale, and hath again revived the Vardingale from Death, and placed it behind, like a Rudder or Stern to the body'.[64]

Even Puritan critics, like the author of *Englands Vanity* find their attacks on dress, however spirited, to be out of keeping with the tolerant, cynical, luxury-loving taste of the times. To add to the usual arguments about the inherent pride and vanity involved in too much concentration on finery, he brings into play the despoliation of the earth's resources to meet the demands of the 'proud Peacocks' of fashion.

> we rob and spoil all Creatures almost of the world, to cover our back and to adorn our bodies withal; from some we take their wool, from many their Skins, from diverse their Furrs, from sundry their very Excrements, as the silk which is nothing else but the very Excrement of the worm; not content with this, we come to Fishes and do beg from them their Pearles to hang about us, we go down into the ground for Gold and Silver.... And having borrowed all this of other Creatures, we jett up and down, provoking men to look upon us, as if ... all that beauty came from us.[65]

He admits, however that the fashion industry is all important to the economy, and that the definition of class through dress is vital – these themes are also to feature in the eighteenth century – and in any case, to denounce pride is a thankless and 'unprofitable' task, for 'what have we gained, but as if we had preached but Fables?'.

6
The Vanity of Human Wishes

The most improper things we commit in the Conduct of our Lives, we are led into by the Force of Fashion.

Richard Steele, *The Spectator*, 1711

Fashion – a word which knaves and fools may use,
Their knavery and folly to excuse.

Charles Churchill, *The Rosciad*, 1761

How is the whole scope of our fancy continually on the stretch, in designing and contriving this drapery of the species. How do we travel from east to west, and ransack the several elements for materials to decorate these our corruptible bodies. To please a vitiated imagination of our own, or attract the eyes of the beholders, and provoke their envy, how content are we to forego our own ease ...

Samuel Fawconer,
An Essay on Modern Luxury, 1765

In a century which placed a high esteem on reason and moderation, we are right to expect some lessening in the fervour of moral rebukes; Puritanism, which in the previous century had been one of the major forces attacking dress as sinful, was no longer of major importance (though it did re-emerge as Methodism) – in any case, enthusiasm was unfashionable. Moderation, however, is certainly not to be seen in some of the very extreme fashions which appear, for women in particular, in the eighteenth century. Men, on the whole, apart from a last flourish in the 1770s, entered their Puritan inheritance, with an increasingly sober appearance in the second half of the century.

As we have seen, sumptuary legislation had fizzled out in the early years of the seventeenth century; the mood of the eighteenth century was best expressed by the great jurist Sir William Blackstone, who found it 'a doubtful question how far private luxury is a public evil'.[1]

Lack of officially ordained clothing coupled with a real increase in real wages, led to a widening consumer market and produced considerable social emulation, which, as one economic historian has remarked:

was taken further in England than in any contemporary society. It was facilitated by growing wealth, increasing urbanization, and especially by the growth of London and the increasingly dominant role that the metropolis came to play in English society.[2]

Views about social emulation in dress were mixed. Some, like Bernard de Mandeville, thought it was not always a good thing, for women in particular were prone to dress above their station:

The poorest Labourer's Wife in the Parish, who scorns to wear a strong wholesome Frize, as she might, will starve herself and her Husband to purchase a second-hand Gown and Petticoat that cannot do half the Service, because, forsooth, it is more genteel.[3]

Eighteenth-century novels are full of references to the social disasters that might ensue if the dress was not appropriate to the situation or the class of the wearer. Fine cast-offs, in particular if worn unaltered, were equated with immorality by a deeply conservative working class; when in Fielding's *Tom Jones* (1749), Molly, the slatternly game-keeper's daughter, attends church in a fine silk gown, unaltered, which had been given to her by Sophia Western, she is physically abused by the congregation.

On the other hand, Pamela, the eponymous heroine of Richardson's novel of 1740, although obsessed with dressing suitably to her station in life, which is quite humble, finally gains caste when she can prove through her demeanour and her good taste in dress that she is worthy to be the bride of the elegant and refined Mr B.

In the eighteenth century dress was considered a crucial part of good manners, and contributed to civilized behaviour. When Joseph Baretti in 1760 heard at Exeter a sermon preached against dress, he angrily noted that although extremes in dress were no doubt ridiculous, they could scarcely be called sinful; 'I have observed that people well dressed have in general a kind of respect for themselves, and whoever respects himself, does a very good thing'.[4]

Novels and periodicals played a key part in the dissemination of ideas of gentility and good manners in the eighteenth century, and they also made frequent comments on dress. 'How much Cloaths contribute to make us agreeable Objects', was the theme of an article in *The Spectator* (8 September 1712); one might complain of the time spent on fashion, but:

> Consider how far the Vanity of Mankind has laid itself out in Dress, what a prodigious Number of People it maintains, and what a Circulation of Money it occasions ...

Much of this money ended up in France, and there is much comment throughout the eighteenth century that the English were too keen to abase themselves before 'a Country which has infected all the Nations of Europe with its Levity'.[5] *The Spectator*, for example, poked fun at English dress-makers who rushed to examine the 'French babies' or 'wooden mademoiselles' – the dressed dolls which were sent over from Paris – which had made the journey in spite of the difficulties caused by Anglo–French hostilities; assuming the persona of Betty Crossstitch, *The Spectator* says:

> You cannot imagine ... how ridiculously I find we have all been trussed up during the War, and how infinitely the French dress excells ours. The Mantua has no Leads in the Sleeves, and I hope we are not lighter than the French Ladies, so as to want that Kind of Ballast; the Petticoat has no Whalebone, but sits with an Air altogether gallant and dégagée ...[6]

The *mantua* which is referred to above was originally a loose informal gown with a casually draped overskirt, but by the beginning of the eighteenth century, it had become a formal gown with stylized back drapery, worn with a heavily decorated skirt (known as a petticoat) and over a tightly boned bodice. It was a style which remained popular in England far longer than elsewhere, for English ladies felt both physically and morally comfortable in a gown which fitted the upper part of the body so tightly. One German visitor found that one of the main reasons for Englishwomen 'dressing to their disadvantage' was their love of heavily whaleboned stays.[7] Such corsets were criticized on grounds other than those of aesthetics; they were dangerous to health because they constricted the waist and the torso. The author of the anonymous poem *The Art of Dress* (1717) declared that in the past, when women wore 'Skins around their Middles', they did not suffer 'Torture for a slender Waste'; too much tight-lacing could cause women to swoon and,

> Mean while, an Am'rous Youth may steal a kiss,
> Or snatch, unfelt, perhaps, a greater Bliss.[8]

While too much bodily constriction could lead, perhaps, to a fate worse than death, women were also urged to beware of the immorality of loose garments which hid the shape of the body. One such garment was the seemingly innocuous hooded cloak which was a popular outdoors covering; due to its capacious shape, we are told by the author of *Female Folly: or The Plague of a Woman's Riding-Hood and Cloak* (1713), women of ill-repute found it useful for hiding stolen goods and even pregnancies. Respectable women are urged not to wear it, lest they be tainted by its bad reputation, for its was commonly worn by harlots to hide their slovenly and dirty dress.[9]

Another mode singled out for criticism was the loosely-fitting *sacque* gown from France, which flowed unrestricted from pleats at the shoulders to the hem. With the known English antipathy, already noted in the seventeenth century, towards loose gowns – especially those coming from France – it was inevitable that *The Guardian* (1713) described it as a 'Dishabille. Everything is thrown on with a loose, careless air'. Moral disapproval was not limited to the English, for a French magazine of 1718 described women strolling in the public promenades in Paris wearing such loose sacques with

> 'an air of coming pleasures ... The déshabillé, which is the usual dress of these ladies, gives their bodies such remarkable freedom to expand and thicken'.[10]

Such freedom was even greater when the *sacque* (sack to the English) was worn over a hooped petticoat which could distend the shape of the dress even more. Hoops appeared in fashion in about 1710, and by the following summer *The Spectator* found that such petticoats 'are now blown up into a most enormous Concave and rise every Day more and more'; the writer Joseph Addison claimed to have thought the first woman he saw dressed in this way was pregnant, but he then discovered that 'all the Modish Part of the Sex (were) as far gone as her self'. It is useless, he continues, for women to say such hoops are 'airy and very proper for the Season', for 'this I look upon to be only a Pretence, and a piece of Art, for it is well known we have not had a more moderate Summer these many Years, so that it is certain the Heat they complain of cannot be in the Weather';[11] is the implication here, perhaps, that women may be trying to find an excuse for their sexual heat?

The early full-length hoops, made of rings of cane or whale-bone, were fairly modest in dimension, assuming a conical shape. By the 1730s they were round and circular, and in the following decade vast and square-shaped. By the middle of the century they were no longer worn, except for court, in the fashionable world outside England, and a French visitor to London in the later 1740s was amazed at the English fondness for extremes – 'they do not seem capable of being moderate in anything'.[12]

The fashionable magazines of the 1740s are full of accounts of the accidents which befell women in what Mrs Delany described as 'the tubs of hoops'. Women had to practise walking in them, and those less skilled in the careful deportment required, would, said *The Female Spectator* (1744), enter public assemblies with 'a kind of frisk and jump (and) throw their enormous hoops almost in the faces of those who pass them by'.[13]

The most comprehensive attack on hoops came in 1745 with the publication of a tract entitled *The Enormous Abomination of the Hoop-Petticoat* by a certain 'A.W.', who begins somewhat defensively by saying he is neither an old man nor a Quaker or Methodist – categories presumably synonymous with the disapproval of extremes in fashion – but that he feels compelled to write about the hoops which are 'now past a Jest'. His complaints are as follows: that they take up too much room – 'women are by this prodigious Garment become a perfect publick Nuisance' – in the streets, in coaches and at church; that they are costly – he itemizes 'the vast foolish Expence of so much Silk and other costly Materials'; that they are unhealthy – 'Females have skrew'd and moulded their Bodies into a Shape quite contrary'; and finally, that they are indecent when a woman lifts her skirts out of the mud, or when the wind, or an accident causes them to be thrown up over her head.[14] He does not, as some men did – rather tongue-in-cheek – defend the hoop by saying that it encouraged virtue in women as it kept men at a distance ...

In any case, according to many critics, some of the more foppish young men were less keen on paying court to women, than on attending to their own appearance. The early-eighteenth-century beau, the direct descendant of the Jacobean gallant and the Restoration fop, is summed up in *The Beau's Character* of 1706:

> A wig that's full,
> An empty skull
> ....
> A snatch of French,
> And none of sense,

49 The Garter (detail) 1724.
J. F. de Troy.
The loose sacque gown in its early form so deplored by the moralists as indicating equal looseness of mind (not to mention the fact that it could hide a multitude of sins), seems the perfect costume for this scène galante.

50 'Taste A-La-Mode 1745'.
Engraving by F. Patton after L. P. Boitard.
The inconvenience and indelicacy occasioned by the wearing of the vast hoops of the mid-1740s is underlined here, although the artist takes care to point out that some of the fashionable beaux ape female fashions in the stiffened swinging skirts to their coats.

> ....
> A foreign tour,
> Domestick whore,
> And mercenary marriage.[15]

Such a man of fashion, with his mistresses (divorce was virtually impossible), his Grand Tour which had given him a few French phrases and nothing much else, and his passion for the latest modes, is a stock character – some might say caricature – of the eighteenth century. He is popularly supposed to spend as many hours on his appearance as a woman does; indeed, in a somewhat dubious compliment to the female sex, the author of *The English Theophrastus, or*

The Manners of the Age says such a beau is 'a Creature who under the appearance of a Man, has all the Folly, Vanity and Levity of a Woman ...' At his mirror in the morning, 'he licks his Lips, paints his Cheeks, and strives to outdo Kneller ... in counterfeiting the lovely Eyebrow. He is two long Hours in tying his Garters, Careening his Wig, tiffling the Curls, tying and untying his Cravat'. Having completed his dressing, and 'scented like a Perfumer's Shop', he goes by chair to his favourite seamstress 'who takes care of his Linnen and manages his Intrigues', and with whom he 'enters into a profound Chat about the newest

Fashion for Cravats, what colour'd Ribband is most proper for that Season, how deep Men wear their Ruffles'.[16] A brief sojourn at White's Chocolate House is followed by a visit to the theatre where he gives a running commentary on the play, the audience and their clothes – the 'entertainments' of the thoughtless and fashionable man-about-town had not changed radically since the days of Shakespeare, when Dekker in his *Gull's Hornbook* had outlined a day similar in content.

As the shape of men's suits changed relatively little during the first half of the eighteenth century, tailors (and their critics) had to concentrate on details of cuff, pocket, cravat etc. *The Spectator* has fun with a 'Will Sprightly' who boasts of being 'the Author of the frosted Button ... I produced much about the same Time the Scollop Flap, the knotted Cravat, and made a fair Push for the silver-clocked Stocking ...'[17]

The predominant feature of the formal coat was the wide side-pleats which were stiffened with horsehair or even wire, so that they echoed the hoops worn by women; at court in 1722 Sarah Osborn found such coats 'like our Mantuas', stating that 'I believe the gentlemen will ware petty-cotes very soon'.[18] For attendance at court, and at any formal function, silk suits trimmed with lace, braid or embroidery were worn; Sarah Osborn thought the coloured coats she saw – silver, pink and pale blue – 'prodigiously effeminate'. They would almost certainly have been made of imported silks, from Italy (if velvets) and France (for woven silks) and one of the main complaints of patriotic critics was of the immorality of preferring foreign luxury to native simplicity.

One poetic comment has a beau asking rhetorically:

> Shall I wear clothes in awkward England made?
> And sweat in cloth, to help the woollen trade?
> In French embroid'ry and in Flanders lace
> I'll spend the income of a treasurer's place.[19]

Flanders produced the finest lace which was often smuggled in to avoid the duty; officers returning to England from the wars against France, according to Farquhar's play *The Recruiting Officer* (1706), 'every year bring over a cargo of lace, to cheat the Queen of her duty, and her subjects of their honesty'. In addition to Flanders lace, the beau would order his linen from the Low Countries, and his suit and wig were either made in France, or by a French tailor and wig-maker in England. It was a hopeless task to dissuade the Englishman from the patronage of foreign finery, however much learned clerics like the Bishop of Llandaff published attacks on French modes; in his *A Treatise upon the Modes: or, a Farewell to French Kicks* (1715) the bishop urged men to wear native woollen cloth and modest wigs, instead of Lyons silks and large, powdered, effeminate French perukes.

Another cleric – better known perhaps as a philosopher – Bishop George Berkeley, joined the attack on foreign imports; his own particular campaign was to encourage the consumption of Irish silks and linens. This would, he believed, help the English as well as the Irish economy, for, he wondered in *The Querist* (1735) 'Whether it be true, that Two Millions are yearly expended by England in foreign Lace and Linnen?'[20]

By the middle of the century, the growing influence of the middle classes had helped to encourage a greater simplicity of taste in men's dress; many Englishmen, except on the most formal occasions, wore small neat wigs (some were even beginning to wear their own hair) and suits of plainly trimmed woollen cloth. It was all the more irritating, said the novelist Tobias Smollett, that when an Englishman travelled to France, where silks were worn on most occasions, he had to undergo a 'total metamorphosis'; 'he must even change his buckles and the form of his ruffles; and though at the risque of his life, suit his cloaths to the mode of the season. For example, though the weather should be never so cold, he must wear his *habit d'été* or *demi-saison,* without presuming to put on a warm dress before the day which fashion has fixed for that purpose.' The Englishman, clad in the moral approbation of his 'beau drap d'Angleterre' must in Paris 'provide himself

51 *Pantin a la Mode*, 1748, attributed to J. June. This is a satire on French fashions in which the elegant company play with pantins or puppets. The verse decries the 'Gallic Influence' as seen in the 'false Delights of Ease and Dress', which is particularly manifest in the two foppish young men with their affected poses, patched complexions and modish costume.

with a camblet suit trimmed with silver for spring and autumn, with silk cloaths for summer ... or velvet for winter', all of which 'frippery' is useless on his return to London.[21]

One wonders how far Smollett, described aptly by Sterne as a 'splenetic Traveller', actually accommodated himself to the much more formal French society, where fashion was a highly revered ritual in which all who could afford it, played a part.

Smollett would perhaps have been sympathetic to the revival of Puritan religious sentiment which appeared in mid-eighteenth-century England with the crusading zeal of John Wesley and the Methodist movement. This strain of thought had firmly remained in sections of English society (notably the working and middle classes), deriving its inspiration from the early seventeenth-century divines, from works like Bunyan's *The Pilgrim's Progress* (1678), and the hymns of Isaac Watts (1674–1748). Watts in his sermons urged 'moderation and decency in apparel' in language very similar to that of the early-seventeenth-century Puritan moralists:

> Nor, while you are dressing, should you forget that you are sinners, and therefore should put on shamefacedness; for all our ornaments and clothing are but a memorial of our first sin and shame, and when we take a pride in our garments, it looks

THE VANITY OF HUMAN WISHES

52 The Rake's Progress 1735.
W. Hogarth.
Disorderly dress to the eighteenth-century mind was an indication of disorderly and immoral conduct. Nowhere is this more clearly expressed than in the work of Hogarth, and in the Tavern Scene we see the Rake himself with his clothes awry, and a number of prostitutes in various states of undress.

as if we had forgotten the original of them, the loss of our innocency.

Christians should see themselves as on a pilgrimage towards a heavenly goal; like Bunyan's pilgrim, they cannot avoid the sight of Vanity-Fair, but they should resist the temptations it contains:

it is below the glory of our character, and the dignity of our calling, to have our thoughts uneasy, if every pin and point that belongs to our apparel be not placed in the most fashionable manner; to fret and rage, if every fold of a garment be not adjusted in perfect conformity to the mode.[22]

In the next generation, John Wesley and his Methodist field preachers spread 'vital religion' to the poor; Wesley himself over half a century delivered the astonishing sum of about 40,000 sermons as he travelled all over the kingdom. In one such sermon, he shows himself in sympathy with the mainstream of Puritan thought in believing that although 'a moderate difference of apparel between persons of different stations' is to be tolerated, the actual wearing of rich clothes is morally harmful, for 'nothing is more natural than to think ourselves better because we are dressed in better clothes'; fine clothes 'have a natural tendency to make a man sick of pride'. The logical extension of spending large sums of money on dress is to steal from God, for it means we have less to spend on His children, the poor. Most of Wesley's remarks are directed at women's dress (his male listeners would, on the whole, be soberly dressed); he wishes them to avoid 'a bold, immodest look' which can be created by 'the profusion of ribbands, gauze or linen about your heads'. Before he dies, his hope, he tells them, is to see:

> a Methodist congregation, full as plain dressed as a Quaker congregation. Only, be more consistent with yourselves. Let your dress be cheap as well as plain. Otherwise you do but trifle with God, and me, and your own souls. I pray, let there be no costly silks among you, how grave soever they be. Let there be no Quaker linen, proverbially so called for its exquisite fineness; no Brussels lace, no Elephantine hats or bonnets, those scandals of Female Modesty. Be all of a piece, dressed from head to foot, as persons professing godliness.[23]

Although quick to condemn fashion as part of the 'irrational, sinful customs of a frantic world', Wesley, like most such critics, can find no really positive suggestions for what 'godly' women can actually wear.

Mid-eighteenth-century London was certainly full of 'sinful customs', and the Methodists (like the Salvation Army over a century later) tried to curtail, if not to banish totally, some of the prevailing vices like prostitution and drunkenness. With the great size of eighteenth-century London – it was the largest city in Europe with a population of a million – prostitution was very much a growth industry. By the 1780s, a Prussian visitor declared that there were 50,000 such women in the capital, some organized by 'matrons' whose supervision was strict; so much so that some of the girls 'escape from their prison with their little wardrobes under their arms, and trade on their own bottoms'[24] – never has there been such an apt phrase. Prostitutes were to be distinguished both by their demeanour and their clothing, the latter by general consent, a kind of tawdry finery, uncorseted slovenliness. In Richardson's novel *Clarissa Harlowe* (1748) we are taken to a bagnio (a brothel) where the inhabitants, to the horrified gaze of the heroine, were 'all in shocking dishabille and without stays ... their gowns made to cover straddling hoops, hanging trollopy, and tangling about their heels'.[25]

The author of *Satan's Harvest Home* (1749) found London 'overstock'd with harlots', and attributed the rise in prostitution to the careless and slovenly upbringing of girls, who were allowed to rise late in the morning and slop around the house in 'a loose Petticoat, Night-Gown and Slippers'.[26] Neither stays nor chemise are mentioned, a sure sign of immorality, for a clean white shift and tightly laced corset were indispensable items for a respectable, even if poor, girl. Underwear, being directly next to the body, retained its medieval symbolism of chastity; it is when the rather rakish Mr B. in Richardson's novel *Pamela* gives the pretty maid the cast-off underwear and stockings of of her recently deceased mistress, his mother, that she realizes that he is trying to seduce her.

It was a common belief (*pace* Satan's Harvest Home), that women who spent too much on their clothes might be inclined to a life of idle frivolity which could lead to even worse excesses. Bishop Berkeley was also of this opinion; he wondered how far the 'Folly' of fashion might 'produce many other Follies, an entire Derangement of Domestic Life, absurd Manners, neglect of Duties, bad Mothers, a general Corruption'.[27]

Among the other follies which tempted

53 Pamela rising from her bed c. *1750*.
P. Mercier.
For a novel that prided itself on its 'morality', Richardson's Pamela *gave rise to a number of singularly immoral works, both literary and artistic, in which the heroine is depicted in deliberately provoking 'undress'. Mercier takes one of the bedroom scenes from the novel as an excuse to show Pamela in a most revealing night shift.*

---

fashionable women (and men) in the eighteenth century was the masquerade, which gave ample grounds for criticism, for its opportunities for intrigue and disguise. It was, said *The Female Spectator*, a 'love of Company... that makes our Ladies run galloping in Troops every evening to Masquerades, Balls and Assemblies, which ... as it were, prepare the way for other more vicious excesses'.[28]

Introduced from Italy in the early years of the eighteenth century, the masquerade flourished in theatres, private houses and in the pleasure gardens of London. The fact that the participants came in disguise and masked, and that masquerades were likely places for vice to flourish (prostitutes found good custom at such events) ensured the popularity of the diversion with the masqueraders, and its denunciation by the authorities; the great earthquake which devasted Lisbon in 1755 was attributed to God's wrath at masquerades (in a similar vein, the Emperor Justinian had, in the sixth century, stated his belief that earthquakes were caused by homosexuality), and they were, rather ineffectively, banned for a year in England. Richardson's heroine Pamela, arbiter of middle-class morality, was tempted to one masquerade, and was horrified by the 'Liberties of Expression and Behaviour', the 'Levity and Indecorum' that she witnessed; there were very real dangers, as Fielding warned in his novel *Amelia* (1751) of 'riot, disorder and intemperance' there.[29]

As well as frequent complaints about the mingling of classes at masquerades, which could lead to unnerving encounters, there were attacks on some of the costumes worn on the grounds of indecency. Costumes that revealed the shape of the body were regarded as especially indecorous; one man, for example, at a masquerade in 1770, disgusted his fellow-revellers by 'the unavoidable indelicacy of the dress, flesh coloured silk with an apron of fig-leaves' that he wore as Adam.[30] For women, Turkish costumes, which were low-necked and unstructured (Turkish women wore no corsets), had a pleasing air of indecorum about them, and were very popular at masquerades; at one such occasion at the Haymarket theatre in 1724, we find 'Lucretia, a Prude', amazed at the choice of dress worn by 'Hilaria, a Coquet':

O Jesu, – Coz. – why this fantastick Dress?
I fear some Frenzy does your Head possess;
That thus you sweep along a Turkish Tail,
And let that Robe o'er Modesty prevail.[31]

The 'indecency' of the Turkish costume probably resided more in its indolent and exotic associations than in any really revealing dress; even the loose trousers which were properly part of oriental costume did not excite much criticism, for it was perfectly possible to wear the clothing of the opposite sex at masquerades.

The masquerade was, however, blamed by some moralists, for encouraging the wearing of *négligé* gowns, usually loosely draped, tying at the waist with a sash, and possibly based on Turkish fancy dresses. *The World* for 1763 noted that 'it is the fashion for a lady to UNDRESS herself to go abroad ...',[32] and *The Connoisseur* attributed 'the propensity of our modern ladies to get rid of their cloaths' to the notorious Elizabeth Chudleigh, who appeared at a masquerade in 1749, in the words of Mrs Montagu, 'as Iphigenia for the sacrifice, but so naked, the high priest might easily inspect the entrails of the victim'.[33]

One suspects that this open display of the lady's charms was disapproved of for its unsubtlety, for the eighteenth century was certainly not prudish about laying emphasis on the shape of the body. The figure was much more the centre of beauty than the face.

By the middle years of the century, under the prevailing influence of the French rococo, a world of sensuality and a language of coquetry could be conveyed through the rituals of dressing and undressing at the formal toilette; it was a kind of witty strip-tease. Rococo dress involved a love of light-reflecting silks, covered with three-dimensional ornamentation such as lace, ribbons and flowers; scraps of these fabrics mixed with feathers and jewels formed tiny headdresses called pompons, after Madame de Pompadour.[34] 'There is not such a thing as a decent old woman left', was the opinion of Lady Jane Coke; 'everybody curls their hair, shews their neck, and wears pink'.[35] As well as these sins (which she attributes to the French) she might have included the popular *sacque* dress, with its flowing back pleats, which was widely worn by Englishwomen; although they wore a version made tight to the bodice, to critics like a writer in *The Connoisseur* (1754), they 'appear with their cloaths huddled on ... loosely and indecently. This manner of dressing, or rather not dressing, was brought from Paris'.[36]

A similar moan came from 'Adam Fitz-Adam' in *The World*, in the previous year, when he lamented not just that his food was 'disguised in the dressing by a French cook', but that his womenfolk too had taken to French red (he means rouge), 'shreds and rags of velvets, feathers, and ribbands, stuck with false stones ... and placed awry' (this is his description of a pompon), and 'scraps of dirty gauze' (this is a reference to the popularity of silk gauze which lost its shine when washed, so that it usually remained dirty).[37] By the mid 1750s hoops were left off in fashionable dress, so that the gown

54 'Miss Chudley in the Actual Dress as she appear'd in the Character of Iphigenia, at the Jubilee Ball or Masquerade at Ranelagh', *1749*.
Anon. engraving.
Elizabeth Chudleigh's daring 'see-through' costume excited both amazement and criticism, and proved a fitting portent of her later career as an adventuress.

often trailed on the ground gathering dirt, another source of criticism. In Oliver Goldsmith's novel, *The Vicar of Wakefield* (1766), the daughters of the Primrose family are reluctant to give up their fashionable ways – 'their hair plastered up with pomatum, their faces patched to taste, their trains bundled up into a heap behind, and rustling at every motion' – even though the vicar found such finery 'very unbecoming in us, who want the means of decency'.[38]

Women's hair had begun to rise in the 1760s and pomatum, a kind of scented paste, was needed to hold the increasingly high edifice together, along with the false hair which was, especially in the 1770s, added to give the necessary bulk. By the 1770s, a decade of extravagance generally in dress, hair was piled enormously high with feathers completing the *tout ensemble*; in the mid 1770s Mrs Delany found such 'waving plumes, preposterous Babylonian heads towering to the sky', a vogue she attributed to 'an influenza of the brain', to be 'more suited to the stage or a masquerade than for either civil or sober societies'.[39] Lady Louisa Stuart remembered that these ostrich feathers were attacked as 'seriously wrong and immoral ... the unfortunate feathers were insulted, mobbed, hissed, almost pelted wherever they appeared, abused in the newspapers, nay, even

55 'La Folie pare la Décrépitude des ajustemens de la Jeunesse'.
Engraving by L. Surugue after C. Coypel, 1745.
A constant theme in satire, both literary and artistic, is the attempt made by older women to recover their youth by adopting a battery of artificial aids. In this case, patches, jewellery and fine lace are used to disguise old age.

preached at in the pulpits and pointed out as marks of reprobation'.[40]

With the powder that covered fashionable hairstyles from the middle of the century, more cosmetics were needed than before in order that the complexion should not appear too pale. The thick white paint of an earlier period, which was

107

TOILETTE DE LA DUCHESSE DES PLUMES OU LE TRIOMPHE DE LA FOLIE DU SIECLE

Le Peintre a bien saisi le gout de sa coeffure ;
L'or le Pon, le Dindon, par leur triste aventure,

Montre que ce beau sexe n'en fut jamais d'autre
Il prend l'orgueil de l'un et la sottise de l'autre.

56 Toilette de la Duchesse des Plumes ou Le Triomphe de la Folie du Siècle.
Anon. French engraving.
This satire is typical of many published in the later 1770s, when the craze for towering hairstyles was at its height. The peacock had long been a symbol of pride, an apt choice to illustrate the vogue for feathered headdresses in this period.

57 'Grown Ladies taught to dance by Monsieur Allemande from Paris'.
Anon. English drawing c. 1778.
The artist satirizes both the mincing French dancing master and his pretentious pupils, in their over-dressed finery, soaring hairstyles and patched complexions, as they learn the arts of polite society.

necessary to some extent to cover the ravages caused by small-pox, was no longer (with the gradual spread of the practice of inoculation) needed as much; make-up was also safer, and many brands were advertised as being free from mercury or other metallic substances, which had eaten into the skin if used copiously enough. Whiteness was now achieved with pearl powder, and red with 'Spanish and Portugal wool', which gave 'glorious Colour to the Cheeks and Lips'.[41] In addition, the middle years of the century saw a revival of the habit of adding patches to the face and bosom, the placing of each one having a meaning of its own, a signal of sex-appeal; the *Lady's Magazine* for 1759 declared that more than one patch was vulgar (or at the most, one large patch on the temple and one tiny patch close by it was permissible): 'Common women stick little patches about their mouths, prudes upon their cheeks, and those who are a little better than the first, about their eyes'. With this veritable battery of cosmetics, it was no wonder that in 1770 an act of Parliament was mockingly proposed in which women were to be urged not to 'impose upon, seduce and betray into matrimony, any of his Majesty's subjects, by scents, paints, cosmetic washes, artificial teeth, false hair, Spanish wool, iron stays, hoops, high-heeled shoes and bolstered hips . . .'[42]

As we have seen in earlier periods, men, too, were often accused of using cosmetics to improve their complexions, a custom which was still in evidence throughout the first half of the eighteenth century, though increasingly subject to ridicule. *The Female Spectator* in the mid 1740s poked fun at the 'coxcombs' (successors to the beaux) who, in spite of 'wars, . . . threatened invasions, . . . popish pretenders', are not inspired to assume manly airs, but appear in public wearing rouge, perfumes, lip salves, complexion creams, and masks to prevent freckles

58 'The Beauties of Bagnigge Wells'.
Anon. engraving c. 1778.
The pleasure gardens of London were popular places for assignations. The young man, dressed in fashionable sporting style, looks interested at the advances of the modish prostitute, whose over-elaborate toilette (like that of her fellow practitioner with her back to us) indicates her status.

and sunburn.[43] Also depicted wearing a mask to protect his complexion is Smollett's risible Captain Whiffle, in the novel *Roderick Random* (1748); he wears red velvet breeches and a white silk coat lined with pink, a combination rather light and 'feminine' for mid-eighteenth-century male attire, and ill-suited to his nautical vocation. Until the rise of the macaronis in the 1760s, the name 'Billy Wiffle' was synonymous with an effeminate man. Some commentators like the author of *Satan's Harvest Home,* attributed 'the Growth of Sodomy' to the cosmetics and the clothes that men wore; picked out for attack as 'effeminate' are over-laced clothes, low-heeled pumps, and hair 'strok'd over before and cock'd up behind, with a Comb sticking in it, as if it were just ready to receive a Head-Dress'.[44]

Another custom which he dislikes, is men kissing each other, a habit imported from Italy, along with the opera. By the middle of the eighteenth century, the Grand Tour was well established, the high-light being a visit to Italy to study classical art in Rome, and enjoy the varied entertainments of Venice. From Italy, in the 1760s, some of these fashionable young men introduced the term 'macaroni', to mean anything exceptionally stylish and elegant. Although the word could be applied to popular plays and pastimes, a macaroni soon came to be synonymous with a very effeminate young man, in a brightly coloured tight-fitting coat (the inside pocket was invented so as not to spoil the line), a nosegay of flowers, and a huge, powdered wig on top of which perched a tiny hat, called a Nivernois after the French ambassador in London. Such coxcombs, sneered *The Town and Country Magazine* (1772) were 'essenced and perfumed', and wore their 'coatsleeves so tight, they can with much difficulty get their arms through their cuffs'; their legs (both tight-fitting breeches and stockings) are 'covered with all the colours of the rainbow'.[45] Dressed in this way, and with their rather mincing walk (partly due to their clothes being so tight), they were a gift to the caricaturists during the 1770s, the decade which saw the first great flowering of this artistic genre. Such exaggerated fashions could hardly be taken seriously, so that instead of heavy moral denunciations of their sin and folly, they were laughed out of countenance. Caricature was, one suspects, especially pleasing to the English, for it combined their love of the extreme and the grotesque with their fondness for preaching and moralizing; to some extent, the caricature took the place of the pulpit for the next fifty years.

59 'Welladay! is this my son Tom!'
Coloured mezzotint c. 1770.
The old gentleman, arriving in London, exclaims in horror at the transformation of his son into a fashionable 'macaroni'.

The macaroni fashions were a defiant last fling of frivolity, for the tendency in male dress in the second half of the century was for a sober middle-class simplicity, a fondness for cloth suits in shades of blue and brown, and for wearing one's own hair instead of a wig. As early as the 1740s we find Lord Chesterfield warning his son against the fashion for looking like 'grooms, stage-coachmen and country bumpkins', with 'brown frocks, leather breeches ... hats uncocked and ... hair unpowdered'.[46]

Some twenty years later, the tendency was in full swing; a dark coloured frock coat (a

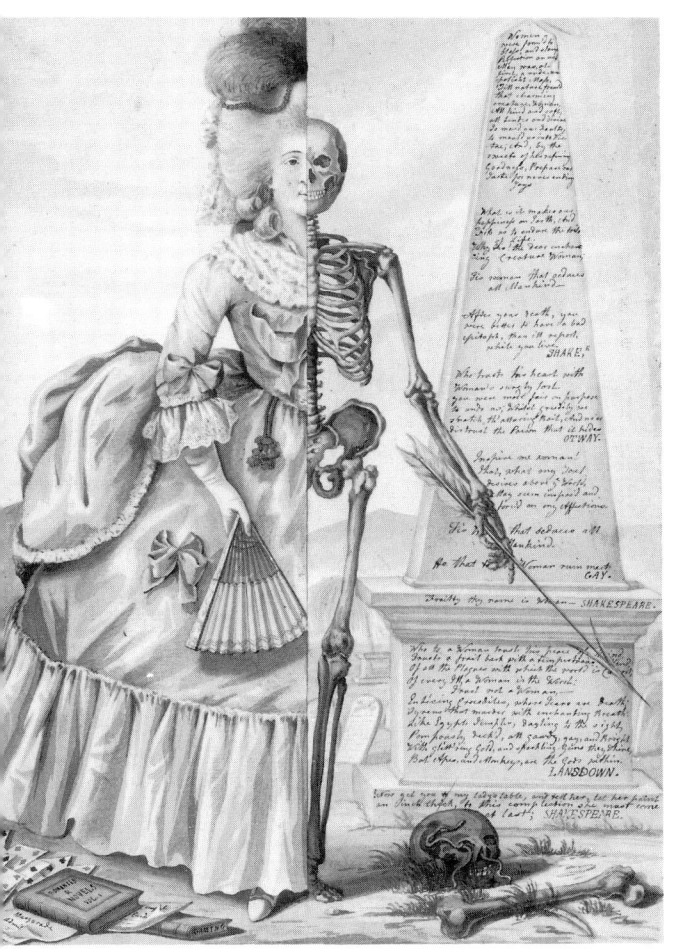 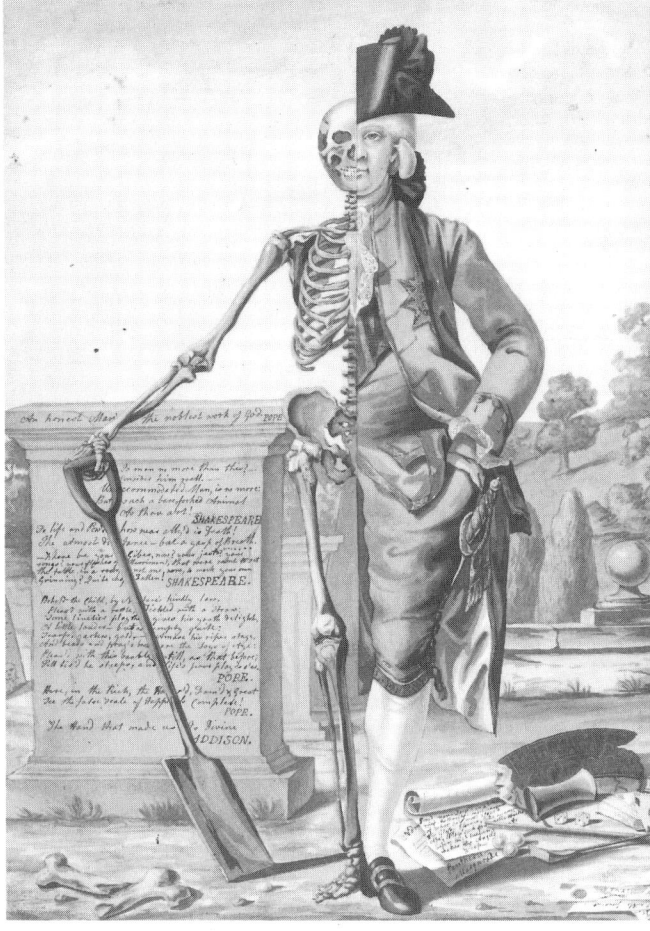

60 'Life and Death Contrasted, or – An Essay on Woman'.
'Death and Life Contrasted, or – An Essay on Man'.
R. Dighton c. 1784.
This is a reinterpretation of the medieval notion of the Dance of Death and the futility of human vanity. The inevitability of death should dissuade men and women from fashionable, trivial pastimes such as card-playing, novel reading and attending masquerades.

simple style with minimal side pleats, plain cuff, and turned-down collar), a short waistcoat, and simply styled natural hair, were the elements of everyday dress. By the mid 1760s, the wig-makers were beginning to panic and petition the authorities for a sumptuary law compelling men to wear perukes. *The St James's Chronicle* (1765) printed an anguished letter from a wig-maker equating the flourishing of England with the wearing of perukes; English gentlemen should avoid wearing their own hair, for this was the custom of the Pope, and because Archbishop Laud in the seventeenth century had been 'Popishly affected, and wore his own Hair, ... he deservedly lost his Head'.[47]

This writer believed that all rank and order would be lost without wigs, which were a visible sign of status; his complaint, that it was increasingly difficult to tell the master from the servant by the clothes they wore, was part of an increasing chorus of such moans in the years before the French Revolution. Indeed, many contemporaries – both French and English – linked the events of 1789 with a general decline in manners and standards of dress, as men rushed to wear garments which were in origin working class, such as the trousers or pantaloons. However proletarian in origin, pantaloons, when adopted into the fashionable man's wardrobe, and worn with fine leather boots, a dark cloth coat excellently cut, and pristine white linen, were far removed from what a working-man would wear. Such a process of 'gentrification' was inevitable, as men distanced themselves (even aristocratic sympathizers with the Republican cause) from the working classes. Cleanness and whiteness of linen was, in particular, a luxury which few of the poor could afford. There was a general feeling, however, that cleanliness was, in Wesley's phrase, next to godliness, and that the poor should be encouraged to wear clean, locally produced homespun instead of the cast-offs which many relied on; it was increasingly felt to be morally reprehensible to wear old clothes instead of having the industry to make one's own. This was the view expressed by Sir Frederick Eden in his important survey *The State of the Poor* (1797); he found the northern poor to be better dressed in their home-made clothing than the more indolent southerners who bought second-hand clothes in the shops catering for this trade.

Cleanliness of attire and of the person was the ideal in all classes of men. A reprobate like Boswell, for example, was out of step with the times in his love of bright, fancy, dress and lack of personal hygiene; he 'looked very badly when dressed, for as he seldom washed himself, his clean ruffles served as a striking contrast to his dirty flesh'.[48]

Although many Englishmen had sympathized with the outbreak of the French Revolution in 1789, they changed their minds when events took a more violent turn with the advent of the Terror in 1794. In this 'Æra of Jacobinism and Equality', as Sir Nathaniel Wraxall called it, 'Pantaloons, cropped Hair, and shoe-strings, together with the disuse of Hairpowder, characterized the man'; he regretted the disappearance of 'Fetters ... of Dress, Etiquette, and Form', for they had served to distinguish the upper from the lower classes.[49]

Although the English denounced the turn that political events had taken in France, equating the deliberately slovenly costume of the *sans-culottes* with the violent anarchy of the times, many young men of fashion aped the *Incroyables* of Paris. These were elegant young men who adopted extreme versions of English country clothing, very tight breeches or pantaloons, cut-away coats with huge lapels, vast starched linen cravats, and carefully dishevelled hair; a popular, if rather morbid style adopted by some *Incroyables* (the term was an expression of astonishment rather than a precise label) was to have the hair long at the side in 'spaniel's ears', and then either combed up or cut short at the back, 'in imitation of what was called *la toilette de la guillotine*, when the back locks were cut off by the executioner'.[50] These *élégants*, who tactfully claimed to be republicans, although they were anti-Jacobin, were really a French version of the outrageous macaronis; they affected a lisp and called themselves the *jeunesse dorée*.

Since the English had, in a sense, invented the fashion, they too wore similar exaggerated styles, to the alarm of their many critics; they

> are distinguished by a hat shaped like a sugarloaf, their locks copiously besmeared with pomatum, and hanging down to their shoulders; a large, thick neckcloth which conceals all the lower part of the face; a wide gaping mouth, both hands in their pockets, and a very unbecoming gait.[51]

In spite of the war between England and France, there was considerable communication of the fashions between the two countries. This was mainly by means of fashion magazines, which had been regularly produced, with illustrations, from the early 1770s; from this time onwards, changes in fashion were immensely speeded up. From this point, real fashion as we understand it today, with regular, speedy and seasonal changes, begins to have a real impact. The range of fabrics available, with the variety of accessories which a fashionable woman required, led to the expansion of the dress-making and couture trades in Paris, which remained a Mecca for the well-dressed visitors, although

61 'A Jessamy'.
Anon. engraving from The Follies of Man, *1790.
In his effeminate, exaggerated clothing, he is the direct descendant of the 'macaroni', although he 'assumes a military air and places a cockade in his hat'.*

It was a more robust version of this costume which inspired the French Incroyables *later in the decade.*

---

men were increasingly turning to London tailoring.

For women, the decade of the 1780s sees a growing divergence between the formal and the informal in dress. Attendance at court demanded a silk *sacque* gown, ornately trimmed, and worn over a hoop; the sack, earlier criticized for its looseness, had now become a respectable garment, and – like much formal or official dress – it became increasingly fossilized, and derided as old-fashioned. With the growth of fashion journalism, it soon became positively shameful to be seen to be behind the fashions.

Developments in fashion took place in less formal gowns, such as the masculine-inspired riding costumes and great-coats. When, in the 1660s, men, as we have seen, started to wear a three-piece suit, women adopted a version of this for riding, but with a skirt instead of breeches; some even wore a man's periwig. This was seen as a deliberate aping of men's costume; Anthony Wood notes, disapprovingly, that 'women ... strive to be like men' in their periwigs and 'riding coate of a red colour all bedaubed with lace which they call vests'.[52] The novelist Samuel Richardson also found such a dress to be offensively unfeminine; in a letter headed '*Against a young Lady's affecting manly Airs; and also censuring the modern Riding-habits*' (1741), he claims to find 'that one cannot easily distinguish your Sex by it. For you neither look like a modest Girl in it, nor an agreeable Boy'.[53]

By the 1780s, women were also wearing greatcoats with long tight sleeves and caped collars, in imitation of the masculine mode; they were also accused of being ungainly in their attempts to copy a male gait. Mrs Montagu, observing such attire in Bath, commented: 'A quiet sober woman is a rarity in these times. How the misses waddle, and straddle, and strut, and swagger about the streets here, one arm akimbo, the other swinging'.[54]

Almost in order to counteract accusations of masculinity in dress, women emphasized their feminine features by amplifying bottom and bosom; cork hip pads or back bustles created a full, bouncy effect over the buttocks, and to enlarge the bosom women wore either false rubber bosoms, or starched linen or gauze kerchiefs. *The Morning Herald* for 29 May 1786, advised women who planned to visit Vauxhall, 'to omit wearing their anterior and posterior protuberances, alias the patent bosoms and Sestini bums, and depend only on the elasticity and rotundity of nature'; the complaint was, as with hoops some forty years earlier, that women took up too much room with such artificially enlarged dresses.

There was, in any case, a movement away from artifice, towards a more natural line, with increasing criticism of tight-lacing. Those opposed to tight-lacing felt, with Rousseau, that there was absolute moral virtue in the natural body shape; this was to be a constant theme of moralists for the next hundred years, although they had no real conception of what the truly 'natural' body might look like, warts and all.

Tight-lacing was also attacked on medical grounds; it was thought by an increasing number of doctors to be the cause of chest complaints, and consumption, among other maladies. Heavily boned stays, said Dr Leroy, in a work published in 1772, were 'un vêtement barbare et dangereux'; they hindered proper breathing, they were bad for pregnant women, they deformed the chest, and by revealing too much of the bosom, they were also immodest. In addition, such a formidable boned structure gave women the appearance of being encased in armour; so that even on aesthetic grounds, corsetry was abhorrent.

Pondering on the question as to why, with all the reasons listed above, women should still wear stays, Leroy can only assume that it is due to the prevailing fashions of dress which highlight a rigid torso and a prominently displayed bosom. He himself, believing that women's charms are best veiled, would prefer the loosely draped cross-over gowns which some actresses wore in oriental roles.[55]

Such styles, being both exotic and comfortable, were very popular in the 1770s and 1780s, although some men like Horace Walpole complained that they looked like dressing gowns. More serious critics stated that such gowns, often made of flimsy muslins or fine silk gauze, were too thin and figure-revealing to be decent. One commentator (writing in 1801, as a republican with a political axe to grind) stated that the most popular of these light gowns, the

62 'Tally Ho' c. 1788.
R. Dighton.
The inelegant and somewhat masculine pose of the fashionable lady in her riding habit was probably what Mrs Montagu had in mind when she complained of the 'misses' who 'strut and swagger about the streets'.

chemise, which was popularized at the court of Marie-Antoinette, was the dress of prostitutes.[56] The chemise dress, made of white muslin and fastening with a sash at the waist, was *the* sartorial success story of the 1780s; as its name implies, it was based on the chemise or shift which women wore as their main undergarment. It was this that made it scandalous (for there had previously been simple cotton and linen gowns worn informally throughout the

63 'The Bum Shop' *1785*.
Engraving after A. Rushworth.
The artist pokes fun at the way in which a fashionable woman, in order to assume a modish rotundity, has to wear absurd, padded protuberances on bottom and bosom.

---

century), especially when worn by a queen. When Marie-Antoinette's portrait by Vigée-Lebrun was exhibited in the Salon in 1783, it caused an outcry as being far too intimate and informal a dress to be depicted in, and it had to be withdrawn. This may have only served to enhance its popularity, and by the mid 1780s, the editor of the *Lady's Magazine* declared that all women from fifteen to fifty were wearing this style which it called 'girlishly juvenile'; it was, she said, 'an undressing age'.

The more transparent and revealing forms of the chemise appear to have been worn more in France than in England. When the American Abigail Adams visited Paris in 1784, she found fashionable Parisians to be 'not averse' to 'a state of nature'. In particular she was shocked to find the widow of the celebrated philosopher Helvétius in a very revealing tiffany chemise; 'after dinner, she threw herself on a settee where she showed more than her feet'.[57] Other than light petticoats, women wore little underwear and certainly no pants. What also amazed the rather severe Mrs Adams, was the overriding importance attached to fashion, an obsession, as we have noted, which was encouraged by the flood of fashion magazines. Many moralists wished women to denude themselves of their false sophistication, and return to the imagined simplicities of Nature; this was also in line with growing demands at the end of the eighteenth century for women to be better educated. The most fervent propagandist for female education was Mary Wollstonecraft; in her *A Vindication* of the Rights of Woman (1792) she argued that women should exercise their minds as well as their bodies. Not surprisingly, with her revolutionary sympathies, she links fashion with frivolity. It is a belief which many feminists today hold dear, agreeing that 'an air of fashion is but a badge of slavery'.[58] What is much more interesting, though somewhat difficult to disentangle, is her discussion of manners and morality; a true morality should be based not on decorum, but on sensibility and reason – otherwise it 'becomes an empty name'. While enlarging on the hypocrisy of men's treatment of women in this respect – that standards of morality and behaviour are vastly different for the two sexes – she does not enlighten us further by discussing morality in the context of dress; one suspects that she would find it somewhat ignoble, stating, as she does, that 'an immoderate fondness for dress' is the 'passion of savages'.[59]

This is rather a pity, for Mary Wollstonecraft was writing in perhaps the most revolutionary of all decades, in terms of politics and dress. By the mid-1790s, in imitation of a revered, heroic, classical past to which the stirring events of the Revolution were linked, many fashionable French women had adopted short-sleeved white muslin gowns, sandals and cropped curls; even though fashion magazines were banned during the Terror as incurably frivolous, immoral and aristocratic, fashion did not stay still. By the end of the decade an even more extreme neo-classical look appeared, described in detail by that most useful of commentators on dress and manners, Louis-Sébastien Mercier. Women, he says, were dressed *à la sauvage*, with clinging semi-transparent muslin gowns, worn over flesh-coloured body stockings, with naked breasts, bare arms and bare feet.[60] Such a costume, worn by the raffish demi-mondaine society thrown up by the Directory, was a direct mockery of established morality and the almost bourgeois virtues advocated by Robespierre during the Terror. The inspiration for the extreme classical look came from statuary; white muslin, artistically draped, looked like marble. It was Mercier's belief that since many of the statues in

64 'The Fashionable Mamma, – or – The Convenience of Modern Dress' *1796.*
J. Gillray.
The new freedom which many women enjoyed in wearing the loose-fitting chemise dress was a source of comment, usually derogatory, by many contemporaries. Gillray perhaps implies that this freedom might be related to a more casual attitude towards maternity.

museums and public gardens were either naked or semi-naked, they encouraged immodesty in women's dress; 'It cannot be doubted that the immodesty of our women is to be attributed to the immodesty of our statues.' He urged the authorities to 'deposit in your museums these lascivious Venuses', or else women would soon show such 'excessive nakedness, they [might] become offensive even to themselves'.[61]

117

65 'Full Dress' 1799.
Anon. English engraving.
It was inevitable that caricaturists should seize upon the classically inspired dress of this period, to suggest that fashionable women would adopt revealing and transparent costume.

People in England watched with fascinated horror the events of the French Revolution, in much the same way they viewed the progress of the Russian Revolution earlier this century. It was easy for moralists to link the laxness of manners and the licentious dressing of the French with an alien, republican political system; caricaturists were quick to point out the possible moral and political decay which might be the consequence of adopting Gallic modes. In spite of the exaggerations of the caricaturists, however, it seems that Englishwomen did not on the whole adopt the semi-naked neo-classical dresses which were, in any case, only worn in France by a fairly small *demi-mondaine* circle of *élégantes*; moral inhibitions, fear of public abuse, and the weather, might be contributory factors.

Writers in the predominantly middle-class English fashion magazines (which appear decidedly frumpy and unstylish compared with their French counterparts) however, found these dresses to be highly immoral. One example, from the *Lady's Magazine* for 1794, will suffice; a young man walking one evening in the Strand accosted a girl he thought was a prostitute, for she was 'dressed in an elegant white muslin gown, (with) to all appearance ... no stays, was far gone with child and with her breasts fully exposed to view'.[62] Being sharply rebuffed, he was chagrined to discover the next day that the 'prostitute' was the girl it was arranged he should marry. The interesting part of the story is the editorial comment that the girl was more to blame than the young man, having almost become *déclassée* by her 'immoral' costume.

It was no wonder that to many contemporaries the world seemed upside down in the last years of the eighteenth century, when respectable women could dress like whores, and men adopt the costume and manners of the Third Estate.

7
The Great Divide

> Fine taste in apparel I have ever seen the companion of pure morals, while a licentious style of dress is, as certainly, the token of the like laxity in manners and conduct.
>
> *The Mirror of the Graces,* 1811
>
> The best dressers of every age have always been the worst men and women.
>
> *The Habits of Good Society,* 1859

> How true it is that the general style of the dress is a sign of the times, and an indication of the morals of society.
>
> Charles Blanc, *Art and Ornament in Dress,* 1877

The nineteenth century sees a number of major developments in dress, which sharply distance it from the past. It sees, for example, a growing divide between the costume of the sexes, by which I mean that men's dress becomes sober, plain and very 'masculine', and women's dress becomes ultra-feminine. In contrast to much of the eighteenth century where wealth was equated with idleness, nineteenth-century man shows by his dress that he is a worker; he does not, on the whole (apart from the early years of the period), reveal his body, or place much value on ornamentation. Woman, on the other hand (or rather one should say 'lady', with all its connotations of gentility), becomes an expensive consumer of increasingly complicated and luxurious dress and accessories which indicate a life of comparative idleness, secluded in the home. It is partly as a reaction to this, that from the middle of the nineteenth century we find the beginnings of the dress reform movement. After a somewhat faltering start, dress reform – the first real anti-fashion for women – allied to the growing influence of sport and the fact that women begin to work outside the home, helps to produce by the end of the century a more practical everyday costume.

It is women on the whole who during the nineteenth century bear the brunt of attacks on their clothing, for male dress – apart from the exaggerated styles worn by the dandies – did not encourage the display of sexuality.

A divide, or at least diverging notions of morality, can be seen in attitudes to dress in the nineteenth century, a period of intense and excited discussion about the implications of new inventions, new communications, and new thoughts about the universe. In the eighteenth century, although the established church was fairly indolent and *laissez-faire*, there was no real doubt about the existence of a God who had ordained an almost immutable class structure. This all changed with the French Revolution, and as the century progressed, a number of philosophers and political writers began to question social, religious and political beliefs. This was bound to affect moral standards, and we tend to find that attacks on dress on the grounds of indecency based on a biblical code give way to some extent to a new secular morality based on practicality, health and hygiene. In the same way, with regard to a firmly entrenched class system and the growing horrors of urban industrialization, it was seen that a basically religious philanthropy was insufficient to help the lot of the poor, and new political concepts such as socialism, resting on the equality of all men and women, were at least discussed at all levels of society, even if their impact was not to be fully effective until the following century.

The French Revolution, which had, in a limited way, tried to put some of these ideals into practice, was the most important influence on dress as the nineteenth century began. It was the Revolution which had been inspired by the relative simplicities of English country clothing to make the formal link between dress and democracy. Silk was the sign of aristocratic indolence, whereas wool and washable linens and cottons – in theory the dress of the less well-off – were suitable to the supposedly less luxurious tastes of the true republicans. As we have seen, garments like trousers (and their tighter-fitting, more elegant version, pantaloons), were seen to be proletarian in origin; with such potentially revolutionary connotations, that they were sometimes banned in countries which feared Jacobin infection.[1]

It was the tight-fitting pantaloons which also attracted criticism on grounds of their indecency; they were often made of light-coloured nankeen (a closely woven cotton, often buff in colour), or stockinette, or fine doeskin leather, or cut on the cross, the better to show off the shape of the legs. This kind of imitation 'nude' look served to lay emphasis on the genitals, particularly as the coat was cut away at the sides. J. P. Malcolm in his *Anecdotes of the Manners and Customs of London* (1808) found that whereas with regard to the dark coat, nothing much had changed since the end of the previous century, men were now stretching 'their Pantaloons almost to bursting'.[2] It was a fashion which was repeatedly denounced by the Papacy, by both Pius VI (d. 1799) and Pius VII (d. 1823). By the time that the latter died, however, looser trousers had taken the place of tight pantaloons.

Clothing that was too revealing was the main complaint with regard to early nineteenth-century female dress. The fashionable woman wished to look like a statue of Parian marble, with her dress hanging in sculptural folds, but very often the dress was cut so low and the fabric was so thin, that it was the shape of the body, rather than the classical effect, that the viewer noticed. J. P. Malcolm declared that 'some thoughtless females indulge in the license of freedom rather too far, and shew their persons in a manner offensive to modesty'.[3] Other critics, more specifically, found that it was the bosom which was too exposed; 'The man of delicacy', according to the editor of *The Mirror of the Graces* (1811), 'turns from the couch of sensuality ... and with celestial rapture clasps to his warm and noble heart the unsunned bosom of the chaste and vestal-enwrapped fair'.[4] The high-waisted chemise gown pushed up the bust, which, with the aid of the newly introduced corset called a 'divorce' (because for the first time it separated the breasts), made 'a sort of fleshy shelf, disgusting to the beholders'.[5]

Although caricaturists like Gillray averred that women wore nothing beneath their flimsy dresses, it seems that they wore 'invisible petticoats ... woven in the stocking loom, ... like straight waistcoats, .. only drawn down over the legs instead of over the arms, so that when walking, you were obliged to take short and mincing steps.'[6] Even so, the dresses were very skimpy (compared to the amplitude of eighteenth-century gowns), and further underwear, in the form of drawers was needed. Yet such essentially decent coverings were only introduced after prolonged opposition; this was mainly due to the fact that they were associated with prostitutes and – this was almost the same in the eyes of many – professional dancers. By

66 'An Englishman in Paris' *1807*.
T. Rowlandson.
The Englishman revels in the sight of scantily dressed Parisian girls of easy virtue.

the early nineteenth century, actresses, dancers and singers wore flesh-coloured silk knitted tights, or what Captain Gronow called 'gauze inexpressibles'.[7] More modest frilled cotton drawers were worn by young girls in England, sometimes reaching to well below the knee, but it was well into the second half of the century before the majority of adult women adopted such bifurcated underwear.

The reluctance to wear drawers stemmed also from the fact that they were seen as 'masculine' garments, and that they were thought of as French in origin. Anything French in the way of dress or pleasures was greeted with a kind of horrified relish. Masculine visitors to Paris during the short-lived Peace of Amiens (1802) made great play with the scantiness of female attire there, and the notion of 'gay Paree' with its vices and opportunities for indulgence of all kinds, became part of the mythology of the city for Englishmen. No matter that many such accounts and guide-books relied on the well-known publications of Mercier for their stories of semi-naked women; this was the story that the public expected to hear, even if the various authors had not observed this state of affairs for themselves. So, we read that France is 'the gay land of trifles and dissipation', that its people pursue 'sensuous or frivolous pleasures ... with a devotion to the shrines of luxury and vanity unknown at any former period', and that women in particular parade in public places 'in a state of undress really immodest.'[8]

One visitor to Paris in 1802 was Joseph Farington, who was pleased to find that the French had a 'want of propriety in dress', which did not surprise him, having met the celebrated beauty Madame Récamier, whose dress he found 'very bare both back and front'.[9]

Many contemporaries found what Farington describes as 'the latitude in female dressing' to be a sign of falling moral standards. It seems clear by this, that some critics, like Lady Susan O'Brien, equated morality with pre-revolutionary civility in dress and deportment, finding in the present age 'a certain rudeness or

67 'The Mirror of Fashion'.
T. Rowlandson.
Rowlandson reworks the medieval notion that a vain woman looked in her mirror and saw the Devil, by showing Death holding her mirror as she vainly tries to stem the advance of age by a battery of potions and cosmetics.

carelessness of manners'.[10] At the same time she notes an over-refinement in language which she finds pretentious and coy; the words 'breeding' and 'lying in', for example, have been replaced by 'in the family way' and 'confinement', and euphemisms like 'small-clothes' for breeches, and 'unmentionables' or 'inexpressibles' for trousers, are current usage.[11]

It is difficult to estimate the extent of 'immorality' in any society; although Regency England has the reputation for being licentious, this is probably only applicable to the upper classes. Evangelicalism with its concentration on high personal moral standards, and domestic virtues, had made great inroads into the middle and working classes by the turn of the century, when England was already well-known abroad for its prudery, or hypocrisy, in matters sexual.

Based as it was on Puritanism, there was considerable emphasis in the Evangelical movement on plainness of dress. One pamphlet published in 1815, *An Appeal to the Consciences of Christians on the Subject of Dress* asks the reader (who is presumed to be female) to justify the self-gratification of 'her curls, frills, beads, brooches, or any part of her dress'.[12] This called forth a reply by 'Honestas' in the following year, who attacked the first tract for its 'bogus humility', its author as being 'a straight-laced soul', and who stated his belief in the unimportance of dress as a guide to one's destination in the next world.[13]

Evangelicism undoubtedly helped to encourage self-respect among the poor; allied to an increase in 'godliness' was an increase in cleanliness both of the person and the clothes, mainly caused by the greater availability of washable and cheap fabrics which meant that the poor relied less on dirty cast-offs. The philanthropist Francis Place, whose recollections span the years from the later 1770s to the 1820s, contrasted the pitiful state of working class women in the earlier period 'without gowns on their back or handkerchiefs on their necks, their leather stays half-laced and as black as the door posts', their skirts 'standing alone with dirt', with their much improved appearance fifty years later, 'with their clean, or cleanly cotton gowns, made pretty high round the neck'.[14] Compared to the loss of civility which Lady Susan O'Brien lamented – presumably in the upper classes – Place found far greater civility among the lower-class population, far less street violence and drunkenness.

Although the claim has been made at the beginning of this chapter that sexual stereotypes in dress were the rule in nineteenth-century England, an exception must be made for the rather effeminate dandies of the second and third decades of the period. They really were the last gasp of the male peacock before the ensuing triumph of middle-class sobriety in dress which is still, to a large extent, with us today. Beau Brummell in the early years of the nineteenth century had advocated an elegant

THE GREAT DIVIDE

68 'The Dandies Coat of Arms' *1819*.
G. Cruikshank.
The monkeys, representing dandies, are dressed in the height of fashion, except for their fools' caps decorated with bells. Cruikshank describes it as: 'The sexes impaled improper between two butterflies ... three pairs of stays argent, the sinister flaunch charged with Royal Pomatum & smell (ing) Bottle ... a frill rampant ... Crest a pair of stays full padded supporting an elevated collar rampant holding a blackhead ... winged with asses ears proper'. Suspended beneath a pair of trousers with the motto is a puppy dog under which is written 'Order of Puppism, suspended in French stiffness'.

simplicity of dress, high quality materials with superb tailoring, which followed the natural lines of the body; he was careful to avoid what he called a 'mountebank appearance', by which he meant the wearing of brightly coloured and exaggerated clothes. No such inhibitions prevented the dandies from distorting their figures with tight-lacing, and padded trousers which gave them a feminine appearance. The author of *The Whole Art of Dress* (1830) while declaring that such styles indicated 'effeminate foppery', waxed quite lyrical about loose trousers called Cossacks (after a visit made to London by the Tsar of Russia in 1814), and quite openly advocated the use of stays (which he calls a belt) under military uniforms; as a cavalry officer himself, he may have been referring to a common practice in the army.[15] Dandies also used cosmetics, and were lampooned for it as the macaronis had been fifty years before. The satirical magazine *The Ton* (1819) describes a dandy's morning toilette; one of his first tasks is to make-up for the day with 'a little of the light brown and a touch of rouge', then to be laced into his stays, and to try on cravats, fourteen in number, until the perfect one is produced. He perfumes himself with musk, puts 'Huile Antique' on his hair, and tells his tailor, 'how to pad my coat on the breast and on the shoulders, to put very thick lining and padding in the sleeves in order to give me an athletic look'.[16]

The satirists had a field day with the dandies, the last time they were ever able to poke so much fun at male fashions.

> No wonder in the present race.
> Great crime pervades the Nation,
> When in her Dandy youth we trace,
> A stiff-neck'd Generation.[17]

This collection of cautionary verses about the 'Singularity and Folly' of the dandies mentions their literally 'stiff-neck'd' style, for men wore

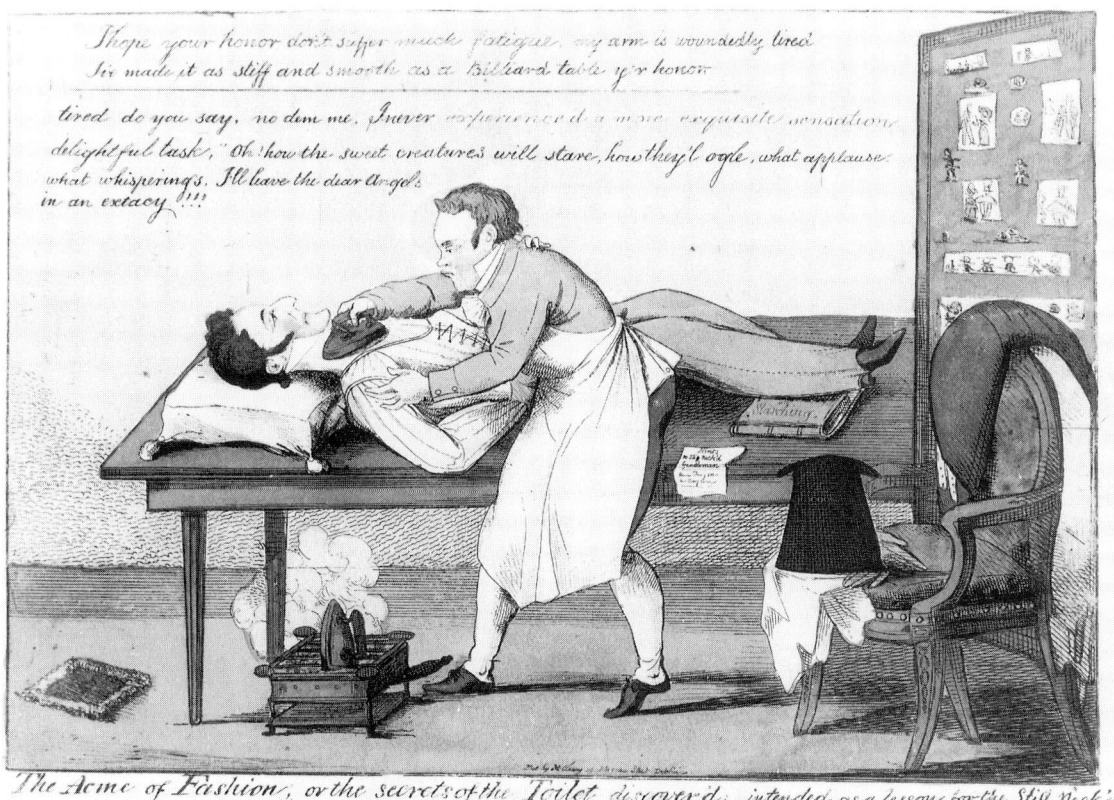

fiercely stiffened collars and elaborately tied cravats or neckcloths. According to the satirical *Neckclothitania* (1818) the starched collars and neckcloths were the only way, in a world where male dress was all levelled out, to distinguish the upper class from lesser beings. Starch, in particular, gave the wearer 'a look of hauteur and greatness ... the air of being puffed up with pride, vanity, and conceit ... indispensable qualifications for a man of fashion'.[18]

The 1830s was really the last time that the upper classes could display a sense of colour in dress; the unrivalled leader of fashion in this decade was Count D'Orsay, an elegant man of somewhat dubious manliness who dazzled the eye with his 'white coat, blue satin cravat, primrose gloves scented with jasmine, and patent-leather boots which would almost enable a man to dispense with a mirror'.[19]

D'Orsay, some might say, was able to shine in London society in this way because he was a foreigner and thus able to make sartorial eccentricities a matter of elegance. Although the idea of the dandified man continued well into the nineteenth century, he never lost sight of his masculinity; from this time onwards, as Quentin Bell puts it, 'the merest hint of femininity in a man's wardrobe was regarded with deep visceral aversion'.[20] Among the upper and middle classes, the only acceptable touch of colour was the waistcoat until the 1860s; from then onwards even that was abandoned and men wore a dark three-piece suit on most occasions, except for evening wear when a white waistcoat was *de rigueur*. A French visitor to England in the 1860s found the moral sobriety of the English best expressed in the sight of the City workers in their black suits and rolled umbrellas like an army in uniform. Such costume was so irreproachable, that for the rest of this chapter we will mainly be concerned with women's dress which had to bear all the criticism on moral grounds; not until the end of

69 'The Acme of Fashion'. *Engraving by McCleary. This tightly laced dandy goes to enormous trouble to have his starched collar 'as stiff and smooth as a Billiard table'.*

70 'Fashions for Fast Men'.
Punch, *1847.*
On the right is a typical example of the 'gent', in his 'short, odd coat' and 'large check trowsers of the true light comedian pattern'.

the century do we see men's dress discussed in critical terms, and that is on the grounds of aesthetics.

Noisy combinations of colour, however, existed into the middle years of the century, in the dress of the 'Gents'; rather flashy middle-class types, fond of the sporting life, and who were certainly *not* gentlemen. Albert Smith in his *The Natural History of the Gent* (1847) describes their pursuits – they like dancing though they do it badly, peforming 'fandango atrocities' in the polka, they like to ogle the actresses in the theatre, they stare at women bathers at Ramsgate, and they accost respectable women in the street – and their costume, 'a short odd coat', 'large check trowsers of the true light comedian pattern', loud cravats and tie-pins, and bright yellow kid gloves over which are worn lots of rings.[21]

It may have been with this deplorable class of men in mind that mid-nineteenth-century etiquette books warn their male readers against glaring colours and extravagance in dress, signs, according to *The Habits of Good Society* (1859) of 'a sin against taste', and only suitable for successful Australian gold-diggers. Gentlemen are especially cautioned to avoid trousers 'as loose as a Turk's', and jewellery which is 'an ornament to women, but a blemish to men'.[22]

With overt masculinity being the ideal, many commentators found the custom of being clean-shaven somewhat 'feminine'; Alexander Walker declared that clean-shaven epochs in the past were periods of 'general effeminacy', which led to 'the decline and fall of states'.[23] Another author composed a poetic tract entitled *Beard-Shaving, and the Common Use of the Razor, An Unnatural, Irrational, Unmanly, Ungodly, and Fatal Fashion among Christians* (1847) in which the Devil appeared and gave Woman a razor which she then presented to her husband,

> and ever since then,
> The Razor disgraces and mutilates men.

While other religions encourage the wearing of beards,

> ... Christians, of paramount pride and pretence,
> In morals, religion and 'plain common sense',
> Shave daily, devoutly, lip, cheekbone and chin,
> Protesting that Nature, not Fashion, doth sin.[24]

No complaints, on the other hand, could be made about 'masculinity' in women's dress in the first half of the nineteenth century, even if there were criticisms about its occasional impropriety. Towards the end of the reign of George III (1820), women's dress had become more modest, with a higher neckline and fuller skirts with a greater number of petticoats. A new feeling of gentility and decorum was in the air, and the role-model for the times was certainly not the outrageously vulgar Queen Caroline, estranged wife to George IV, with her 'black wig, ... her eyebrows painted black, her cheeks .. plastered with rouge', who attempted unsuccessfully to be crowned with her husband. Prior to this occasion of supreme bathos – 'Fate wrote her a most tremendous tragedy and she played it in tights', was Max Beerbohm's apt comment – she had travelled on the continent where a Frenchwoman saw her, in Genoa, in 1815 in a very low cut pink dress, so short that she showed 'two stout legs with pink top-boots'. She was seated in a phaeton shaped like a sea-shell which was drawn by two piebald horses driven by a child 'dressed like an operatic cherub with spangles and flesh-coloured tights'.[25]

By the 1830s women were becoming far more hindered by their constricting and elaborate costume than they had been for many years; with huge sleeves – one fashion magazine stated sarcastically that air balloons were fixed to each shoulder – increasingly wide skirts, and a tiny waist, the fashionable woman looked rather like a wasp. To crown this slightly grotesque costume, a woman of fashion had her hair arranged in elaborate sausage curls, and wore a vast bonnet. In the next decade, however, dress quietened down; the outrageous hairstyles and sleeves disappeared, to give way to a simple, straight coiffure with central parting, and sleeves more akin to the shape of the arm beneath, although, as the shoulder seam was set very low, a woman could only with difficulty lift her arms. This of course was the desired effect, that a woman should not appear to be capable of any physical effort; her main role in life was to be the centre of her home, and to run her household efficiently. She was encouraged to do this by a flood of publications in the 1840s, with advice on domestic duties (including the control of servants inclined to unsuitable finery), and the most appropriate dress for any given occasion. One American publication of 1843, quoting Alexis de Tocqueville, that 'women are the protectors of morals', em-

71 'The Fashion Behind but not Behind the Fashion' *1829*.
'P. Pry' i.e. W. Heath.
The artist pokes fun both at the huge ribboned hat, the vast balloon-like sleeves, and the wide skirts lined with horsehair (or a similar stiffening) which immodestly reveal so much of the ankle.

---

phasizes their role as moral guides, by avoiding excess in dress, by eschewing cosmetics (only the lightest of pearl or rice powder was acceptable for evening), and by taking care not to over-exert themselves and thus bring on a taste for stimulants like strong tea or coffee, wine or even 'the small dose of opium'.[26]

Servants were a particular problem, for they would spend their wages on unsuitably fashionable or frivolous clothes. 'Menials' unless positively discouraged, would spend two to three months' wages on a fine bonnet or a silk dress, whereas they should have spent it on good underclothing or sturdy shoes; this passion for finery could, it was stated, easily lead to crime, wretchedness, and 'the lowest degradation'.[27]

This was the message hammered home by a number of tracts issued by the Religious Tract Society, which had been founded in 1799; servants cannot resist temptation unless constantly warned against the moral evils of 'fine ribands and caps' which can lead to 'idle and dissolute habits' and maybe even to prison.[28] It was not just the servant classes who were in danger, but all women who tried to ape the dress of those above them, and thus brought their households to moral and financial ruin – this is the message of a number of contemporary publications. Morality was equated with cleanliness of attire (soiled and tawdry dress was a sign of a depraved woman), modesty of deportment, and avoidance of excessive finery. On a practical note, a girl was urged not to dress up too much in public, for it might lead a prospective husband to think her wealthier than in reality she was, 'and what prudent man would think seriously of uniting himself with a young woman so likely to spend his fortune ... upon the decoration of her person?'.[29]

Most etiquette books content themselves with lurid descriptions of female frivolity, without enquiring as to why women felt the need to express themselves in this way. One exception was Mrs A. J. Graves in her book *Woman in America; being an Examination into the Moral and Intellectual Condition of American Female Society* (1843), in which she states that girls were brought up from infancy to think that dress was important, they were given dolls dressed up in frills and furbelows, and were themselves shown off to adults in unnecessary, fussy finery; much the same arguments had been used by Mary Wollstonecraft some fifty years before. The words refinement and gentility were used approvingly of the perfect lady; the worst possible term of abuse was vulgarity. This was equated with showing off in public in

THE GREAT DIVIDE

AN IRRESISTIBLE ARMING FOR CONQUEST.

La! my Lady, you make the Gentlemen so___ so what Mrs Lucy?
so Stand, & gape my Lady.___ ha! ha! ha!___ thats all.

72 'An Irresistible Arming for Conquest' c. 1828–30. Anon. engraving.
The tight-lacing so deplored by moralists, aesthetes and doctors, produced a prominent bust, and a tiny waist which was further emphasized by a flounced bustle tied at the back over the petticoat. The attendant maid comments knowingly that the gentlemen will 'Stand & gape my Lady – ha!ha!ha! ...'.

---

unsuitably expensive and luxurious dress: 'The lady who walks in the streets in a showy dress suitable only to a fête; who comes to a quiet social gathering with a profusion of costly jewellery', and those generally who 'are always over-drest for the occasion, may be set down as vulgar'. This was not only evidence of bad taste, but such 'indulgence in personal luxury in women has an injurious effect on the moral tone ... the first symptom, if not the cause, of a relaxation in virtue'.[30]

One of the main complaints about women's dress was our old friend the extreme décolletage; it was indeed a paradox that although women dressed during the day with a high-necked gown, in the evening low-cut frocks were worn. *The Young Lady's Friend* (1845) warned against the moral dangers of this custom: 'No woman can strip her arms to her shoulders and show her back and bosom without injuring her mind, and losing some of her refinement; if such would consult their brothers, they would tell them how men regard it'.[31]

From the late 1820s metal eyelets were used in corsets, enabling very tight lacing; corsets had gussets for the bust, and at the sides for the hips, producing an immensely seductive shape which emphasized bosom and hips. With such advances in corsetry techniques came renewed criticism on the familiar grounds of distortion of the body and hazards to health. Some doctors, however, realizing that women would continue to wear corsets in spite of being warned of their dangers, argued for the wearing of medically approved models. A Dr Tilt, for example, in his *Elements of Health and Principles of Female Hygiene* (1852) recommended the stays made by Madame Roxey Caplin. This 'anatomical corset manufacturer' had a business in Berners Street, and provided stays, as she claims in her book *Health and Beauty* (1856), which actually supported the figure; she was also one of the first writers to advocate the use of exercise for girls and women to improve their posture.

The majority of writers, however, were in the anti-tight-lacing camp, disliking such garments as artificial; Mary Merrifield in *Dress as a Fine Art* (1854) stated that tight-lacing was a violation of the Laws of Nature, as indeed were cosmetics: 'We seek to repair the ravages of time on our complexions by paint, when we substitute false hair for that which age has thinned or blanched, when we pad our dress to conceal that one shoulder is larger than the other'; some defects, she goes on to say, 'are so carefully concealed by the dress, that they are only discovered after marriage'[32] – a clear case of *caveat emptor*!

She finds another example of distortion in the 'present .. practice of wearing hoops to make the dresses stand out at the base'.[33] This is a reference to the crinoline, literally the most prominent part of a woman's dress in the 1850s. This device, originally with the practical purpose of keeping the weight of petticoats off the legs, attracted a vast amount of criticism. By 1856 the first whalebone hoops had given way to a cage crinoline made of wire, which was considerably lighter, but which could also more easily blow up in the wind and even over the head, making drawers really necessary. When, in a celebrated account, in 1859, the Duchess of Manchester fell over a style on a country walk, her cage crinoline flew up to reveal scarlet tartan knickerbockers; the response of a fellow walker, the duc de Malakoff, – 'c'était diabolique' – seems particularly apt.

Few Englishwomen could walk elegantly in the huge crinolines which reached their greatest expanse in 1859; nor were they as adept as the Empress Eugénie and her ladies in imbuing the swaying movement of the crinoline with a delicate sexual quality. *The Habits of Good Society* (1859) laid the blame for the introduction of the crinoline on the French Empress; this was erroneous, for Eugénie as a member of

73 'Pic nic' c. *1860*.
Anon. engraving.
A demonstration of the problems involved with the early uncollapsible form of the crinoline.

a somewhat parvenu royal family, had to be careful not to be the first to adopt such an extreme or 'immoral' fashion.

The crinoline was criticized on the grounds of the yardage of silk and ribbons which it entailed; *Punch* (which had had great fun in describing some uses of the crinoline, as a bathing machine, a tent for the Crimean war, etc.) stated solemnly in 1857 that the crinoline had to be regarded as a depopulating influence, for it took so many yards of silk and was covered with lace, ribbons and all kinds of furbelows, that 'ladies have to choose between a fine dress and a family, for no income but a Rothschild's can provide for both'. Queen Victoria, in a letter addressed *To the Ladies of England* in 1863, stated her strong disapproval of the 'wearing of the indelicate, expensive, dangerous and hideous article called Crinoline.'[34] Fairly minor dangers entailed being entangled in carriage wheels, and blown under horses in the streets; far more serious was the danger of fire, such as the occasion in 1863 when two thousand women burnt to death in the cathedral of Santiago when candles ignited their light flimsy dresses worn over crinolines.

Because the crinoline was so extreme a fashion, it required a light hand with colours and accessories, a subtlety of touch which the English on the whole lacked. A French visitor to England in the 1860s, Hyppolite-Adolphe Taine, found the dress of Englishwomen totally devoid of taste, and striking for its use of harsh and glaring colours; he found it particularly irritating that although the English denounced the French for their supposed immorality of dress, they (the English) liked the 'exaggerated and violent . . . flaunting and overdone' costume more suitable for women of suspect virtue. They wore:

> bonnets resembling piled-up bunches of rhododendrons . . . with packets of red flowers or of

enormous ribbons, gowns of shiny violet silk with dazzling reflections, or of starched tulle upon an expanse of petticoats stiff with embroidery; immense shawls of black lace, reaching down to the heels ... the glare is terrible ... The crinoline is like a tub at the bottom, the cloaks are tucked up in clumsy and pretentious puffs ... Thus bulged out, they walk along rustling, their dress follows and precedes them like the ticking of a clock ... energetic, discordant, jerking, like a piece of mechanism.[35]

Rarely can there have been such a comprehensive and utterly damning account of women's clothing. Yet in an age when novelties in dress and bright glaring colours (aniline dyes came out in the late 1850s) were admired in England as a sign of their love of inventions, an indication of an up-to-the-minute modishness, it was sometimes difficult to tell the virtuous woman from her impure sister.

This was particularly the case in France, where an opulent vulgarity, to many critics, appeared to be the *leitmotif* of the Second Empire, with its extravagant court infiltrated by expensive harlotry. It is the world of *Nana* which Baudelaire describes in his essay *The Painter of Modern Life*, in which woman is a kind of idol, bewitching but stupid, her only real talent being for dress, 'the muslins, the gauzes, the vast iridescent clouds of stuff in which she envelops herself'. It is the world of the almost aristocratic courtesan in her prime, striving after patrician airs, proud at once of her youth and the luxury into which she puts all her soul and all her genius, as she delicately uses two fingers to tuck in a wide panel of silk, satin, or velvet which billows round

74 'La dame au canapé'.
C. Guys.
No other artist depicts so well the hot-house sexuality of the Parisian demi-monde in the Second Empire. This fashionable prostitute allows her vast billowing skirts to reveal nearly all her charms.

her, or points a shoe whose over-ornate toe would be enough to betray her for what she is, if the somewhat unnecessary extravagance of her whole toilette had not already done so.[36]

Baudelaire (and Constantin Guys who is the subject of his essay) concentrates on the more 'artistic' qualities of the high-class prostitute, rather than on the lowest class of whores, 'the poor slaves of those filthy stews', which seemed to form the profession in England. English prostitutes with talent and a fine dress sense could make a better career on the continent. Taine was shocked by the brutalized state of the urban poor in London, among whom were the prostitutes long known to be 'filthy in their dress, openly brutal and indecent in their advances'; one historian has found that with regard to the working classes, the period of greatest immorality was the mid-nineteenth century.[37]

Some prostitutes and a number of poor people wore second-hand clothes, a custom which Taine found 'uncomfortable. To wear these old clothes is degrading; in doing so the human being shows or avows that he is the offscouring of humanity'.[38] The vast production and over consumption of finery, which is characteristic of mid-nineteenth-century England, led to the revival of the old clothes trade, whose dealers were 'superior scavengers whose duty it is to relieve us of our rejected garments, and to put them into circulation among different classes of the population'.[39] Compared to the eighteenth century, when even the upper classes had relatively few clothes, in the nineteenth century with huge technical advances in the machinery for making fabrics and clothes, women were able to possess huge wardrobes. They were able, in the words of a satirical poem *Nothing to Wear: An Episode of Fashionable Life*, to have:

> Dresses for breakfasts and dinners and balls;
> Dresses to sit in and stand in and walk in;
> Dresses to dance in and flirt in and talk in;
> Dresses in which to do nothing at all.[40]

This publication provoked a sharp reply, *Nothing to You; or, Mind Your Own Business*, in which the author of the first poem was taken to task for the double standards practised by men:

> We talk of morality – practise the vices,–
> Make rules for young ladies, but none for ourselves.

Men, it continues, make women 'a play toy and not a companion', encouraging their interest in dress so that they become just exquisitely dressed puppets.[41] A similar theme was expressed a few years later by Frances Power Cobbe, who advocated higher standards of education for women, insisting that true women were formed by expanding their minds, and 'not by pinching her in mental stays.... Such processes produce Dolls, not Women'.[42]

Some of the first steps towards a more practical costume for the 'progressive' woman were made in the early 1850s, with the introduction of the 'Bloomer' costume, named after the American Amelia Jenks Bloomer, active in the fields of temperance and women's rights, and founder of *The Lily* – a paper devoted to the interests of women, including dress reform. Mrs Bloomer shot to fame – or at least to notoriety – when in 1851 she popularized the wearing of a reformed dress which consisted of a knee-length tunic and loose Turkish trousers. The idea of such trousers, as a more practical alternative to long skirts which entrapped dirt, had been mentioned as early as 1819 when *The Ton* referred to 'belles in Turkish trowsers'; it is not clear whether this meant bloomer-like garments, or just long drawers.[43]

Although Mrs Bloomer's trousers were voluminous enough not to reveal the shape of the legs, and were gathered in modestly at the ankle, they provoked a storm of critical and amused comment; linked as this costume was to women's rights, its wearers were depicted as bossy harridans assuming masculine airs. Dr Tilt found it worrying that if women wore trousers, they would assume 'our masculine manners, which would not enhance their charms',[44] and Mrs Merrifield who liked the idea of 'light and roomy' clothing along oriental lines, had some rather hypocritical reservations about trousers on the grounds of propriety, objecting 'not to this article of

A QUIET SMOKE.

(BEHIND THE COUNTER THERE IS ONE OF THE "INFERIOR ANIMALS.")

75 'A Quiet Smoke'.
Punch, *1851*.
The cartoonist John Leech speculates on the changes in manners were women to adopt the 'masculine' Bloomer costume.

---

dress being worn, ... but to its being seen'.[45]

Fear of social disapproval was the main reason why in England 'Bloomerism seems to be making little headway', but, said *The Family Herald*, 'most people agree that the costume is neat, and likely to be both economical and serviceable'.[46]

A number of women in the major cities in the United Kingdom, stated the same paper, had appeared in the Bloomer dress in public, but they had been 'unnerved' by the 'persecuting curiosity excited by the transatlantic garb'.[47]

One brave girl, however, faced with ridicule and accusations of immodesty, rose to the challenge with spirit, when at a ball, 'the gentlemen admired her neat and comfortable dress, but several ladies accused her of being immodest. She turned to some of them, whose dresses were quite low in the bosom, and replied "If you will pull up your dresses to a proper place about your necks, your skirts will hang no lower than mine do".'[48] Much more importantly, the Bloomer costume had an impact on the dress of some working women in dirty manual occupations; the Wigan pit brow girls, for example, by the late 1850s, were wearing fustian or corduroy trousers, a mode of dressing which provoked accusations of immoral, coarse and mannish behaviour.[49]

The accusations of immodesty levelled at the Bloomer costume were mainly on the grounds that it was worn in public; for some years before the ballyhoo of 1851, women had sometimes worn bifurcated garments for gymnastics and in sanatoria – although these were, of course, worn in privacy away from male eyes. By the end of the 1850s, a version of the Bloomer

76 Wigan Pit Brow Girls c. *1860*.
Photograph by *J. Cooper*.
This costume which to the twentieth-century eye seems functional and unprovocative, excited a great deal of criticism mainly on account of the trousers worn.

---

costume 'consisting of jackets shaped variously according to taste, and loose trousers reaching to the ankle', was being recommended for female beach wear instead of the cumbersome and possibly immodest – the skirts could float up in the water – flannel bathing dress.[50] Whereas mixed bathing was the custom on the continent, in England the sexes bathed separately, for men bathed naked. One unfortunate Frenchman, bathing *à l'anglaise* at Brighton, found that the sea had receded between him and his cabin, and right in his path were three ladies; unable even to find some seaweed to cover himself with, he had to walk the gauntlet, finding out later that the ladies 'disapproved of bathing on Sundays, and had adopted that unexpected method of discouraging Sabbath-breakers'.[51] *The Observer* noted that at Ramsgate some women quite unashamedly gazed on the naked male bathers; its belief was that 'the authorities ought to compel gentlemen to wear, as in France, *caleçons*, and the ladies dresses should at least be so constructed as to prevent a wholesale exposure of their natural perfections or imperfections'.[52] By the mid 1860s, women generally had adopted bifurcated bathing costumes, either made in one piece or consisting of a blouse and knickerbockers, but it was not a universal practice for men to wear bathing costumes until the Edwardian period.[53]

By the end of the 1860s the rounded silhouette created by the crinoline had disappeared, to be replaced by a new tight-fitting dress with back fullness, which placed a new emphasis on a tightly moulded torso from bust to hips. Such a dress which outlined the bust and the shape of the thighs was eagerly taken up by ladies of the *demi-monde*, and courtesans such as Zola's heroine Nana, who longed for the chance to show off their figures released from the billowing draperies of the crinoline. Some fashion writers claimed that the back drapery of the new gowns, created by the kilting up of the overskirt, was a revival of eighteenth-century styles; the French gave them names like 'Pompadour' and 'Marie-Antoinette', indications of *Ancien Régime* decadence which critics like Harriet Beecher Stowe found to be inspired by 'a certain class of women in Paris ... They are women who live only for the senses, with an utter and obvious disregard for any moral or intellectual purpose'.[54]

An air of hot-house femininity pervades fashions of the late 1860s and 1870s, with their tiny waists, moulded busts, curved hips emphasized by a bustle, and a mass of elaborately styled and sometimes false hair. In the late 1860s the corset known as the 'Grecian bend' was introduced, which pushed back the legs and thrust forward the bust; outlined by steam-moulded corsetry, the bust was the focal point for a woman of fashion, who, in the words of Charles Blanc (*Art in Ornament and Dress* 1877), 'displays the beauty of her figure above the waist'.[55]

The pros and cons of tight-lacing raged in the pages of popular periodicals in the later 1860s, notably in *The Queen* and *The Englishwoman's Domestic Magazine*. Some of the correspondence, advocating in purple prose the almost sexual delights of tight-lacing (for men as well as women), has a lurid exhibitionist quality. 'Staylace', for example, writing in *The Englishwoman's Domestic Magazine* for 1867, finds 'the so-called evils of tight-lacing to be a mere bugbear and so much cant', and, rejoicing in 'quite a collection of these much-abused objects' (i.e. corsets), 'never feel[s] prouder or happier, so far as matters of the toilette are concerned, than when I survey in myself the fascinating undulations of outline'.[56] The merits of tight-lacing were extolled on almost moral grounds as 'an ever-present monitor indirectly bidding its wearer to exercise self-restraint; it is evidence of a well-disciplined mind, and well regulated feelings'.[57]

Carefully avoiding the murky waters of this possibly spurious correspondence, it seems likely that although to some wearers, tightly-laced corsets provided sexual thrills, to most women they helped to produce the appearance of a good figure and no more; it seems unlikely, in spite of the horror stories of women lacing themselves to death, or suffering miscarriages due to tight-lacing, which the more lurid newspapers related, that there were really serious medical grounds for banning the practice, except for *very* tight-lacing.

Eliza Lynn Linton, for example, in her famous articles on the manners of 'the girl of the period' for *The Saturday Review* during 1867–8, hardly mentions tight-lacing. She is much more concerned with the use of cosmetics and false hair which she sees as evidence of moral degeneracy in women of all ages who copy the fashionable ideal, the woman of the *demi-monde*. She is 'a creature who dyes her hair and paints her face ... Her main endeavour ... is to outvie her neighbours in the extravagance of

77 Lady with a fan c. *1868*.
C. Guys.
Such an elegant lady from the demi-monde *('women who live only for the senses', in Harriet Beecher Stowe's words), shows off her bust in her décolletée gown, which has a fringed overskirt draped in the opulent swags characteristic of the Second Empire revival of eighteenth-century styles.*

fashion ... In the time of crinolines she sacrificed decency, ... now in the times of trains, she sacrifices cleanliness'.[58] Inspired by the French, 'fastness' had swept into English life, manifesting itself in the use of slang, and in grossly artificial aids to beauty. Among the latter are the wearing of false hair, especially huge chignons (made, alleged one writer, from

THE GREAT DIVIDE

136

THE GREAT DIVIDE

78 (opposite) Nana *1877*.
E. Manet.
The inspiration for this portrait was Zola's novel L'Assommoir *(1876–7) in which the precociously immoral Nana first appears, later (1880) to be the subject of his masterpiece* Nana.

It is not hard to imagine why the Salon of 1877 banned the portrait, which is permeated with sensuality, from the softly rounded arms of the young courtesan, to her corset, lace-trimmed underwear, embroidered stockings and high-heeled shoes.

79 (left and right above) 'History Repeats Itself'.
Punch, *1870*.
'Être et Paraître'.
Caricature by Hadol 1869.
Punch *mocks the 'Grecian bend' stance which pushed back the legs and thrust forward the bust.*

Hadol shows us the artifice which made up this look, such as the padded bust improvers and bustles. In addition, the fashionable lady tottered along under a vast chignon and ringlets of false hair.

---

the hair of corpses, fever patients and female prisoners)[59] and the copious use of cosmetics. Although married women were permitted more latitude in the opulence of their dress and the extent of their make-up, Mrs Linton found that mothers set a bad example to their daughters, when they used art to hide the deficiencies of nature. One recent writer on the Victorian period believes that cosmetics were disapproved of, because, in the resulting brilliant eyes and flushed cheeks, critics saw a mimicry of the physiologial changes made in a woman's appearance during the sexual act.[60] This is somewhat of an informed guess, for no Victorian critic would make so bold a statement. However, an over-painted woman was (and to

137

THE FAST SMOKING GIRL OF THE PERIOD.

DESCRIBED BY HERSELF.

I'M a filly just rising eighteen,
  Lots of life I'm determined to see;
Stow "Markham and Mental Improvement"—
  No more of such rubbish for me.
Balls, concerts, 'drums, sensation-novels,
  Are the cheese for us girls of to-day:
And I'll do a mild weed on the quiet,
  For that is the new-fashioned way.

Oh, bother the children! You know
  At South Kensington, Ma, I am due,
That exquisite cast of Apollo
  To draw with my master till two.
"Draw landscape, fruit, flowers." No, thank you;
  Such tame subjects are not in my way:
The glorious masculine figure
  Is the model *I* study all day.

80 'The Fast Smoking Girl of the Period' *1867*.
The 'fast' girl who smokes and who prefers, for her drawing lessons, to copy the 'glorious masculine figure', features frequently in journalism of the late 1860s. It goes without saying that such a girl will adopt the latest and most extravagant fashion, such as the 'Grecian bend', emphasized by bunched-up drapery, short skirts and high heels.

some extent still is) equated with a certain freedom in her sexual favours. Mrs Linton reserved her fiercest attacks for 'la femme passée', who: 'is dressed in the extreme of youthful passion; her thinning hair dyed and crimped ... her flaccid cheeks raddled, her throat whitened; her bust displayed with unflinching generosity as if beauty is to be measured in cubic inches; her lustreless eyes blackened round the lids ... perhaps the pupils dilated with belladonna'. As if this was not enough, she has in her carriage a store of opium and eau-de-cologne, to give herself a 'false and fatal brilliancy'.[61]

Such a woman would no doubt have availed herself of the services of Madame Rachel (originally literally a madam or brothel-keeper) whose shop in New Bond Street offered cosmetic advice and dubious physical aids for the restoration of beauty. Her motto was 'Beautiful for Ever', and she was particularly fashionable for 'enamelling' ladies in the 1860s; involved in criminal activities for many years, she was sentenced to penal servitude for blackmail in 1868.

While Mrs Linton has some, modified, sympathy for the growing intellectual needs of women – she is particularly scornful of women who have nothing better to do with their time than to daub sketches, embroider 'trifles which no-one wants' and put lace frills round piano legs – she dislikes the adoption of 'mannish' elements in dress; among such 'designedly unlovely apparel' she mentions long cloth jackets cut on masculine lines, and waistcoats.[62]

While comments on masculine incursions into female dress are a feature of the journalism of this period, many critics continued to complain about the too lavish display of feminine charms. A pamphlet published c. 1867 entitled *Who is to blame? A few words on Ladies' Dress in its Moral and Aesthetic Aspects*, found 'the low-necked dress' to be, if not a sign of depravity, at least an indication of tasteless indecorum. The novelist Charlotte Mary Yonge went even further, stating firmly that: 'Exposure is always wrong; whatever be the fashion, it is the Christian woman's duty to perceive when indecency comes in and to protest against it by her own example'; she should never 'promote a fashion which is bad for the lower classes'. Fashions picked out for criticism include 'the low corsage, the tight skirt, and some kinds of headgear'. While the thought of 'headgear' being indecent might be hard to grasp, she has in mind the tiny hats (these had by 1870, the time of her publication, replaced the earlier modest and face-framing bonnets), which revealed 'a totally unprotected countenance (which) cannot be modest in itself; nor does a veil coming close over the nose materially alter the matter'.[63]

As with all such criticism, even when made by a well-known author, it appears to have passed unheeded. Indeed, female readers were growing restless with endless moral reproofs, one complaint being made to the editor of a fashion magazine: 'I think you preach a great deal too much about goodness; when it would be far more amusing to hear of some new way of doing the hair . . .'[64]

If goodness was out of favour, a new seriousness about women's role in life was in the air in the 1870s. Questions of female emancipation were discussed and already in 1867 John Stuart Mill had proposed the equal enfranchisement of men and women, although this was not to be achieved for half a century. The standard of female education was greatly improved, both as a desirable end in itself (even the universities, with some reservations, welcomed women students), and as a practical necessity when an increased number of women had to earn their livings. With the constant emigration of young men to the colonies, as many as a quarter of the female population would never marry. It was becoming positively foolish to be an empty-headed frivolous girl; as Mrs Haweis pointed out in her book *The Art of Beauty* (1878): 'However gaily clad in other people's hair, and as many dead birds as a savage, the maiden can never be more than a laughing stock, who believes that Alexander the Great conquered Britain'.[65]

Mary Eliza Haweis was the most important advocate in the 1870s of dress reform, which she wished to base on aesthetic lines. 'The body is so beautiful that it is a pity it can be so little seen' – the problem was, what dress would best enhance it? The answer was certainly not the current fashionable dress with its whalebone, 'immovable arms' and 'scrunched toes', but the flowing drapery of the past, especially 'medieval' styles, in the muted colours – or 'greenery-yallery' shades that critics mocked – admired by the aesthetic circle of which, as an artist, she was a part. Most of the aesthetic dress reformers – a particularly English phenomenon – could only see reformed dress as a reflection of the admired dress of the past, from which they selected the most appealing elements. Mrs Haweis was particularly critical of Charles Blanc whose book *Art in Ornament and Dress* (1877) praised, she thought, contemporary fashionable dress at the expense of 'artistic' costume. Being English, Mrs Haweis brought morality into play, 'for moral qualities may be applied to the fashioning and adorning of a robe . . . they tend to exercise a right influence on the mind; they satisfy, soften, and do not enervate or harass it'.[66]

Another possibility for reformed dress was Turkish costume, which Mrs Haweis approved of for its artistically flowing lines, and because of the modesty of the trousers. Ever since Mrs Bloomer's unsuccessful attempt at introducing trousers, the pros and cons of this costume had rumbled quietly on in the pages of the more thoughtful fashion magazines. In *The Lady's Newspaper* (1863) one 'J.M.' advocated a dress consisting of loose 'Mamlouk' trousers and a knee-length tunic (it sounds rather like the Bloomer dress), which, it was claimed, would be more modest and less cumbersome than the crinoline, and would make a trip in an omnibus less of a public ordeal. This suggestion was

THE GREAT DIVIDE

81 Form versus Fashion *1885*.
G. Steell.
The ghost of Pygmalion's famous statue of Galatea gazes in astonishment at the deformities of fashion in the middle 1880s. To the dress reformers, high fashion seemed absurdly far from the ideal and idealized dress of ancient Greece.

speedily opposed by 'A.H.T.' who listed all the reasons why such a dress would be unsuitable; the climate was too cold, the costume would be the first step on the road to 'oriental manners' (such as the harem) and if worn in public such an outfit would be 'a source of anarchy and confusion'.⁶⁷ Another writer, the popular Mrs Oliphant, was quick to equate 'the loose and light garment of an Eastern race' with 'the entire disruption of all Northern habits and principles.'⁶⁸ It was clear that if trousers were to be successfully introduced into the dress of Englishwomen, it would have to be in a clearly unoriental guise.

Throughout the 1880s and 1890s, the arguments and proposals for the perfect aesthetic dress continued, the earlier 'medieval' styles (which don't look very medieval to us) giving way at the end of the 80s to a revival of classical costume, although the high waists of the Regency period were resisted. On the whole, however, the dress of the early nineteenth century with its simplicity and graceful folds, was considered to be supremely artistic, and was enthusiastically advocated in the pages of *Aglaia*, the journal of the *Healthy and Artistic Dress Union*, which was founded in 1890 with the aim of dress reform.

It was recognized that men needed dress reform even more urgently, for contemporary costume was seen to be a dark, hideous and boring uniform. Although some reformers fancied a costume based on the medieval past, the more realistic declared that the eighteenth century would be the most artistic inspiration. *Aglaia* urged its supporters to wear knee-breeches (velvet for evening), silk stockings, silk shirt and a loose jacket. A similar costume had been worn by Oscar Wilde on his US lecture tour in 1882, but inevitably, with his long hair and sometimes deliberately effeminate manners, such a dress did not stand much chance of success outside a very small aesthetic circle. Wilde was probably the source of Bunthorne in Gilbert and Sullivan's send-up of the whole aesthetic movement, the operetta *Patience* in 1881, although the character was also based on Swinburne and Burne-Jones.

Dress reform for men was a non-starter, whether seen as artistic/effeminate in the late nineteenth century, or overtly masculine in the late 1920s; men have been singularly resistant to any radical change in dress which does not evolve naturally from the immediately pre-

82 Oscar Wilde *1882*.
N. Sarony.
Wilde's 'aesthetic' costume, consisting of frogged jacket with eighteenth-century knee-breeches and hose, caused a stir when he visited America.

ceding style. This was maybe why, in the early 1880s there was considerable opposition to the introduction of pyjamas, a novel departure after many hundreds of years of the male nightshirt. Moralists asserted that they were perfect for those who roved the corridors of the newly built, fashionable hotels which were springing up, and Edmond de Goncourt declared

HARROD'S STORES, Limited, Brompton. 841
UNDERCLOTHING AND BABY-LINEN.
No. 17 DEPARTMENT—*GROUND FLOOR.*

LADIES' TEA GOWNS.

'**Princess."**
Very stylish **Black Silk Tea Gown,** handsomely trimmed with Beige Lace of very new design, 4½ guineas.
Orders by Post carefully executed. Patterns of all goods Post Free.

83 Tea Gown.
Anon. engraving from a Harrods Catalogue 1895. This gown with its huge sleeves, follows the line of fashionable dress of the 1890s, and indeed – in spite of worries about its 'immorality' – was by this time worn as an informal dinner dress.

that they were a costume for assignations.[69]

The same claim – that it encouraged immorality – was made about the loose, floating tea-gowns which women had first, in the late 1870s, worn as a kind of dressing-gown in the boudoir, but which, by the end of the next decade, were worn during the afternoon. Made of chiffon, or a similar light silk, they were a becomingly confortable gown, compared to the rigidities of formal, corseted attire. 'Moralists affirm that it must bring in its train all sorts of immoralities, but beauty-lovers of the day laugh at such absurdities. In a Tea Gown a woman will appear just "adorable" and what more can a woman want to be?'[70]

The tea gown was limited to married women; not only did it have an air of sexual languor about it, but it was the informal dress worn by women initiated into the pleasures and problems of the marital state. The married woman, ideally with the opulent charms admired by the Prince of Wales, was the fashion leader of the 1890s; she was often divorced (divorce, though possible since 1857, finally became socially acceptable in the last decade of the nineteenth century), and she was allowed a far greater latitude in behaviour than previously thought acceptable. She could smoke and dine in public, and she could wear cosmetics; in the upper social levels, sophistication, artifice and cynicism were fashionable attributes. In Wilde's play *Lady Windermere's Fan* (1892), Mrs Erlynne found 'a heart doesn't suit me ... Somehow it doesn't go with modern dress', and Max Beerbohm in his *Defence of Cosmetics* (1894) welcomed the return of artifice, 'that fair exile', finding that 'no longer is a lady of fashion blamed if, to escape the outrageous persecution of time, she fly for sanctuary to the toilet-table'.[71]

Beerbohm admitted the fact of woman's 'seizure of the bicycle and the typewriter', two important elements in the movement towards a more practical dress for women, which gathered momentum in the last two decades of the century. Fashionable formal dress during this period remained very artificial, with a very angular bustle in the 1880s which made no pretence at approximating to the female form, and in the 1890s the sleeves swelled out to such enormous dimensions that women had sometimes to go sideways through doors; heavily boned stays continued to thrust forth the bosom in a manner which some critics considered to be unnatural and distorted. It was no wonder that, with the growing influence of sport, and the greater numbers of women seeking employment (mainly in teaching and in offices), there should be some reaction against fashionable dress with its superfluity of ornament and its long, sweeping trains. From the late 1870s, many women began to wear shorter skirts to their dresses, for sports such as tennis, roller-skating and golf; in some cases the dress was made of jersey (either of knitted wool or wool/silk), a fabric which, being elastic in movement, was particularly suitable for sporting activities. By the 1890s, the New Woman (*Punch*'s term for the emancipated woman who worked for her living and was beginning to agitate for female suffrage) had begun to wear clothing based on masculine styles. These included the simply cut, untrimmed 'tailormade' – a jacket and skirt based on the male suit, which was often worn with blouse and tie. 'They are unbecoming and unseemly', said one critic, 'as any imitation of man's attire must be for a woman', but the style found favour with a growing number of young women, who found that, although not necessarily very comfortable (the starched shirt collar caused soreness at the neck), it demonstrated their determination to enter the world of men.

This was made even more apparent when in the 1890s some women took to wearing trousers for the new sporting craze of cycling. Ever since the failure of the Bloomer dress, there had been a number of attempts (especially in the US, where dress reform on practical grounds was taken seriously) to re-introduce a trousered form of dress. In a series of lectures delivered in Boston in 1874 in the cause of dress reform, a number of speakers speculated on what form this might take. One, Mary Safford-Blake, declared that 'the trailing and décolletée dress of the salon is historically one of the relics of

84 Study for the portrait of Madame X 1884 (Madame Pierre Gautreau).
J. S. Sargent.
This portrait of a professional beauty, famed for her love affairs, caused a scandal when exhibited at the Paris Salon, on account of the impropriety of her décolletage, emphasized by one completely bare shoulder, due to a fallen diamond-studded shoulder strap. To remedy this, Sargent painted in another shoulder strap, which appears in the finished portrait in The Metropolitan Museum of Art.

THE GREAT DIVIDE

85 'The "Extinction" of Species: or, The Fashionable Lady without Mercy and the Egrets'. Punch, 1899.
The ultra-fashionable lady, who deforms her body in the name of fashion, is the kind who, according to Punch, *plunders the birds of their plumage in order to decorate her hats.*

the period of lust when women were shut out of the kingdom of thought'; she lamented the fact that although the public were accustomed to see women lifting up the trains of their dresses, if they were to see under the dress 'leggins which fit closely, or Turkish trousers fastening at the ankle, what fears are harbored for the appearance and morals of women'.[72] Other speakers agreed that some form of bifurcated garment was healthier than dragging around layers of petticoats, and they were also of the opinion that it was immoral in any case to spend vast sums of money on ever-changing fashionable dress. It is somewhat of a paradox that, although one speaker described men's dress as 'black as ebony and straight as clothes pins', it was also seen to be more comfortable than women's dress and not subject to violent change. Some of the more radical dress reformers felt that fashion had been used by men to incite lust and degrade women; at best it had ensured that their minds were occupied by frivolity and not by more weighty matters. These were theories to be taken up in the 1890s by the American economist Thorstein Veblen who found that women's dress was conspicuously expensive, wasteful and envy-provoking; ignoring the fact that women – and presumably most men – found it sexually attractive, he declared it to be merely the appalling advertisement of an idle life.

In England, dress-reformers turned from the contemplation of the aesthetic, to the more practical. The Rational Dress Association, founded in 1882, pressed for bifurcated garments either in the form of divided skirts, or trousers; as sport was fashionable, it was decided to introduce such garments in sporting rather than everyday costume. At their 1883 exhibition of examples of reformed dress, the first prize went to a cycling dress consisting of a jacket and trousers, the latter being covered with a skirt for the sake of modesty, and to protect the wearer from verbal (and sometimes physical) attacks. With cycling the most fashionable sport, by the late 1890s, for middle-class and professional women, a costume that emphasized that they had legs and rode astride a bicycle, caused uproar. Mrs Lynn Linton, who in the late 1860s had inveighed against the mannish 'girl of the period', now attacked the vogue for cycling, fearing it would lead to immorality as girls roamed the countryside in search of adventures. Suppose, she wondered,

RATIONAL COSTUME.

The Vicar of St. Winifred-in-the-Wold (to fair Bicyclists). "IT IS CUSTOMARY FOR MEN, I WILL NOT SAY GENTLEMEN, TO REMOVE THEIR HATS ON ENTERING A CHURCH!"
[Confusion of the Ladies Rota and Ixiona Bykewell.

86 'Rational Costume'.
Punch, 1896.
In a confusion of sexual identities, it is not clear if the 'fair Bicyclists' should act like men and remove their hats, or keep them on in church according to the conventions of feminine dress.

such a cyclist had an accident and fell off into the arms of a strange man? *The Lancet* declared that trousers were 'in many ways detrimental to health and morals',[73] and the newspapers reported with relish the confrontations that occurred when hotels refused admittance to lady cyclists dressed in trousers,[74] even when semi-hidden by a skirt which was weighted to stop it flying up. More realistically, recognizing that the style had come to stay, *Punch* was philosophical. Reporting the death of Mrs Bloomer in January 1895 it repented of its ridicule in 1851, finding that nowadays, a trousered costume

> ... 'twould scarce provoke derision
> If worn by pretty girls, and tailor-made.
>
> For by the lady-cyclist, as she plies
> Her pedal, neatly clad in knicker-bockers,
> See Mrs Bloomer, first of Grundy-shockers,
> Now vindicated in Dame Fashion's eyes.[75]

By the end of the nineteenth century women had to some extent overcome much opposition to their adoption of male garments at least for sporting purposes; the battle for the right to wear trousers in a non-sporting context, either for work or play, was not won until well into the twentieth century. But women were moving inexorably towards a life where jobs and sports, education and politics, were to take them increasingly out of the home and on to a wider stage.

8
Dress and Disorder

Suggestive dress means in the end the ruin of a people.

Modest Apparel, 1931

The denunciation of the young is a necessary part of the hygiene of older people; and greatly assists in the circulation of their blood.

Logan Pearsall Smith, *Afterthoughts*, 1931

To a considerable degree, the Edwardian period – which for convenience we will take up to the First World War, an event which changed the course of history and ushered in a new age of political and social attitudes – is a postscript to the late Victorian era. It was an age of luxury, of lavish entertainments, and – in spite of the well publicized activities of the suffragette, the successor to the emancipated New Woman – of the still very wide gulf between the lives, attainments and expectations of men and women.

Superficially, then, there appears no abrupt break in the habits of 'Society' with the death of Queen Victoria in 1901. But some critics were convinced that there was a definite acceleration in the decline of moral standards in the last years of the old century, as the pleasure-loving Prince of Wales officially sanctioned such pastimes as racing, gambling, and visiting French resorts.

The twentieth century dawned with what some considered to be an unhealthy passion for novelty, in particular the craze for motoring and the rage for new American dances, like ragtime, of dubious morality. The author of *The Sin and Scandal of the 'Smart' Set* (1904) found that motoring provided an opportunity for 'inventing or wearing an entirely novel, wholly hideous, and correspondingly expensive costume': by this she means that because of the dust and/or rain – for the early cars were open-topped – women had to wear a waterproofed voluminous coat and goggles. Even worse, the Americans had, along with slang and 'free and easy manners' introduced jazz, 'a negro medley of indecent postures and exaggerated steps' which sets men and women 'barking, leaping, floundering about on all fours, trailing costly gowns and crumpling dress shirts, in the endeavour to recapture the lost art of apes'.[1]

Other sensation-seekers took drugs (a 'Society' problem since at least the mid-nineteenth century) such as morphia or cocaine, 'to restore their jaded senses, weakened nerves and fatigued bodies'. This was a habit which the Jesuit Father Bernard Vaughan seized upon as one of *The Sins of Society*, the title of his book of sermons published in 1906, which castigated those in the 'Smart Set' whose craving for sports, pleasures, travel and immodest dress indicated a reversal to paganism. Those who

DRESS AND DISORDER

87 'Primum vivere, deinde philosophari'.
Punch, 1905.
Smoking and gambling are accepted pastimes among these ladies of the Edwardian 'smart' set. Father Vaughan would perhaps say that such dissipations go hand in hand with the custom for wearing such low-necked evening gowns.

flocked to his sermons in Farm Street (for some of his listeners they served as serialized extracts from the racy novel of their own lives) heard him denounce the immorality indicated by some aspects of female dress: 'It is not what women put on, but what they take off, that matters. There are not a few houses from which society ladies are permanently excluded because of their want of decent clothing'.[2]

Thinking of the rather upholstered and firmly corseted Edwardian lady, this statement is somewhat surprising, until we remember that no age is exempt from thinking some of its modes to be indecent. In this case, it is probable that the reverend author was thinking of the low-necked gowns for evening wear, or the flimsy tea-gowns (now worn much more in public) in pale pastel colours, which some late nineteenth-century critics had castigated as immoral. *Punch*, too, in the early years of the twentieth century found an equation between light dresses and light morals[3].

Male critics in particular disliked the fast woman for being too 'knowing'; she was often a gay divorcee (a potential wrecker of households) who knew about contraception, and who knew most of all how to enhance her experienced charms and display her sexuality through dress.

No doubt such a woman would have gone to Lucile, the most fashionable dress-maker of the pre-war period. Born Lucy Kennedy, and entering the dress-making business after a divorce and with a small daughter to care for, she eventually achieved social and financial respectability by marrying Sir Cosmo Duff Gordon in 1900, and setting up a salon in Hanover

88 Evening Gown *1900*.
Fashion plate from The Queen.
At Redmayne's of Bond Street, the fashionable customer could find this gown of embroidered satin and chiffon, frivolous and feminine enough to appeal even to Mrs Pritchard in her campaign to persuade her countrywomen that seductively luxurious fabrics were not necessarily a sign of sinfulness.

Square. In her lurid autobiography in which the word hyperbole comes most often to mind – 'I was the first dressmaker to bring joy and romance into clothes' – she lays great emphasis on the sensuality of her gowns, which some of her critics had described as too immodest and diaphanous. These tea-gowns, in popular shades of Parma violet and soft sweet-pea colours, were all given names which expressed, presumably, the mood of the wearer and the viewer; one example was 'The Sighing Sound of Lips Unsatisfied', '... a dress of soft grey chiffon, veiling an underdress of shot pink and violet taffeta ... rather like an opal'.[4]

Tea-gowns, not surprisingly, had a somewhat risqué reputation, and Mrs Pritchard in *The Cult of Chiffon* (1902) advised her readers, before setting off on a visit, to check with their hostess to see if such a dress could be worn at an informal dinner, for some women 'consider the tea-gown as a sign of the indolence and degeneracy of the times'.[5]

Mrs Pritchard finds this rather irritating, for her book is a propaganda exercise to persuade more Englishwomen to wear beautiful and luxurious fabrics, especially in their underwear; 'the cult of Chiffon has this in common with the Christian religion – it insists that the invisible is more important than the visible'.[6]

For most of the nineteenth century, underwear was plain and white; if coloured or luxuriously trimmed, it was often declared to be the sign of a woman of easy virtue. Like the Queen of Spain, women supposedly had no legs, so their drawers and combinations when shown in fashion magazines were drawn folded up so that their bifurcated nature was not seen. By the 1880s, however, a more rational mood prevailed, and women's pants (now called knickers), were depicted for what they were – knee-length trouser-like garments, either fully closed or open at the crotch. Pierre Dufay, in *Le Pantalon Féminin* (1916), an erotic excursion into the delights of female underwear, devotes a whole chapter of his lengthy book to the open and closed types of knickers, coming to the not very surprising conclusion that the former could be seen as an invitation to a sexual encounter; the excitement of the can-can lay in the promise of this titillating form of underwear, as well as the display of layers of frills in both petticoats and pants.

By the early twentieth century, Mrs Pritchard was still finding that some Englishwomen looked on expensive and luxurious underwear as unnecessary and even 'suggestive of evil', a state of affairs which she found absurd. Why, she asked, should beautiful underwear be 'the preserve of a class of woman less favoured than ourselves?' (i.e. prostitutes); if the underwear is well chosen (she finds the black underwear favoured by American women to be 'curiously effective'), then it might be used to rescue a failing marriage.

So important was underwear that Mrs Pritchard urged women to spend as much as one-fifth of their income on it. If one could not afford Lucile's 'underclothes as delicate as cobwebs and as beautifully tinted as flowers', then one could buy from the big department stores; most of the household names we know today were in existence by the beginning of this century, the last major one to open being Selfridges in 1909. These huge retail outlets catered for all classes, selling ready made and partially made clothing, and a vast range of luxury items. One critic, Hugh Stutfield, in *The Sovranty of Society* (1909) found luxury, aided and abetted by 'snippety light journalism' to be a cancer eating away at society; others found vanity and a taste for material possessions to be a reason for the decline in the British Empire, as it was, they averred, in ancient Rome.

Another sign of the decadence of the times, so such critics argued, was the custom accepted by a growing number of respectable people, for women – and not just married women – to wear cosmetics; by 1910 there were make-up parlours in London and the major cities. Make-up was not permitted for girls, for there was still a wide dividing line between adolescence and adulthood, a distinction which since the Second World War, we have largely lost. Gwen Raveret, writing in 1952, recalled Rupert Brooke telling a story of a Cambridge friend who dreamt one night of a recently deceased girl cousin, aged seventeen, of whom he had been very fond; she was standing before a mirror trying to cover up the ravages of death, and he woke 'to the dreadful knowledge of mortality. It was in 1912 that Rupert told us that story, but you could not tell it now. The point of it – the impossibility of a young girl making up before a mirror – would be entirely missed'.[7]

By 1912, the time of the story, change was in the air, both political and sartorial. The suffragette movement (they were the militant wing, the suffragists were law-abiding) was in full cry, and although some critics like Father Vaughan tried to link the movement with the mannishly dressed New Woman of the late nineteenth century, this was far from the case; they were often very fashionably dressed women, said the author of the pamphlet *Is the British Empire ripe for Government by Disorderly Women who smash windows and assault the Police?*; in their 'pretty costumes, big hats, carrying flowers and artistically man-designed bannerettes'.[8]

Many of the supporters of female suffrage would have found their activities greatly helped by the introduction, towards the end of the first decade of the century, of shorter skirts and a high-waisted dress that required far less corsetry. Edwardian languor was increasingly out of favour, and the 'refinement' of its pastel colours was reeling under the onslaught of the new, 'barbaric' colours, inspired by the exhibition of *Les Fauves* in Paris (1905) – artists such as Matisse and Derain – and the Russian ballet in Paris (1909) and London (1911). The leading light of the new movement was Paul Poiret, possibly the greatest couturier (and self-publicist) of all time; inspired by avant garde artist friends, and the clashing colours and eastern exoticism of the *Ballets Russes*, he designed dresses which appeared stunningly different, brightly coloured, and – above all – youthful. The opulent curves of the Edwardian lady, with her stately piled-high hair in art-nouveau curves and her huge hat covered in birds' plumage, were no longer required. The ideal now was a young, slim girl with short hair fitting close to the head, and an ability to put together seemingly clashing colours with artistic skill. Over the next few years the skirt remained short, sometimes being quite tight at the ankles, so that it had to be slit for walking, or with a pleated insert. Lucile designed dresses where the skirts were draped to reveal the lower leg, but modest women were warned that although they might be tempted 'by the wild tendencies of the moment', they should keep on at least one petticoat. Movement at the ankle was needed most of all for dancing, especially for the energetic swooning which the tango, the most fashionable of dances, demanded. Much more practical would have been the 'harem' costume which Poiret devised in 1910, loose Turkish trousers with a tunic top, but this never quite took off as a fashion in spite of its impeccably exotic credentials.

Poiret was sometimes accused by his rivals of being a vulgar showman, and there were many critics who found it 'demoralizing' to view 'the streets of great cities (which) present humiliating spectacles of a mad riot of colors and a tag-rag of stuffs'.[9] Flaunting colours, a silhouette that drew attention to the legs, strange and barbaric jewellery such as slave bracelets, and a virtual absence of corsetry – no wonder that many moralists found a new air of dangerous excitement in dress.

The rage for dancing, far more than the influence of sport, led to the introduction of easier undergarments, and a more natural body shape. The early Edwardian straight-fronted corset created an egg-shaped thrust-forward torso, which was emphasized by a blouse pouched in loose folds over a tiny waist; pads under the arms and at the hips served to reduce the apparent size of the waist. This was the ideal figure, the 'Gibson girl' created by the American artist Charles Dana Gibson, and personified on the London stage by Camille Clifford in *The Belle of Mayfair*. Such solid charms were, however, by 1910 quite out of fashion, a much more modish idol being the French dancer Mistinguett with her bobbed hair, slim figure and high-waisted Poiret dresses.

Young women, at least, replaced the boned corset with a much softer, less structured garment, called a brassière, which revealed the midriff. Originally a bodice of white cotton worn in the nineteenth century to keep the corset clean, the brassière was claimed as the invention of a number of designers, Lucile among them, but – no matter to whom it should be credited – it aroused considerable opposition. Many older women felt that the boned corset improved posture and contributed to self-discipline, and the manufacturers lamented the fact that at dances there were to be seen 'a number of women who affect an excessive unconstraint ... (and) have abandoned all support; the bust undulates to the rhythm of the dance in a loose fashion'.[10]

Equally startling to those brought up on late Victorian and Edwardian strictures with regard to the covering of the neck in the daytime, was the introduction of a modest V-shaped neckline c. 1913. Denounced by doctors as the 'pneumonia neckline', it joined the list of 'immoral' fashions, such as thin blouses and short skirts, which some Catholic clergymen saw fit to attack. The Bishop of Laibach's pastoral letter of January 1913 stated that:

> The newest fashions in clothes are designed to serve the cause of lust. They are sad evidence of the moral depth to which the modern spirit has fallen and at the same time a still sadder proof of the power and tyranny of the mode, before which women and girls ... bow the knee.

Other clerics of the same persuasion joined the protest, and in 1914 some of the Catholic unions in the garment trades declared that they would refuse to make 'garments which contravened Christian morality and propriety'.[11]

---

89 'Resource'.
Punch, *1913*.
Finding that a modest 'tailor-made' suit is not fashionable at Monte Carlo, Miss Browne 'made herself inconspicuous' by removing her blouse (thus creating the modish V neckline), shortening and tightening her skirt, and sticking her umbrella in her hat in imitation of the fashionable 'oriental' aigrette.

RESOURCE.
(How Miss Browne whose simple appearance attracted too much attention made herself inconspicuous at Monte Carlo.)

This must have been as useless a gesture as the declaration by the state of Illinois in 1914 that women were to wear dresses no more than six inches off the ground; short sleeves, low-cut necks for day dresses, and see-through blouses in the style called 'Peek-a-boo ... (which) displays the lines of the female figure too pronouncedly' were strictly forbidden. Offenders could be fined up to twenty-five dollars, and they could even run the risk of imprisonment if they wore 'provocative' bathing costumes.[12]

By 1914 the fashionable world had more pressing concerns to worry about, with the declaration of the war which was to have a major impact on all classes of society, not least on women who from 1917 were joining the armed services, and before that working in what were traditionally 'men's' jobs. From 1915 women began to work in munitions factories, on the buses, and on the land, and many of them for convenience and comfort began to wear trousers. There were some complaints of indecency, especially by the older women, and many of the 'munitionettes' from the respectable working class were sensitive to the ridicule and hostility which the wearing of trousers sometimes called forth. Yet the public generally became as accustomed to see women dressed like this, as they became used to women in that other traditionally masculine costume, the uniform. Although women were only supposed to wear their uniforms at work, many of them found it more comfortable than fashionable dress, and they were often to be seen in restaurants dressed in this way.

To many old-fashioned critics, the sight of women dining on their own in restaurants was as bad, if not worse, than their appearance in uniform, an indication of the hectic and fast life they were pursuing – dancing, smoking and indulging in sexual adventures. For the first time, a far greater number of women were employed and had wages to spend. While the majority prudently saved, some had their first, heady taste of such pleasures as jazz and going to revues–pleasures which before the war had been mainly limited to the upper classes. It is probably true that many women, aware of the carnage in Flanders as the full horror of the war became known, were more receptive to the advances of their young men, fearing that they might not survive.

This shift in moral attitudes had profound effects on post-war England, and the great topic of the 1920s was the so-called decline of morality as a result of the war. We would probably say that it was not so much a period of decline, as a time of moral upheaval, as previously widely accepted beliefs about religion, politics and society were questioned. While there had been, from the last quarter of the nineteenth century, a growing scientific and rationalist approach to religion amongst the middle-class intelligentsia, the appalling and wasteful casualties of the First World War, a time when God was seemingly oblivious to the bloodshed in the world He had apparently created, forced many people in all classes away from religion towards more humanist, secular ideals. Educated to a higher standard (after the Education Act of 1870), and with mass production of cheap newspapers and periodicals, it was possible to read and absorb, for example, works on socialism, philosophy, and even sexuality. Paradoxically, the London Council for the Promotion of Public Morality, which had begun in 1898 with the aim of getting rid of the sex-shops, massage parlours, sex shows (or 'living statuary') and the lewder music hall acts which the capital offered, was by the outbreak of the First World War quite openly discussing the various kinds of sex and associated vices available, and it helped to promote a much freer climate for discussion after the war. The fact that people now talked far more in public about subjects

---

90 'Glorinda: A Portrait'.
Punch, *1922*.
With the passion for youth dominating the fashions of the 1920s, older women who wished to be à la mode had to do far more than use cosmetics to achieve this end. Glorinda, aged forty-nine, not only is 'plastered with carmine on her cheeks and lips', but 'diaphanously clad, with purple locks', she has to keep up with changing intellectual tastes, to follow all the 'new, bizarre, sophisticated things'.

GLORINDA: A PORTRAIT.

Resolved from earliest youth to shock and shine,
Glorinda, at the age of forty-nine,
Still drinks with thirst insatiate at the springs
Of new, bizarre, sophisticated things.

Goaded by all the demons of unrest,
Pursuing pleasure with ferocious zest,
Though growing daily longer in the tooth
She leads the revels of rebellious youth,
Sitting, for choice, cross-legged upon the floor
While neo-Georgian lions round her roar;

Though none can drown her piercing peacock tones
As she denounces Browning or Burne-Jones,
Dismisses Wells or Bennett to the ranks
Of fogeydom along with Squire and Shanks,
Or holds it less a blunder than a crime
When the dear Sitwells deviate into rhyme.
As the fit climax of a hectic day
She loves to patronize the horror play,
In ecstasy succumbing to the lure
Of scenes a scavenger could scarce endure;
And in the realm of music knows no joys
Save those provided by "deliberate noise."

In old Victorian days a game was played
Wherein young ladies their "confessions" made,
And wrote their answers to the *questionnaire*
In albums cherished with religious care.
Some still survive, and one of them enshrines
Glorinda's creed in forty lurid lines,
Showing, in all its cultivated kinks,
The mental outfit of the super-minx.
Most I pass over, but a few may serve
As illustrations of her taste and nerve.

"*Your favourite virtue*—Perfect self-expression.
The vice you most abominate—Discretion.
Your favourite heroine—Queen Jezebel.
Your pet aversions—Beethoven and Dell.
Your favourite authors—'Aldous' and James Joyce.
Your favourite animal—My big Rolls-Royce.
Your favourite diet—Gin and gorgonzola.
Your favourite female names—Locusta, Lola.
Your favourite composers—Bliss and Bax.
Your favourite sport—Riding on flapper-racks.
Your favourite artists—Poy, Picasso, Lamb.
The Heaven you hope for—One prolonged Grand Slam."

Nor are her ardent energies confined
To championing the mutiny of mind,
Or wallowing with rapture unalloyed
Deep in the ectoplasmic mire of Freud.
No, in the elastic ambit of her code
The modern Mænad has a place for Mode,
And in the streets the very motors shy
When, dressed to kill, Glorinda passes by,
Alert, self-conscious to the finger-tips,
Plastered with carmine on her cheeks and lips.
But whether you behold her in her box,
Diaphanously clad, with purple locks,
Or jazzing with contortions that outdo
The gestures of a boxing kangaroo,
Tarantulated by the fearsome tunes
Played by a band of epileptic coons—
Glorinda holds the centre of the stage,
The most "conspicuous monster of our age."

THE PLATITUDINARIANS.

If we took our stand near to the parish pump in some sequestered village, and heard Gaffer Brown talking gravely of the weather to his crony, Master Bellows—"And what I say is that it's always raining or else it's shining. And when it isn't raining or shining, belike it's soon going to do ayther the one or t'other"—we should probably say to ourselves, "The dear old fellows seem to think that they're in Westminster."

But if we took our place at Westminster and heard our rulers talking gravely about the state of trade—"And we have every reason to cherish the sanguine hope that within the next few months—the next few months, Mr. Speaker—we are likely to witness a considerable change in the outlook, taking into account the well-established economic law that periods of depression are usually followed by periods of trade revival"—we should probably say to ourselves, "The dear old things seem to imagine that they're round the parish pump."

New Profession for "Knuts."

"Small Walnut Telescopic Diner Wanted; good condition and at reasonable price."—*Advt. in Daily Paper.*

It seems an excellent idea. He would be there when required and take up very little room at other times.

"The Bishop visited us on his 'Pilgrimage Tour,' and though the men could not, owing to agriculture, attend, there were several kind and Sacrificing Spirits amongst the women able to appreciate the short service."—*Parish Magazine.*

We trust his lordship appreciated their sacrifice.

which were previously taboo, did not, in spite of a torrent of criticism, mean that they practised what they discussed.

However, women *looked* more immoral in the eyes of those who had been brought up in the relatively well-padded and covered Edwardian period. The 1914–18 War did not, curiously enough, really affect fashionable dress; there was no clothes rationing, and although by 1916 some newspapers were urging women to dress plainly, dresses remained quite long, full in the skirt and often ornately trimmed. It was as though women wanted to be especially feminine, out of uniform, for when their men returned from the trenches.

The knee-length 'flapper' dress which we associate with the 1920s did not really appear until *c.*1925, but by the early years of the decade, women's dress was often quite flimsy, shapeless, and worn with a minimum of underwear such as a corselette held up by shoulder straps, which flattened the bust and ignored the waist. Dresses which were basically tubular – the *Daily Sketch* for 21 October 1924 found women's fashions to be 'designed by a plumber and a cubist meeting in Bedlam' – and made of cheap materials such as rayon, were simple enough to be made by even the most amateur dress-maker of any class; high fashion appeared to be democratically open to all, quite appropriately when by 1928 all women over 21 had won the right to vote.

It was during this year that Aldous Huxley published *Point Counter Point*, in which the lascivious middle-aged Sidney Quarles itemizes the charms of his mistress, her cropped hair, her thin dress through which he could see 'just below her shoulders, the line where the underclothes gave way to bare skin', and her stockings 'the colour of sunburnt flesh'; brought up

> in an epoch when ladies apparently rolled along on wheels, Mr Quarles was peculiarly susceptible to calves, found modern fashions a treat, and could never get over the belief that the young women who adopted them had deliberately made themselves indecent for his benefit, and because they wanted him to become their lover.[13]

Indecency, for Mr Quarles, comprised short skirts – by 1925, when they were banned by the Pope, they were a few inches below the knee, but by 1927 they had reached knee-length – the revelation of silk underwear, cropped hair, and flesh-coloured stockings. By 1927, dubbed by the *Daily Express* 'leg year' and outstanding for its 'parade of bronze and sand-coloured limbs', nearly all women had adopted artificial silk stockings in 'nude' or flesh colours. These had been pioneered before the war by Poiret, but the public had not really taken notice of them until 1922, according to Beverley Nichols, when the Trix sisters appearing at the Ritz startled their audience with a sight of their beige stockings, 'and a number of elderly ladies felt that the country had taken another step towards the Pit'.[14] Never before had female limbs been so openly displayed, and attention drawn to them by the fashionable slouch; furthermore, said one commentator,

> No nice girl in pre-war days crossed her legs in public. No nice girl lifted her hands to rearrange her hair in public, for the pull of the arm brought the pectoral muscles into play and featured the breasts; that indicated a mind offering a body. So the little girl pal slouched in her chair, went in for the cult of the leg, and lifted her arms frequently. How else could she light her cigarettes?[15]

The 'little girl pal' was a curious mixture of sophistication and boyishness, the latter quality reflected in her short hair and her coltish demeanour. 'What is a modern girl?', was the question put in 1925 to Lady Walpole by a reporter from the *Weekly Dispatch*, to which she replied:

> She is an inane, insane, Eton-cropped, useless, idle, mannish young woman who smokes doped

---

91 'The Insurgence of Youth' *1924*.
Max Beerbohm.
The cartoonist picks out the difference between the somewhat effeminate young man, legs decorously together, and the slouched girl whose shapeless gown reveals a boyish torso. Smoking, drinking and bad language were, to many moralists, further signs of the decadence of the young.

92 'Rouge à lèvres'.
K. van Dongen.
Moralists were seemingly unaware of the contradiction implicit in their complaints about the short 'masculine' bobbed hairstyles, and the copious use of cosmetics as worn by the fashionable woman. While many were reconciled to the widespread use of cosmetics, making up the face in public was still frowned upon.

cigarettes, uses bad language, wears practically no clothes, and is an abomination to her fellow creatures.[16]

Part of the mannishness consisted in the short haircut; the Eton crop of 1925 was shorter than a man's hair. Some avant-garde women, such as Colette, had cut their hair well before the war, and Chanel had bobbed hers some years later, setting a vogue, as some critics called it, for copying the *poilus*; the razored recruits to the French army. This was somewhat of an exaggeration, for women who cut their hair kept it well below ear-length, a modest style compared to the very short 'shingle' of the early 1920s. Moralists lamented the loss of a woman's crowning glory; no matter how much it had been eked out with false hair (something they had been very quick to complain about in earlier periods), it was feminine, which the short bob was certainly not. To quote Beverley Nichols again, when one recalls the spate of attacks on short hair, 'one would think that "bobbing" and "shingling" were pseudonyms for the penchants of Sodom and Gomorrah'.[17]

Moralists were quick to state that the whole of fashionable society was riddled with homosexuality; novels and newspapers entered into somewhat breathless discussions of lesbianism in particular, free to tell in print what had previously been forbidden. The heroine of Victor Margueritte's novel, *La garçonne*, the *succès de scandale* of 1922, is described as taking drugs and lovers (of both sexes) with equal ease. Postwar Paris is seen as a totally cynical and decadent society, where all moral restraints are pushed aside to gratify the sensual impulses of the moment, and nowhere is this more reflected than in dress:

> Each body, whether beautiful or otherwise, flaunted its nakedness from the shoulder to the hips, revealed through the cutaway sides of the light dresses. It might have been a slave market, conducted under the practised eyes of the merchants and private fanciers, who appraised with a glance the contours of the bodies, the arms rejoicing in their nakedness. The array of coiffures, ranging from blue-black to a reddish blonde, the paint on lips and cheeks, all gave to the show of peacock faces a fictitious brilliance as of painted masks.[18]

The discreet Edwardian use of cosmetics was swept away by garish make-up; novels written in the 1920s, like Michael Arlen's celebrated *The Green Hat* (1924) have their heroines starkly made up with white faces and bright red lips. Not until the later 1920s did the vogue for sun-bathing – helped by the knowledge that the production of vitamin D was encouraged by sunlight – dispel the use of heavy, artificial make-up. By the end of the decade, so important a market was being opened up by mass holidays at sea-side resorts, that many designers turned their attention to bathing-costumes which became short and tight-fitting to the figure. The author Raymond Mortimer, discussing, on the whole with approval, the new freedom in women's dress, declared that 'Today there is little of our bodies which we are not ready to exhibit on the beaches of the Mediterranean'.[19] And a fashion writer defending the modern girl found that 'Women have the right, if not to *be* less virtuous than their grandmothers, at any rate to *look* less virtuous'.[20]

At this point we have to note the last really fierce religiously-inspired attack on dress, a last blast of the trumpet against the monstrous regiment of immodesty. This occurs in a pamphlet by a Mr T. I. W. (who describes himself as 'a Christian Business Man'), entitled *Modest Apparel. An Earnest Word to Christian Women* (1931). The author, who is particularly incensed by 'women in bathing attire [who] pose in immodest or indecent positions for the photographer', and by those who wear sleeveless short dresses and even shorts, had waited in vain for 'some godly sister in Christ' to condemn this 'dressing like harlots' – but in vain. He thus takes upon himself the burden, stating that, as women have always been the instruments of Satan, it is not surprising that by their dress they should tempt hapless men to crimes of passion:

> Remember the girl who dresses in an alluring way cannot condemn anyone but herself if the lure of her dress brings her the treatment which is usually accorded to women of questionable morals.[21]

Where one man sees 'nudity' in dress, another man sees freedom, and many men by the end of the 1920s were beginning to envy women for their liberty of movement and relative freedom from convention which they saw in the wide variety of costume at their disposal.

Ever since men could remember they had been warned against any eccentricity in dress, which was regarded as not only incorrect but as insulting to society. Compared to the dramatic changes which had taken place in women's dress since the beginning of the nineteenth century, hardly any changes seemed to have occurred in men's dress. True, the frock coat had vanished and the morning suit was reserved only for very formal occasions, but these were only minor changes in usage, not style, and with regard to all types of dress, the rules were very strict. One etiquette book of 1926 exclaimed in horror, 'I actually saw a man in the Carlton Hotel entrance hall one night last summer, wearing brown shoes, a dinner jacket, and a straw hat. He was presumably an American, but even so ...!' Other prohibitions included the wearing of patent leather shoes in the daytime, tan boots in London, a bowler hat with evening dress, and a jumper with a town suit.[22]

One wonders if the conventional Englishman envied the apparent sartorial freedom which Americans enjoyed, or if he relished the moral superiority which 'correct' clothes gave him. George Bernard Shaw declared in *Man and Superman* (1903) that such 'morality' was just discomfort – 'An Englishman thinks he is moral when he is only uncomfortable'.

This was a statement which the dress reformer J. C. Flügel agreed with. The problem which the men's dress reform movement at the end of the 1920s had to face was how to overcome the 'moral' associations of men's conventional clothing without being accused of effeminacy.

For many contemporaries agreed that, no doubt as a result of the war and the increasingly masculine role played by women, some young men were showing unhealthy signs of effeminacy in their appearance. Quite what these were, it is difficult to say, for the critics were not specific; they were probably nothing more than an unusually wide lapel to the jacket, the admittedly voluminous Oxford bags of 1925 which, said Beverley Nichols, were 'somehow connected with atheism, effeminacy',[23] an unconventional colour of tie, or a polo jersey – an informal style which was, according to Doris

93 'Manners and Modes: Crossing the Road – 1925'. Punch, 1925.
Beverley Nichols' comment that the wide Oxford bags were a sign of effeminacy, is perhaps echoed here by Punch, *as the fashionable gentleman lifts his trousers to cross the muddy road.*

Langley Moore, particularly popular with homosexuals.[24] In an age in which the staid and conventional expected to be shocked by the dress and behaviour of the young, the latter obliged by adopting the fashionable pose of crossing the sexual divide. Among Evelyn Waugh's Bright Young Things in *Vile Bodies* (1930), 'Miss Runcible wore trousers and Miles touched up his eyelashes in the dining room of the hotel where they stopped for luncheon. So they were asked to leave'.

There was perhaps a feeling that such incipient effeminacy could be disciplined by dress reform of a patently masculine kind, so that although some dress reformers and artists like Eric Gill argued for beauty and colour (he wanted a vaguely 'medieval' tunic and hose), the preferred costume turned out to be an open-necked shirts, shorts and sandals for the day and for the evening – though there was considerable disagreement about this – black knee breeches and a silk blouse. Supported by an impressive list of those eminent in the fields of medicine and the arts, the *Men's Dress Reform Party* was founded with great optimism in 1929 in order to convert the male public to a more comfortable, rational and attractive dress. It did not meet with any great success, the majority of Englishmen agreeing with the comments made by a (conventional) tailor at a Dress Reform Dinner Debate in 1932 that those men who rejoiced in unusual or exotic attire were 'sexually abnormal . . . soft, sloppy clothes are symbolical of a soft and sloppy race'.[25] Furthermore, he went on, although free and comfortable clothes were all right for sport, they were out of the question at work; even informally, it seems, the reformed dress was not welcome in the public rooms of some hotels, and the MDRP had to publish a list of places where the open-necked shirt and shorts were acceptable.

Another campaign which they waged was to encourage sea-side resorts to allow men to wear bathing slips, i.e. trunks, instead of the bathing costume which covered the chest as well. Most resorts had, by the outbreak of the First World War, accepted that mixed bathing was here to stay, but many – at least half those questioned by the MDRP in 1930 – regarded the slip as 'indecent exposure of the person'. Gradually, however, during the 1930s, bathing trunks were accepted for men, rather more due to a disregard of local bye-laws than to any pressure exerted by the men's dress reform movement. It was a very slow and painful process for men to reveal that they had bodies beneath their heavy, constricting suits; it was even more of a break with the Victorian and Edwardian past to begin to think of wearing brightly coloured clothes, and even to adopt elements of women's dress – the latter is a battle still to be won if men wish it. For women, however, the 1920s was the decade of triumphs; the battles which had been raging for centuries – the right of women to reveal virtually all their bodies and to wear an almost complete masculine wardrobe if they wished – had been won.

Having proved their point, the 1930s sees a return to a more ostensibly feminine look, with longer dresses cut on the bias to reveal the figure, and dipping alarmingly at front and back. Typical quotations from the fashion magazines are: 'In the evening you can show everything except ankles' (1933), 'Nudity is the new hue and cry in fashions' (1934) and 'Bare your bosom as low as your figure will allow and your conscience will permit' (1935). After a decade or more of hiding the figure, it was seen that a woman now had a bust and hips, very much in evidence beneath the erotic, clinging fabrics like slipper satin which were in vogue. The bottom – what the Victorians had called 'the hips at the back' – was emphasized by an elastic roll-on girdle, and the bust helped by the up-lift brassière; even 'falsies', i.e. false rubber bosoms, were brought to the aid of the woman who was not well endowed by nature (or who had lost her shape during the twenties). One brand called 'Very Secret' was 'blown up with a straw, as if you were sipping crème de menthe'.[26]

All this the critics appeared to have taken lying down; were they punch-drunk after the extremes of the 1920s and ready to welcome feminity back at any price, or had they, as a breed, disappeared? The only major complaints appear to have been about the increased expenditure which women had to make on their clothes, jewellery (real jewels instead of the fakes made fashionable by Chanel in the '20s were back in vogue) and cosmetics. Women, who were allowed to make up their faces in public for the first time without attracting censure, spent in one year (1933), according to *Punch*, as much as £40m on make-up.

Looking back in 1939 on the fashions of the previous decade, Antonia White, in *Picture Post*, remembered: 'It is was so easy to look smart when everyone from duchess to mill girl wore exactly the same type of clothes. And you didn't have to bother with perms and elaborate hair-dos, when you only had to cram a little felt hat well over your ears ...'

In spite of the element of untruth contained in this statement (even in the twenties the duchess would be distinguished by the quality of the fabrics), it was certainly true that in the

94 The Twin Sisters of Castor and Pollux. *Drawing by Thomas Lowinsky in Raymond Mortimer's* Modern Nymphs *1930.*
A less than perfect figure could no longer be hidden under the dress as it had in the shapeless twenties. The new fashions revealed the body in the same way as did the neo-classical styles of the early nineteenth century, but without generally exciting the same volume of criticism.

MANNERS AND MODES: THE LATEST LINES.
She. "That's a pretty woman."
He. "Which? The one in the bath wrap or the one in surgical bandages?"

95 'Manners and Modes: The Latest Lines'.
Punch, *1931*.
Complaints about women's dress were not so much about their 'immorality', although the fashions were often very revealing, but because of their risibility. It was obviously all too easy for the fashionable bias cut gowns to take on the appearance of a 'bath wrap' or 'surgical bandages'.

1930s a woman needed a much larger wardrobe. She needed long-skirted evening dresses and short-skirted day dresses; she needed practical suits to work in, and a whole range of sporting clothes to play in. Ever since the end of the 1920s, Chanel had included trousers in her collections both for sport, everyday wear and the beach; such garments were essential wear for the fashionable woman. Sport, most of all, coupled with a growing health and body cult, helped to break down old-fashioned conventions regarding exposure of the body. When semi-nudity was the rule at revues and bare limbs an everyday sight in the streets, the public was no longer easily shocked at bare flesh.

So much were designers themselves bored at the end of the 1930s with the *sportif* semi-nudity of informal dress, and the athletic figure-hugging dress for evening, that by 1938 they were experimenting with huge crinolines and boned corsets, the kind of flirtation with the past which the English in particular admired. Queen Elizabeth helped to popularize the style, but, said *Picture Post*, it was rather costly – the whaleboned petticoats could cost as much as £60, and the skirts took up to eighteen yards of material – and cumbersome; 'if universally adopted, the whole paraphernalia of modern life, from railway-carriage and cars to telephone booths, would require to be almost entirely reconstructed'.[27]

Picture Post need not have worried, for almost as soon as the Second World War began in 1939, austerity hit the world of high fashion. Women were either in uniforms in the armed services, or bound by the strict clothing regulations which came into force in 1941. In order to control consumer spending to release clothing workers for more important work and to make more factory space available, clothes were rationed with increasing severity as the war continued. Unlike the 1914–18 war which did not really affect the development of fashion, the 1939–45 war ensured that fashion virtually came to a full stop. The civilian clothes which women could buy with coupons or make for themselves from rationed material, were casual, practical and often with a military flavour, such as duffel jackets, trench coats and square-shouldered suits.

The only way a woman could show her individuality was in cosmetics and elaborate hairstyles; these served to keep up morale and to reassure women of their femininity. There were those who criticized some women who bleached their hair to a film-star platinum blonde appearance or – and this was infinitely the greater crime to their menfolk – who took for favours the nylon stockings offered by the American soldiers who came over to England from 1941 when the U.S.A. entered the war. To some extent (although it must not be exaggerated) there was some relaxation of sexual morality during the war; this was hardly surprising when men were away for years, and women, the majority of whom were involved in war-work of one kind or another, had considerable social freedom. While a sexual invitation could not be expressed through glamorous clothes, it could be hinted at by the wearing of a gold anklet chain on the left leg.

During the war it had been fashionable to be unfashionable, and women had accepted the need for wearing practical masculine clothing as part of the camaraderie of the war effort. While acceptable if women were in the armed services, it was less appreciated in civilian dress, and in a letters column on the subject of modesty run by the *Daily Mail* in the autumn of 1945, most men claimed to dislike the 'slackness of behaviour of the war years'. One man stated that: 'I would refuse to be seen in public with a female wearing shorts or slacks and dangling a cigarette between her lips'.[28] Because of their comfort and practicality, women would never relinquish their trousers, but by the end of the war they were increasingly tired of uniforms and uniformity, and of the rather squat square-shouldered, short-skirted styles which rationing and the military mood of the times had imposed on them. To meet the demand, from a shattered and demoralized Europe, that femininity should be revived, in 1947 Dior introduced the New Look, a tiny-waisted dress with a long full skirt. It amazed a public used for many years to utilitarian brevity of cut, and provoked considerable controversy both on economic and aesthetic grounds. It was an immensely extravagant style which could take up to twenty-five yards of fabric, and which relied for best effect on a tiny waist which had to be created by a boned wasp-waist corset, an item which in a still-rationed England was classed as a 'luxury garment'. Although it was claimed that 'the British Corset Manufacturers will never disturb a woman's organs' (i.e. making the heavily boned 'waspies' which the new style demanded) they had to move with the times and produce them; a year after the introduction of the New Look, it was worn all over England. Labour politicians in particular found the New Look economically immoral; while Harold Wilson thought it 'damn silly', Bessie Braddock declared that it was 'the ridiculous whim of idle people', and Sir Stafford Cripps wanted it outlawed.[29] The *Daily Herald*, sympathetic to this point of view, stated that not only was the style difficult to cope with on public transport, but that hard-pressed clothing factories did not have the facilities – nor should they be made to, was the implication – to meet the demand.[30] The public were divided on the issue. To begin with, in the autumn of 1947 the *Mass Observation Bulletin* reported that most were against

96 *Dior's* New Look 1947.
Harper's Bazaar.
In the context of a dreary post-war world, the New Look, with its tightly-corsetted waist and an abundance of fabric in the skirt, added a touch of welcome frivolity and feminity to the scene. In spite of some misgivings expressed on moral and economic grounds by the new Labour government (Puritanism is a constant strain in the Labour Party), the style came to be widely adopted, proving that fashion nearly always triumphs over politics.

long skirts, although some of those questioned expressed a belief that they would help to improve the manners of post-war Britain by improving politeness: 'Women determine the morals of a nation, and longer skirts create a far more composed state of mind, which has the same effect on men'. By 1949 most women were wearing long skirts to their dresses or suits (by this time rationing had a negligible effect on clothes), although not as long as those of the original New Look. Anne Edwards in the *Daily Express* found that 'the ideal skirt should be like a good speech, long enough to cover the essential parts, and short enough to be interesting'.[31]

The 1950s was in many ways the most interesting decade of the post-war period, with some startlingly divergent styles. The cult of youth was not yet firmly established, and to a large extent girls wished to look like glamorous adults, with high-heeled shoes, hair either permed or back-combed into a fashionable 'beehive' style, and faces expertly made up. Head teachers at some schools fought a running battle against some of their more rebellious pupils who wished to incorporate some of these fashion elements into their school uniforms. Paper nylon petticoats crashed under school skirts and particularly daring girls wore heavily stitched pointed bras to emphasize their breasts.

During the war, in America in particular, the bust had been the area of maximum sexual appeal; favourite pin-up girls of the period, such as Lana Turner and Jane Russell, were famed for their bust measurements, especially when displayed under a seemingly demure sweater. 'I'd like to see her in a sweater', was the caption to a 1945 cartoon of an American soldier ogling a bare-breasted beauty on a Pacific island. Jane Russell in the film *The Outlaw* (1943) wore a bra designed to create pointed uplift; the film was banned for some years because of its overt sexual display.

At about the same time the mail order firm, Frederick's of Hollywood, began offering elaborate contrivances by which the perfect pneumatic figure could be achieved – 'blow yourself

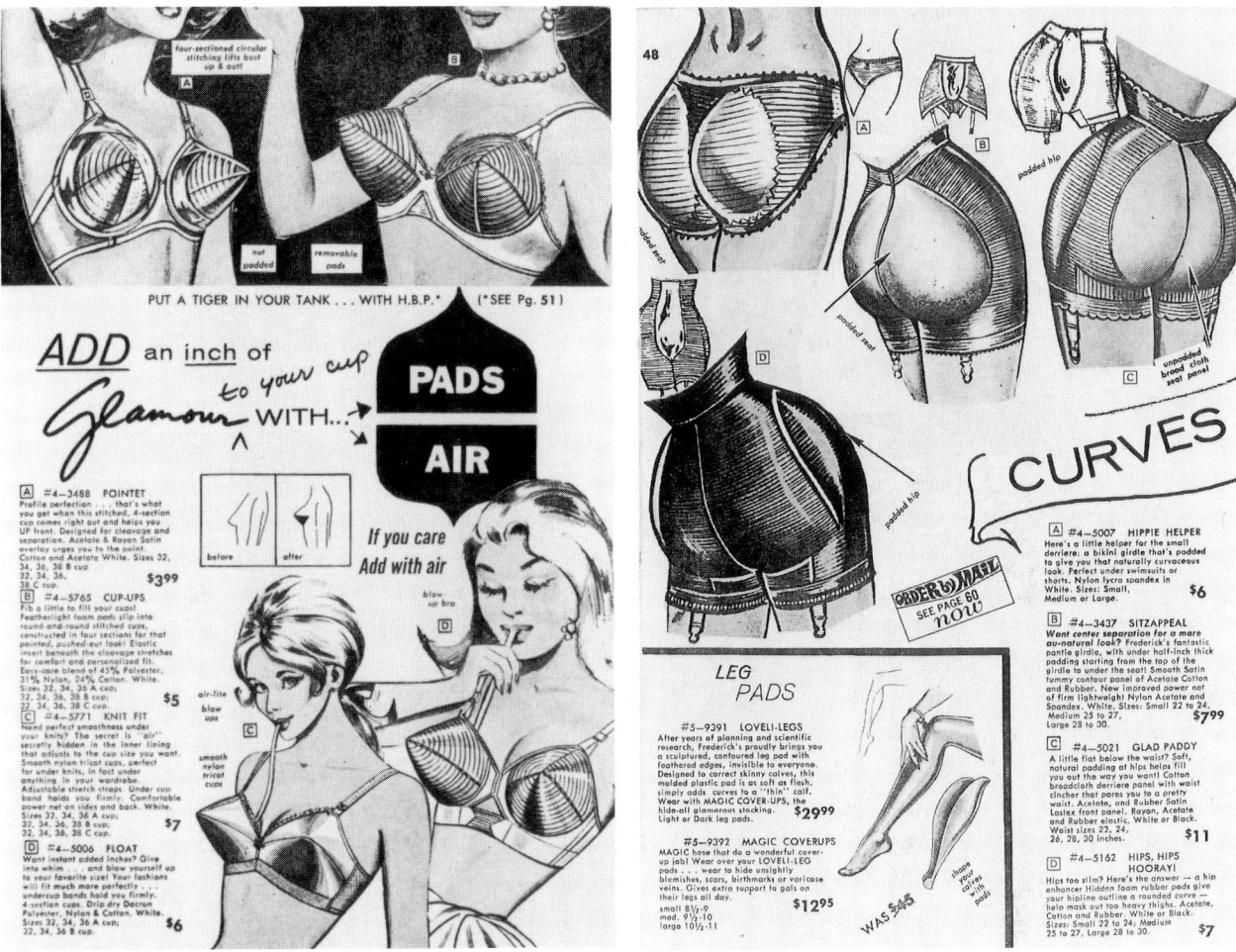

97 *Advertisements for Frederick's of Hollywood, 1968 and 1969.*
The latest in a long tradition of correcting the deficiencies of nature with regard to the female body. All that is missing is the figure of Death or the Devil to remind the readers of the vanity and ultimate futility of their endeavours.

up to your favourite size' bras, girdles with cut-outs at the buttocks to let the bottom wobble, tightly laced corsets and leg-pads ('Lovelilegs') to correct skinny calves. With its emphasis on ultra-femininity, cleavages, handspan waists and rounded hips, the firm is, in its delight in artifice almost a throw-back to the world of the Victorian tight-lacers, and perhaps somewhat of a paradox in the late twentieth century. Still going strong, it represents either the fantasy world of the tired provincial housewife, or the more dubious arena of the fetishist male, a market which is also catered for in the small advertisements of today's Sunday papers.

An overt display of feminine charms, whether by firmly cantilevered bras, or by revealing bathing costumes and sun dresses, aroused some criticism by the clergy during the 1950s. Two-piece swimming costumes had been seen on the beaches as early as the late 1920s; by the early 1950s such bathing suits were quite cut-away and often made of new synthetic stretch fabrics which emphasized the figure – they were given the name 'bikini' after an atoll in the central Pacific where U.S. atom tests took place. Some sea-side authorities made half-hearted attempts to ban the bikini, but to no effect, and it ruled supreme through the 1960s and 1970s.

It was probably one of the garments to which the Catholic Church took exception, when in 1955 Cardinal Ciriaci of the Vatican sent a letter to the bishops of every diocese deploring recent trends in women's dress:

> particularly in the summertime, and not only on the seashore and at country resorts, but almost everywhere... and not infrequently in buildings consecrated to God, there has come to prevail an unworthy and shameless manner of dress, by which the soul, particularly the soul of youth that is easily turned to sin, is placed in very serious danger of losing that innocence which is the greatest and most beautiful ornament of mind and body.

Catholic women in America were urged to boycott 'designers and manufacturers who go to extremes in exploiting "femininity for profit"'; instead they were asked to buy 'Marylyke Modest Dresses' with the slogan 'Dare to be different for our Lady's sake'.[32] These dresses, which were presumably fairly ample in cut and did not reveal the shape of the body, were at least a positive response to complaints about immorality in dress, although one suspects that fashionable Catholic women preferred sleeveless sundresses to 'Marylyke Modest Dresses' in the summer.

The first half of the twentieth century was noted for papal denunciations of 'immodest' dress; it appeared to have taken over the mantle of earlier Puritan invective in this respect, as it weighed in against sun dresses and short skirts. In all fairness, it did not have a monopoly with such criticism, for in 1955 the evangelist Billy Graham preaching in Toronto declared:

> It is as bad as murder to entice others to immorality. Many of you women have dressed in such a way as to bring impure thoughts to the minds of men.[33]

Christian religions which demand a total commitment to doctrine and unquestioning obedience to authority – like the Catholics and the more fundamentalist Protestant churches – are today most likely to demand 'decency' in the dress of their congregations even if they have difficulty in defining it. The more tolerant (or indifferent?) Anglican church, since it has relaxed the sartorial standards of many of its own clergy, cannot demand propriety in dress from all its worshippers. In any case, the voice of the church in post-war England was becoming considerably muted in reaction to a largely indifferent public more motivated by material pleasures. Young people in particular in the 1950s had more money to spend, and fashion was an obvious choice. Girls could spend their money on the very feminine well-groomed styles popularized by fashionable film stars like Grace Kelly, or on skin-tight jeans and loose sweaters – fashions taken from American youth. As early as 1944 *Life* magazine reported, as though about some far-away tribe, that teenage girls in America were wearing men's shirts and jeans, a fashion frowned on by parents and teachers who 'find it shockingly sloppy. This makes the custom exciting ... and keeps the girls firmly united against all protests'.[34] It was a style which showed off the body in the athletic movements of such popular dances as the jive and, later, rock and roll, which swept England in the 1950s.

For men, the first major attack on post-war sartorial austerity came at the end of the 1940s with the introduction of the loose 'drape' jacket and wide trousers pleated in to the waist; this was the middle-of-the road style adopted by men of all classes throughout the 1950s. Some more fashionable men-about-town had also begun to appear in a kind of 'Edwardian' costume, a long velvet-collared jacket, a patterned waistcoat, and tighter trousers. In the early 1950s it was taken over by working-class youth, becoming more exaggerated in the process; the 'Teddy-boy' was identified by his drape jacket, tight 'drain-pipe' trousers, fancy waistcoat, luminous socks, large crepe-soled shoes called 'brothel-creepers', a bootlace tie and long oiled hair. The sense of outrage which the style evoked and its palpable aura of criminality made it immensely popular. One writer comments:

DRESS AND DISORDER

98 *Cartoon by 'Sprod'.*
Punch, *1958.*
The girl with her pony-tail, swinging jewellery, tight skirt and high heels, attracts the attention of the Teddy Boys with their equally overtly sexual clothing and love of display.

The baroque complexities of their costume, the tightness in the thigh and crotch, and their rituals of attraction like the hair-combing in front of women – all of this was in the classic peacock tradition of direct sexual display.[35]

Sexual flamboyance in dress had returned, at least to a section of the working class, and new cult heroes were made from American pop stars like Elvis Presley in his very tight trousers and greasy hair, deliberately creating mass hysteria in his audience by the sexual quality of his singing and his wild hip gyrations.

The scene was set for the succession of youth fashion cults which during the next decades flourished in the wake of pop groups. These ranged from the fairly clean-cut image of the Beatles with their relatively short hair and neat short Italian 'mod' suits, to the more unkempt and dangerous-looking Rolling Stones who openly revelled in their sexual exploits and experiments with drugs. The long and dishevelled hair of the Rolling Stones attracted considerable censure, something that should not surprise us when we remember that whole moral tracts were written in the past on hair alone; 'it was their hair, and the murder in their faces peeping out through the jungle ... hair used as a kick in the teeth, as insult and ridicule ... as symbolic of sex, of energy ...'[36]

Many pop groups of the 1960s had middle-class backgrounds – however much they tried to disguise the fact by adopting a somewhat romanticized version of working-class costume – and many were students; by the end of the decade many were drawn towards the

it a sort of gladiatorial circus to go with the bread of economic stagnation, or is it, as its apologists claim, new and good and energetic like a gush of oil in the North Sea?'[37] While anyone could see what these young people wore, there was less agreement about what it all meant; some professed to find it immoral, others disliked the violence, an even greater number found it amazing/amusing, and sociologists and journalists claimed that it was a protest against society – against unemployment and the harsh

100 'Beatnik Flower Power versus the Honey Bee'. *Cartoon by Osbert Lancaster in* The Daily Express, *1967*.
A popular view of the late 1960s 'hippie', with his long, untidy hair, Indian beads, frayed tunic and floral jeans. Nothing was more calculated to make retired military men and/or writers to The Daily Telegraph *urge the reintroduction of national service.*

99 *Cartoon by Emmwood 1962.*
The Daily Mail, *1962*.
By the early 1960s, the colourful flamboyance of the Teddy Boy was giving way to a more deliberately proletarian style where casual clothing was increasingly influenced by working wear. The girl with her heavily made up face produces an effect of some sartorial confusion in her short tight skirt and her sloppy, 'masculine' sweater.

quasi-intellectual qualities – 'beat' poetry of a vaguely anarchic kind, Indian mysticism, and 'artistic' flowing draperies – which they saw in the 'hippie' movement. It was partly in reaction to this that crudely working-class movements like the 'skinheads' developed around 1968, with their crew-cut hair, open-necked shirts, short ankle-length trousers and aggressively large 'bovver' boots. Equally outrageous, although more a deliberate work of art, were the punks who emerged in 1976, with their ripped and tattered clothes, their spiked leather and paramilitary camouflage outfits, and their startling dyed and crested hair. Did this manifestation, asked one journalist in 1980, 'represent Terminal Decadence or a cure for it? Is

realities of a dingy, decaying post-industrial civilization.

Since the war, society has professed itself puzzled as to the meaning of the dress of the young; they seem to feel a sense of personal affront if they cannot work out what it is all about, if indeed it means anything at all. Historians of dress try to search for a pattern among the high fashion, the sub-fashions bounded by class, and the anti-fashions which have flourished in the last few years. Only in the 1960s do they find a coherent story, dominated by the mini skirt and such deliberatively provocative styles as, for example, see-through dresses, which are cited as evidence for the permissive society; a society which, via the con-

102 'Yes, I think I might renew my season ticket after all'.
Cartoon by Keith Waite for The Mirror, *1971.*
While the mini skirt of the 1960s does not seem to have inspired cartoonists, it was a different story with the – admittedly even shorter – 'hot-pants' of the early 1970s. Such a costume, delighting these rail commuters, was in startling contrast to the maxi skirt which was also part of current fashion.

---

101 'New Year Revolutions' (*detail*).
Cartoon by Emmwood in The Daily Mail, *1971.*
Emmwood expresses the popular view that women's charms could be improved with artificial aid in the form of the bra. The feminist is portrayed in shapeless jumper and trousers, while the girl who is seen in male eyes to be more sexually attractive, wears a tight-fitting top, hot pants and boots.

traceptive pill, gave girls in theory the chance to be as sexually active as men, should not throw up its hands in horror at the sight of women exploiting their new-found freedom in their clothes as well as in their sexual lives.

The mini, popularized by Mary Quant in the mid-sixties, was, she declared, worn by a modern girl who took sex for granted, and who was 'lively, positive, opinionated'. The 'fun clothes' which such a girl liked to wear, might include boots and dresses made of shiny wet-look fabrics, fake furs and brightly coloured nylon wigs. The most popular fastening was the zip (a type of fastening first patented in 1917, and used for dresses from the 1930s), often in bright colours and designed to catch the eye. The sexual message in the zip fastener – an invitation to speedy undressing – was not ignored. An even more open sexual invitation was conveyed by the topless dress of the mid-sixties; not many girls were brave enough to reveal themselves in this way, but the threat of such a display caused

103 'Holiday Snaps' (*detail*).
Cartoon by Emmwood in The Daily Mail, *1973. Topless bathing in England still has connotations of immorality, and is technically still illegal on most beaches.*

youth was the most important influence on dress, even as they deplored some of its manifestations, and found the strange mixtures of clothes which the young wore quite perplexing. One fashion historian, while approving of the way in which the dress of the young had helped to bridge the class divide, deplored the sight of girls in:

> a coarse duffle coat, suitable for a lumber camp ... elegant four-inch-high-heeled pointed-toed shoes suitable for a diplomatic reception. They wear their hair long and uncombed together with over-manicured finger-nails, navvy's caps and ski-champion's anoraks, together with transparent nylon stockings – curious sartorial hybrids as culturally mixed up as cockatrices.[38]

Such a girl had contravened the morality of consistency and good taste – these were the canons of acceptability in dress in the late 1950s and early 1960s. By the end of the 1960s, however, 'good taste' – in the sense of a ladylike restraint and an acceptance of sartorial conventions – was almost a dirty word in the struggles of young people against what they considered to be authoritarian and 'establishment' attitudes. Often hand in hand with left wing revolt went a crusading feminist movement which originated in North America and then spread to western Europe. Imbued with the notion that fashion was a sign of feminine weakness or masculine exploitation, some feminists chose to signal their freedom from its rules by getting rid of garments that emphasized their femininity, such as brassières, or by adopting masculine dress, notably trousers or workman's dungarees. It was a curious paradox that – unlike their nineteenth-century predecessors whose feminism was often linked to socialist sympathies – the feminists of the late twentieth century did not interest themselves in dress reform, but chose to wear versions of the costume of their male 'oppressors'. Women who burned their bras and wore nothing under their tee-shirts, did not do so in a spirit of sexual provocation (though sometimes popular newspapers saw it in this light), but as a challenge to accepted conventions. This fashion however,

Mecca dance halls to ban them in 1964, as also did the Mayor of New York in 1967.

The look of the sixties was brash, violent and blatantly sexual; it is perhaps no accident that the dress of prostitutes, partly in reality and wholly so in popular images, derives from the cruder aspects of the dress of that decade – the short skirts, the legs emphasized by fishnet tights, shiny fabrics of the most artificial kind. It is a paradox that such styles have lasted so long, although the signals conveyed are of the 'use-me', 'throw-away' kind. By the early 1960s, commentators on dress agreed that along with that for loose, sometimes diaphanous Indian cotton gowns favoured by 'hippie' girls at the same period, was linked by popular belief to an unconventional existence which incorporated drug-taking, sexual licence, and left-wing (even revolutionary) sympathies. A variant on this tradition of protest through dress has been seen in the 1980s in the form of political slogans on tee-shirts.

As part of the revolt against the accepted conventions regarding male and female behaviour in the late 1960s, there arose the so-called 'unisex' fashion where in theory sartorial differences between the sexes could be almost eliminated. In practice this meant both sexes wearing shirts and trousers i.e. masculine items; the feminine content consisted in flowered or frilled shirts for men as well as for women. It was inevitable that occasionally the results of this style were subject to sniggering comment. The *Sunday Express*, while disliking 'the same sexless shirts, waistcoats, trousers and so on', found it particularly absurd when 'a big tough male descends to frills, chain belt, and fancy pants, and finishes up looking like Danny La Rue on his night off'.[39]

The furthest that most men actually went along the road to feminine dress in the late sixties was to adopt velvet trousers, flowered shirts and ties, and longish hair. While in the early 1980s, some male pop stars chose to wear female dress at times, and some fashion designers showed men in skirts, these seem to be more gimmicks than serious portents of a total sexual revolution in dress. While women in trousers have been accepted everywhere except on the most formal occasions, and certainly not called lesbians, men who adopt elements of female attire are invariably accused of effeminacy. Ever since men, in the early Victorian period, generally stopped wearing bright colours and luxurious fabrics, there has been a firmly entrenched belief that sobriety equals masculinity. Well before the First World War, there were references to 'the effete Boudoir Boys, who give smoking parties to each other in order to display the latest thing in satin corsets and hand-embroidered tea-coats'[40] and it is not too

104 'Min and Friend' *1982*.
J. Brocklehurst.
Punks disturb and alarm not just because of their deliberately outrageous and menacing appearance, but because it is often difficult to know where the sexual boundaries are drawn.

far a step from this to the local council which in 1984 banned homosexuals from its employment, claiming that they had contributed to Britain's moral decline, and 'we are not having men turning up for work in dresses and earrings'.[41]

This statement aroused predictable fury as an example of outrageous sexual stereotyping. In the same way, in the same year, a feminist element in the Greater London Council ran a campaign against what it saw as 'sexist' advertisements for underwear which depicted women

105 *Greenpeace poster 1985.*
Photograph by David Bailey.
The dramatic impact of this poster showing a fur coat trailing blood made people question the morality of killing animals for their fur.

as sex-objects; this met with understandable ridicule, as critics rushed to point out that the late twentieth century was not exactly noted for reticence with regard to the display of the semi-naked body, and that men too were often depicted in the briefest of underpants.

To a large extent, however, it may be true to say that we still look at the dress of men and women with somewhat different standards. With regard to women, it is still the age-old complaint that they reveal too much of their bodies. One intemperate letter-writer in the London *Evening Standard* in 1978 gave it as her view that, 'since the advent of the mini skirt' when 'hind quarters ... thinly clad in nylon knickers' were openly displayed, 'women surely gave up all claims to feminine modesty'.[42] And 'short, figure-hugging apparel', along with punk hairstyles and earrings 'worn six to one ear', were blamed by one newspaper for the rise in schoolgirl pregnancies at a Redditch comprehensive school in 1985.[43]

Topless bathing, though accepted on many Continental beaches, is technically still illegal for women in Britain, except on officially designated nudist beaches; offenders are guilty of the crime of 'insulting behaviour'. A few years ago, a prosecution was brought under this heading against a girl who was walking in the West End of London in a completely see-through blouse; her defence, that her boyfriend was able to walk in public without a top at all, did not avail her, and she was fined £25, and ordered to 'be of good behaviour and to keep the peace for a year'.[44]

With regard to men, the main complaints today are about dishevelment in dress, whether this is the almost artistically contrived disarray of the punk, or the scruffy attire of some working class males. When at a football match in Brussels in May 1985, some Liverpool fans were largely held responsible for the riot that caused the collapse of a wall and resulted in many deaths, some elements in the press rushed to blame the slovenly dress of the British supporters, as an indication of their indiscipline, a symptom of the moral malaise of the country. Equally sharply, some commentators found it lamentable that such a simplistic link could be made between people's moral status and their appearance, and the discussion moved one correspondent to *The London Standard* to say:

> Nowhere in scripture is Christ commended for a smart appearance, which suggests that his violence against the moral hooliganism of the (no doubt well-dressed) money changers in the temple would be condemned as delinquency.[45]

It may be, however, that there is something to be said for a link, albeit tenuous, between dress and behaviour. Ralph Waldo Emerson had an apt comment when he noted that 'if a man have manners and talent, he may dress roughly and carelessly. It is only when mind and character slumber, that the dress can be seen'.[46]

The question which has, in a sense, hung over the whole book, 'How far does clothing reflect sexual morality?', is a difficult one to answer today. Many people feel that as traditional sexual morality (by which they mean a permanent relationship with one person of the opposite sex, or at least with a modest number of partners) has largely disappeared, so too has modesty in clothing. They might also say that sartorial morality has almost gone, that the accepted rules and conventions of dress have been pushed out by excessive individuality – 'anything goes', they cry, in dress. Is this true, or are we caught up so much in our own time that we cannot stand back and look at ourselves dispassionately, in the light of history?

We may, with John Stuart Mill (*On Liberty*, 1859) hold the belief that a free society should have diversity in morals, and that a man should be able to seek salvation his own way, aided by the removal of restraint. We may feel that in some cases our conscience should dictate to us what to wear or not to wear, that our political beliefs and individuality should be seen in our dress; we may scoff at notions of etiquette and custom. But we cannot avoid the dynamism of fashion and style; it is implicit even in the humblest working garment. We find it difficult to be totally at ease in the 'wrong' clothes on particular occasions; Emerson approved of the lady who said to him that 'the sense of being perfectly well dressed gives a feeling of inward tranquillity which religion is powerless to bestow'.[47]

In spite of the breaking of many sexual taboos, and the deliberate cult of the exposed body, which are such characteristic developments in this century, there is still a surprising consensus of what 'decency' in dress means, that there are limits to the display of the primary sexual organs. While we are still

106 *Photograph of Katherine Hamnett 1985. This designer's personal commitment to certain causes – political, social and ecological – made her slogan T-shirts a success story of the mid 1980s; it is debatable, however, if all those who wore them did so because they sympathized with the causes or because they were high fashion. This shirt, which could be interpreted as a plea against nuclear annihilation (a cause which Hamnett had espoused) is in fact an anti-drugs comment.*

bound by our Judaeo-Christian heritage in this respect, one cannot see much radical change in our attitudes, although we may talk incessantly about a Brave New World in which considerations of sex, class and age cannot be distinguished by clothing. Nor is it possible to dispense as easily as we might like with our accumulated traditions and assumptions regarding dress as an indication of morality.

Notes

Introduction

1 W. Lillie, *An Introduction to Ethics*, London 1961, p. 56.
2 J.C. Flügel, *Man, Morals and Society*, London 1945, p. 138–9.
3 Lord Patrick Devlin, *Morals and the Criminal Law*, London 1965, p. 5 *et seq*. The author argues that 'a State which refuses to enforce Christian beliefs has lost the right to enforce Christian morals'.
4 For example, the Hasidic Jews of East London wear virtually a uniform, of black clothing originally derived from the ghettos of eighteenth-century Poland. Like other ultra-orthodox Jewish communities, a married woman wears a wig, because no man other than her husband should see her hair which is a symbol of her sexuality.
5 A. Ribeiro, *If the slogan fits, wear it*, The Times, 14 Aug. 1984.
6 F. Hussain (ed.) *Muslim Women*, London 1984, p. 25. It is later interpretations of the Koran which have made the lot of women worse; a growing asceticism in Islamic communities contributes to the notion that women are morally defective.
7 Q. Bell, *On Human Finery*, London 1976, p. 46.
8 Ribeiro, *op. cit*. The Observer newspaper in January 1984 reported that President Shagari of Nigeria was ousted partly because of his taste for finery; his hand-embroidered national costumes (he was chosen best-dressed man of the year by a local newspaper) cost $2,500 each.
9 Veblen's theories can be found in his *The Economic Theory of Women's Dress*, in *Popular Science Monthly*, vol. XLVI, Nov. 1894, which he expanded into *The Theory of the Leisure Class*, 1899. See also Bell's *On Human Finery* (revised ed. 1976) where he proposes a slightly modified version of the Veblen theory.
10 Devlin, *op. cit.*, p. 15.
11 J. Mudie, *The Felonry of New South Wales*, London 1837, p. 204. Mudie was a magistrate in New South Wales from 1822 to 1836.
12 J. Brophy, *Body and Soul*, London 1948, p. 106.
13 J.C. Flügel, *The Psychology of Clothes*, London 1930, p. 75.
14 C.W. Cunnington, *Why Women Wear Clothes*, London 1941, p. 212.

I

1 Herodotus, *The Histories*, trans. and ed. A. de Sélincourt, London 1963, p. 343.
2 J. Donaldson, *Woman; Her position and influence in ancient Greece and Rome, and among the early Christians*, London 1907, p. 203. This attitude was attacked by Plutarch in his *Lives* (Book I); speaking of Spartan girls, he finds 'modesty attended them and all wantonness was excluded'.
3 S. Pomeroy, *Goddesses, Whores, Wives and Slaves*, New York 1956, p. 142.
4 See M. Scott's unpublished MA report (Courtauld Institute of Art, 1975) on *Dress on Greek Vase Paintings*, for a discussion of byssus.
5 It seems unlikely that silk from China was worn in Europe much before the beginning of the Christian era. Aristotle mentions a kind of wild silk from the Indian tussor moth which feeds on oak trees, and silk woven on the island of Cos, probably from silk imported from India or Syria, unravelled and then re-woven; this 'tissue from Cos' is also mentioned in Ovid's *Art of Love*.
6 Donaldson, *ibid*.
7 Pomeroy, *op cit.*, p. 83.
8 S. Dill, *Roman society in the last century of the Western Empire*, London 1898, p. 98.
9 Juvenal, *The Sixteen Satires*, trans. and intr. P. Green, London 1967, pp. 77–8 (Satire II).
10 A.F. Kendrick, *Catalogue of Early Medieval Woven Fabrics in the Victoria and Albert Museum*, London 1925, p. 27.
11 Suetonius, *The Twelve Caesars*, trans. R. Graves, London 1957, p. 175.
12 Petronius, *The Satyricon*, London 1933, p. 47. Trimalchio's grave clothes, which he shows to the company assembled at his banquet, include a *toga praetexta* or magistrate's toga with a purple border, to which he has no right.

13 Quintilian, *Institutio Oratoria*, trans. H. E. Butler, 4 vols., London 1968. Book IV, pp. 317–25, on dress, states: 'Nam est toga et calceus et capillus tam nimia cura quam negligentia sunt reprehenda' – 'for excessive care with regard to the cut of the toga, or the arrangement of the hair, is just as reprehensible as excessive carelessness' (p. 318).
14 *The Letters of the Younger Pliny*, trans. B. Radice, London 1963, p. 117.
15 Sir. R. L'Estrange, *Seneca's Morals by way of Abstract*, London 1678, quoted in *The Morals of Seneca*, ed. W. Clode, London 1888, pp. 71–2. Seneca's *De Tranquillitate Animi*, from which this quotation is taken, was composed c. 49–54.
16 Juvenal, *op. cit.*, Satire VI, p. 134.
17 Petronius *op. cit.* p. 98. The Roman senate passed a law in 115 B.C. to curb female luxury in dress and specifically the amount of jewellery worn, but it seems, like all such legislation, to have been ineffective.
18 Juvenal, *op. cit.*, p. 146.
19 Ovid, *The Art of Love*, trans. R. Seth, London 1953, p. 88.
20 W. E. H. Lecky, *History of European Morals from Augustus to Charlemagne*, 2 vols, London, third ed. 1877, II, p. 3 and p. 7.
21 Juvenal, for example, in his *Satires*, attacks the would-be Amazonians in Roman society who attend chariot races wearing men's clothes, and those who wrestle and fence in masculine cloak, helmet, arm-guards and thigh-pieces. See J. Carcopino, *Daily Life in Ancient Rome*, London 1941, p. 92.
22 S. de Beauvoir, *The Second Sex*, London 1953, p. 184.
23 *The Writings of Clement of Alexandria*, trans. and ed. W. Wilson, Edinburgh 1869, I, p. 233, p. 258. Tyrian purple was the most expensive dye in antiquity, being extracted from the juice of a species of shellfish; it was an imperial colour, in theory at any rate, and the dyeing of purple stuffs was a state monopoly. See *Ciba Review*, Basle, No. 4, 1937.
24 A. F. Kendrick, *Catalogue of Textiles from Burying Grounds in Egypt in the Victoria and Albert Museum*, London 1920–22, I, p. 20. The museum has a range of textiles from the fourth to the tenth centuries which have been preserved in the sterile sand of their burial places.
25 Clement, *op. cit.*, I, p. 259.
26 Dill, *op. cit.*, p. 113. Courtesans in Constantinople, the seat of the Eastern Empire when the Roman Empire was divided in 395, were forbidden to wear the sober dress of virgins, lest it bring the latter into disrepute – see W. G. Holmes, *The Age of Justinian and Theodora*, London 1905, I, p. 88.
27 Other supporters of the virgin state are:
St Ambrose (340–397) *Ad virginem devotam exhortatio De lapsu virginis consecratae*.
St Augustine (354–430) *De sancta virginitate*.
St Jerome (331–420) *Epistola ad Eustochium de custodia virginitatis*.

The temptations to which St Jerome was exposed, while a hermit in the Syrian desert, included the sight of women dressed like men. Modern psychologists find a note of intense hysteria and sexual hatred in many of the diatribes of the early Church Fathers against women and their finery. For a discussion of such attacks on women, see A. Hentsch, *De la Littérature Didactique du moyen âge s'addressant spécialement aux femmes*, Cahors 1903.
28 St Cyprian, *De Habitu Virginum*, ed. and trans. A. E. Keenan, Catholic University of America, Patristic Studies vol. XXXIV Washington 1932, p. 63.
29 *Ibid.*, p. 59.
30 Clement, *op. cit.*, p. 277.
31 Lecky, *op. cit.*, p. 149.
32 Clement, *op. cit.*, p. 284.
33 Dill, *op. cit.*, p. 13. Clerical concubinage was a problem which beset the early Christian church.
34 J. Lindsay, *Byzantium into Europe*, London 1952, p. 144.
35 Procopius, *Secret History*, trans. R. Atwater, Univ. of Michigan, Ann Arbor, 1961, p. 36.

2

1 Tacitus, *Life of Agricola*, quoted in J. R. Planché, *History of British Costume from the earliest period to the close of the eighteenth century*, London 3rd. ed., 1900, p. 17.
2 F. M. Stenton, *Anglo-Saxon England*, Oxford 1947, p. 1.
3 *The Letters of Sidonius*, trans. and intr. O. M. Dalton, Oxford 1915, II, p. 35. A few items from royal burials testify to Frankish fondness for silk garments. Queen Arnegunde, one of the consorts to Chlotar I (King of Soissons from 511 to 558 and sole King of the Franks from 558–561) was buried in a tunic of violet silk, a gown of dark red silk embroidered with gold and closed with gold brooches, and a red satin veil fixed with gold pins. When Charlemagne's tomb (he died 814) was opened in the twelfth century, he was found dressed in a sumptuous patterned woven silk tunic and dalmatic, as befitting the first Holy Roman Emperor.
4 Planché, *op. cit.*, p. 30. Sharon Turner (*The History of the Anglo-Saxons*, 1807, II, p. 58) gives no authority for saying that Anglo-Saxon women painted their faces red. Strutt (*A Complete View of the Dress and Habits of the People of England* . . . 1775–6), states that the Anglo-Saxons dyed their hair blue, red, green etc., but Planché in his revised edition of Strutt in 1842 (I, p. 38) believed that this was an error due to the 'idleness of the illuminator' of the various MSS which Strutt consulted for visual sources, where the colour is sometimes erratically laid on.
5 William of Malmesbury *De Gestis Regum Anglorum*, ed. J. A. Giles, London 1847, p. 279. This work was probably written in the 1120s.
6 See D. Whitelock, *Anglo-Saxon Wills*, Cambridge 1930.
7 A considerable amount of jewellery has been found in Anglo-Saxon graves; it is listed in detail in G. Owen, *Anglo-Saxon Costume: A study of secular, civilian clothing and*

jewellery fashions, unpublished Ph.D, Newcastle-upon-Tyne 1976. Jewelled objects in graves include belt-fittings, pins, brooches (often in pairs) and armlets which may have also had a practical purpose in keeping long sleeves in place.

8 Planché, *op. cit.,* p. 47. The quotation is from the thirteenth-century chronicle of John Wallingford, printed in Gale's *Historicae Britannicae et Anglicanae Scriptores,* Oxford 1689–91.

9 Quoted in Owen, op. cit., p. 538, from A. W. Haddan and W. Stubbs (eds) *Councils and Ecclesiastical Documents relating to Great Britain and Ireland,* Oxford 1869–78, III, pp. 493–4: 'considerate habitum, tonsuram, et mores principum, et populi luxuriosos. Ecce tonsura, quam in barbis et in capillis paganis adsimilari voluistis.'

10 E. S. Duckett, *Anglo-Saxon Saints and Scholars,* London 1947, p. 63.

11 Turner, *op. cit.* II, p. 63.

12 E. Kylie (ed.), *The English Correspondence of Saint Boniface,* London 1911, p. 190.

13 *De Gestis Regum Anglorum, op. cit.,* p. 279.

14 *Ibid.,* p. 213.

15 C. H. Smith, *Selections of the Ancient Costume of Great Britain and Ireland,* London 1814 (no pagination).

16 *De Gestis Regum Anglorum, op. cit.,* p. 337.

17 Orderic Vitalis, *The Ecclesiastical History,* ed. M. Chibnall, Oxford 1969–78, IV, p. 189. 'summopere comebant, prolixisque nimiumque strictis camisiis inclui tunicisque gaudebant' – 'they loved to deck themselves in long over-tight shirts and tunics'.

18 Eadmer, *Historia Novorum in Anglia,* ed. R. W. Southern, London 1964, p. 48.

19 Eadmer, *op. cit.* p. 229. Orderic (VI, p. 65) believed that only penitents and criminals should wear their hair long, to 'proclaim by their outward disgrace the baseness of the inner man'.

20 Orderic, *op. cit.,* IV, p. 193. On the subject of clerical marriages, a frequent cause for complaint, Papal Councils of 1073 and 1075 forbad it, but in the English spirit of compromise, the *Council of Winchester* of 1076 while accepting the ban on such marriages, recognized the existing marriages of parish priests. But as late as 1237 Matthew Paris records that a Church Council in London passed ordinances against the keeping of concubines. In addition, those appointed to holy orders were to wear 'garments of becoming measure . . .'; bishops in particular were to make sure that clerks observed 'a propriety of dress . . . and a becoming tonsure'. (Matthew Paris, *English History from the year 1235 to 1273,* ed. J. A. Giles, London 1852–4, I, p. 83.

21 Orderic, *op. cit.,* IV, p. 189.

22 *Ibid.,* p. 187.

23 *Ibid.,* p. 190.

24 From the poem La Vie de S. Thais, quoted in J. Harris, *The Development of Romanesque-Byzantine elements in French and English Dress 1050–1180,* unpublished Ph.D.Thesis, University of Manchester 1977, p. 98. Laces were apparently given to young men as love tokens; they had an obvious erotic significance.

25 The twelfth and thirteenth centuries were marked by religious controversies and the determined efforts of Rome to combat heresy. The Waldensians and the Albigensians placed greater emphasis on purity of life than the mere lip service paid to it by some members of the Church hierarchy; they wished a stricter adherence to the teaching of the Gospels and a greater concentration on vows of poverty and simplicity. The teaching of such 'heresies' included attacks on the vanities of life such as fine clothing.

26 M. W. Labarge, *A Baronial Household of the Thirteenth Century,* London 1965, p. 42.

27 C. V. Langlois, *La Vie en France au Moyen Age de la fin du XIIe siècle d'après des moralistes du temps,* Paris 1926 II, p. 223.

28 From a *chanson d'amour* by Adam de la Halle (c. 1250–c. 1288), published in *The Penguin Book of French Verse I: To the Fifteenth Century,* ed. and intr. B. Woledge, London 1966, p. 195.

29 *Ibid.,* p. 212.

30 Quoted in G. R. Owst, *Literature and Pulpit in Medieval England,* Cambridge 1933, pp. 377–8. The quotation comes from the great encyclopedist of the thirteenth century, Vincent of Beauvais.

31 E. Langlois (ed.) *Le Roman de la Rose par Guillaume de Lorris et Jean de Meun,* Paris, 1914–24, III, pp. 114–16.

32 *Ibid.,* II, pp. 13–15.

33 An anonymous sermon quoted in Owst, *op. cit.,* p. 392.

34 *The Summa Theologica of St Thomas Aquinas,* Part II, 2nd Part, vol. XIII, trans. by the Fathers of the English Dominican Province, London 1932, pp. 309–10.

35 *Ibid.,* p. 304.

36 *Ibid.,* p. 307.

3

1 *Froissart's Chronicles,* ed. G. Brereton, London 1968, p. 212.

2 *The English Works of Wyclif,* ed. F. D. Matthew, London 1880, p. 128.

3 M. Scott, *The History of Dress Series: Late Gothic Europe 1400–1500,* London 1980, p. 62. In 1446 'it was proclaimed throughout Paris that prostitutes should not wear silver belts any more, nor turned-back collars, nor lengths of squirrel or miniver on their dresses' (*A Parisian Journal 1405–1449,* trans. and ed. J. Shirley, Oxford 1968, pp. 362–3).

4 Robert of Brunne's *Handlyng Synne,* ed. F. J. Furnivall, London 1862. This is a somewhat free translation (sometimes amplified) by a contemporary, William of Wadington, who in fact mentions the devil sitting on the long skirts of women.

5 *Medieval English Verse,* trans. and intr. B. Stone, London 1964, pp. 108–9.

6 Quoted in G. R. Owst, *Literature and Pulpit in Medieval England,* Cambridge 1933, p. 392.

7 *Grandes Chroniques de France*, ed. A. P. Pâris, Paris 1837, V, pp. 462–3. The word 'fronciées' is rather confusing; it could mean that the tunics were pleated or gathered at the sides, or it could mean that the tunics were so tight that they formed creases at the sides.
8 *Chronica Johannis de Reading*, ed. J. Tait, Manchester 1914, p. 167.
9 Quoted in *Chaucer's World*, ed. E. Rickert, London 1948, p. 336.
10 Owst, *op. cit., p. 404.*
11 See the *Register of Edward, the Black Prince Preserved in the Public Record Office*, trans. M. C. B. Dawes, London 1930–33. The register for 1352 lists, for example, 66 sets of buttons; ten years later the Prince of Wales paid £200 for jewelled buttons for his wife – this would have paid the daily wages of an esquire or master craftsman for ten years. In November 1353 20,000 seed pearls are ordered which cost £80. Rubies and diamonds also figure prominently, even to decorate jousting helms.
12 S. M. Newton, *Fashion in the Age of the Black Prince*, London 1980, p. 52. The fur gris was the fur of the northern squirrel which has a white belly. The white belly fur edged with grey is miniver.
13 For the details of sumptuary legislation in England, see N. B. Harte, *State Control of Dress and Social Change in Pre-Industrial England* in *Trade, government and economy in pre-industrial England,* eds. D. C. Coleman and A. H. John, London 1976, and F. E. Baldwin, *Sumptuary Legislation and Personal Regulation in England,* Baltimore 1926.
14 *Statutes of the Realm* 37 Edward III, Cap. VII–Cap. XII. Punishment for infringing the law was the forfeiture of the offending garments.
15 Owst, *op. cit.* p. 406.
16 *The Book of the Knight of La Tour Landry*, ed. and intr. T. Wright, London 1868, p. 29.
17 *Ibid.*, pp. 62 and 64.
18 *Ibid.*, pp. 67–8.
19 *Sir Gawain and the Green Knight*, ed. R. A. Waldron, London 1970, p. 104.
20 Scott, *op. cit.* p. 44. Deschamps also wrote a *Balade contre les modes du temps*, in which he inveighs against the long pointed shoes lined with whale's tooth (? whalebone) which are so awkward to wear that men have to walk backwards like lobsters.
21 *Chaucer's Canterbury Tales.* ed. and intr. A. C. Cawley. London 1958, pp. 555–6. It has been suggested that the Parson's Tale, with its fear of death and judgement, may have been written in 1400 when Chaucer knew he was dying. Richard II's livery colours were red and white; Chaucer's description of the hose coloured in this way may be an attack on the ultra-fashionable young men who had flocked to his court.
22 Quoted in Baldwin *op. cit.,* p. 78. There were petitions to the Crown early in the reign of Henry IV that no-one should wear garments with cut shapes in the form of flowers, leaves and letters; these were no more successful than petitions to reduce the length of gown sleeves.
23 T. Occleve, *Of Pride and wast clothing of Lordis men,* London 1869, pp. 106–7.
24 Even a historian as considered as J. R. Planché, found that 'the march of foppery was accelerated under the reign of the weak and luxurious Richard of Bordeaux' (*History of British Costume*, 3rd. ed., London 1900, p. 163); the Victorians generally found Richard to be unmanly and too concerned with luxury, comparing him unfavourably with the martial Edward III and Henry V.
25 *Richard the Redeless*, ed. W. W. Skeat, London 1867–1885, III pp. 491–3. The poem has been attributed to William Langland.
26 In 1445 Guillaume Jouvenal des Ursins became Chancellor of France and his brother, an ecclesiastic, wrote to him urging him to tell the king that he should not allow the ladies of his household to wear gowns with front openings that revealed their breasts and nipples. See Scott, *op. cit.*, p. 141.
27 *The Chronicles of Enquerrand de Monstrelet*, trans. T. Johnes, London 1840, I, p. 546.
28 *A Selection from the Minor Poems of Dan John Lydgate*, ed. J. O. Halliwell, London 1840, p. 47.
29 *Le Miroir aux Dames*, intr. A. Piaget, Neuchatel, 1908, p. 56. The poem was attributed to the courtly poet Alain Chartier, but it is now thought to be by a friar concerned to save women from damnation.
30 Chaucer, *op. cit.*, p. 167 and p. 285.
31 Christine de Pisan, *The Book of the City of Ladies*, trans. E. J. Richards, London 1983, p. 63.
32 F. W. Fairholt, *Satirical Songs and Poems on Costume*, London 1849, p. 56.
33 *Historical Poems of the XIVth and XVth Centuries*, ed. R. H. Robbins, New York 1959, p. 138.
34 Statutes of the Realm III Edward IV, Cap. V.
35 Statutes of the Realm XXII Edward IV, Cap. I.
36 *William Gregory's Chronicle of London*, ed. J. Gairdner, London, 1876, p. 238. Gregory was a skinner of the City of London Skinners Company, and Mayor of London 1461. He died apparently in 1466, and the chronicle which continues to 1469 was finished by another hand; the reference to the Pope is dated 1468.
37 See for detail the Statutes of the Realm. By this time, ermine was no longer reserved for royalty, and the most fashionable and expensive fur was sable.
38 *Le Blason des Couleurs en Armes, Livrées et Devises . . .* intr. and ed. H. Cocheris, Paris 1860, p. 101. The treatise was composed probably between 1435 and 1458.
39 *Ibid.*
40 O. de la Marche, *Le Parement et Triumphes des Dames,* Lille 1870 (a facsimile of the 1510 edition). The theme was not introduced by Olivier but was common currency during the fifteenth century. F. W. Fairholt, *op. cit.*, p. 59, quotes from the Scottish poet Robert Henryson's poem *The garment of guide ladyis,* where he talks of the hood of honour, the kirtle of perfect constancy, the hose of honesty etc.

NOTES

41 Antoine de la Sale, *Le Petit Jehan de Saintré*, trans. and ed. I. Gray, London 1931, p. 312. Antoine de la Salle (*c*. 1386–1462) composed this romance in the 1450s. Blue was perhaps the most noble of all colours in the Middle Ages. As the colour of loyalty, it was chosen for the Order of the Garter when it was founded in the mid fourteenth century.

4

1 See Edward Halle's *Chronicle containing the History of England during the reigne of Henry the Fourth . . . to the end of the reigne of Henry the Eighth*, London 1548. This has many entries, with copious details, about the dress worn at masques and tournaments. German fashions with their bright colours were particularly popular, and Halle tells us that at a tournament in November 1510, the king and fifteen of his gentlemen wore such 'almayne' fashion, with 'Jackettes of Crymosyne & purple satyne, with long quartered sleves, with hosen of the same sute . . .' (1809 ed. p. 516).

2 *The Complete Poems of John Skelton*, ed. P. Henderson, London 1931, pp. 144–5. The poem in question is thought to have been written in the 1490s. Skelton was one of the increasing number of critics who attacked the luxury of the court in the early sixteenth century. After the Reformation there was some lessening of critical comment on the 'richly and warm bewrapped' clergy, and the main subject for such attacks became the court and the aristocracy – especially the parvenu nobility.

3 A. Barclay, *The Shyp of Folys of the World*, London 1508, pp. 18–19.

4 Anon., *A Treatise of a Galaunt* in *Remains of the Early Popular Poetry of England*, ed. W. C. Hazlitt, London 1864–6, III, p. 159. Borde in his *First Boke of the Introduction of Knowledge* 1542 (see Note 17) describes dress in the character of a Frenchman: 'My rayment is jagged and kut round a-bout: I am ful of new invencions' (p. 190).

5 From the middle of the fourteenth century there are accounts of masquerades, 'disguisings', and mummings at court and in the country. While those at court were imbued with Renaissance imagery and an increasingly sophisticated visual and intellectual vocabulary, those in the countryside probably were no more than crude buffooneries. During the carnival season between Christmas and the ostensible austerities of Lent, there were all kinds of entertainments, a kind of licensed anarchy condoned by the Church, which often included cross-dressing, and dressing up in exotic costume: Alexander Barclay in *The Shyp of Folys* describes men 'in strange londes gyse' (p. 245).

6 French tailors were sent over to England to supervise the trousseau taken to France by Mary Tudor, sister of Henry VIII in 1514, and the fabrics listed in the wardrobe accounts include, for example, 'tawny cloth of gold of damask . . . furred with hermyns', 'white cloth of silver of damask lyned with crymsyn velvet upon velvet', and so on (PRO SP/1/9/fol. 136, quoted in an unpublished MA thesis by J. Thomas, *Developments in English Dress* 1510–20, Courtauld Institute of Art 1977, p. 62).

7 Sir D. Lindsay, *Works*, ed. D. Hamer, Edinburgh 1931–6, I, p. 120. Erasmus in his *In Praise of Folly* (1526) also attacks – although in a less intemperate way – the court lady who 'reputeth hir selfe the more woorthie of honour and estate, the longer taile she traineth after hir' (Erasmus's book was translated as *The Praise of Folie* by Sir Thomas Chaloner in 1549; see 1965 ed. with intr. by C. H. Miller, p. 95).

8 Quoted in N. B. Harte, *State Control of Dress and Social Change in Pre-Industrial England*, in *Trade, government and economy in pre-Industrial England* eds. D. C. Coleman and A. H. John, London 1976, p. 139.

9 See W. Hooper, *The Tudor Sumptuary Laws*, in *English Historical Review*, vol. XXX, 1915, p, 433 *et seq*.

10 *Ibid*., p. 435.

11 M. E. de Montaigne, *Essays Done into English by John Florio*, ed. and intr. G. Saintsbury, London 1892–3, I, pp. 310–11.

12 Sir T. More, *Utopia*, trans. and intr. P. Turner, London 1965, pp. 86–9.

13 *Ibid*., p. 75.

14 J. Knox, *The First Blast of the Trumpet against the Monstrous regiment of women*, London 1558, p. 17.

15 A. Piccolomini, *Raffaella: A Dialogue of the Fair Perfectioning of Ladies*, trans. and intr. J. L. Nevinson, Glasgow, 1968, p. 46.

16 *Ibid*., p. 49.

17 A. Borde, *The First Boke of the Introduction of Knowledge*, ed. and intr. F. J. Furnivall, London 1870, p. 116.

18 G. della Casa, *Galateo of Manners and Behaviours*, intr. J. E. Spingham, New York 1914, p. 105. Peterson's translation was the first in a number of English translations of this popular book.

19 *Ibid*., p. 43.

20 *Ibid*., p. 104.

21 T. Artus, *Description de l'Isle des Hermaphrodites*, Paris 1605, p. 12 *et seq*. The book was apparently originally published in 1579.

22 Hooper, *op. cit.*, pp. 439–40. Tailors were ordered to use no more than $1\frac{3}{4}$ yards of fabric in a pair of hose, and only to give them one lining, except for the linen lining next to the leg. They were to be imprisoned if they broke the law.

23 *Ibid*., p. 441.

24 *Ibid*., p. 443. This apparently lasted for about fifteen years.

25 Anon., *The Boke of Nurture*, ed. F. J. Furnivall, London 1867, p. 6.

26 R. Ascham, *The Scholemaster*, London 1570, p. 21.

27 J. Marston, *The Scourge of Villainy*, 1598, in K. W. Gransden (ed.), *Tudor Verse Satire*, London 1970, pp. 112–114.

28 F. Thynne, *The Debate between Pride and Lowliness*, ed. and intr. J. P. Collier, London 1841, pp. 9–10.
29 Montaigne, *op. cit.* I, p. 312.
30 P. Stubbes, *The Anatomie of Abuses*, London 1583, p. 30. The book went through five editions between 1583 and 1595.
31 *Ibid.*, p. 27. Stubbes may be referring here to a popular jacket called a *mandilion* which could be buttoned either down the front or down the side seams; when all the buttons were undone it was often worn sideways with one sleeve in front and one behind. This kind of contrived asymmetry was particularly popular at the end of the sixteenth century.
32 *Ibid.*, p. 8 *et seq.*
33 *Harrison's Description of England*, ed. F. J. Furnivall, London 1877, p. 168.
34 The sumptuary legislation was repealed mainly due to a growing irritation by Parliament at the royal claims to legislate by proclamation, and not to a belief that dress should not be dealt with in this way; it lasted in some parts of Europe until well into the eighteenth century. See Hooper, *op. cit.*, p. 449.
35 Harrison, *op. cit.*, p. 170.
36 P. Stubbes, *Anatomie of Abuses, 1583. Part II: The Display of corruptions requiring reformation*, ed. F. J. Furnivall, London 1882, pp. 35–6.
37 Stubbes, *op. cit.*, pp. 22–3.
38 R. Crowley, *One and thyrtye Epigrammes wherein are brieflye touched so many abuses*, London 1550 (no pagination).
39 Hazlitt, *op. cit.*, III, p. 255.
40 Crowley, *op. cit.*
41 Hazlitt, *op. cit.*, III, p. 238. The poem was written during the reign of Edward VI.
42 Anon., *Le Blason des Basquines et Vertugalles*, Lyon 1563 (no pagination). Randle Cotgrave's *Dictionarie of the French and English Tongues* (1611) defines a basquine as a Spanish farthingale; a vertugalle is merely defined as a 'vardingale'.
43 Hazlitt, *op. cit.*, III, p. 257.
44 *Ibid.* Women wore no drawers beneath their shifts; such knee-length drawers were worn by prostitutes, if we can go by the delighted descriptions of Venetian courtesans made by English gentlemen on the Grand Tour at this time.
45 Stubbes, *op. cit.*, pp. 38–9.
46 Hazlitt, *op. cit.*, III, p. 258.
47 Gransden, *op. cit.*, p. 115.
48 Stubbes, *op. cit.*, p. 36.
49 *Ibid.*, p. 35.
50 See, for example, Barnaby Googe's *The Popish Kingdome or reigne of Antichrist* of 1570, a free translation of a Latin work published by Thomas Kirchmeyer in 1553. The book is a savage denunciation of Catholic beliefs and customs, including the carnival. Among the costumes adopted on this occasion which mock accepted conventions – some dress as fools, some as monks, some as kings – he picks out those who assume the clothing of the opposite sex:

> Both men and women chaunge their weede, the men in mayde's aray,
> And wanton wenches drest like men, doe travell by the way.

(See the edition intr. R. C. Hope, London 1880, pp. 47–8.) During the celebrations in England, a Lord of Misrule was chosen to 'rule' over the proceedings; Stubbes calls him a 'grand captain of mischief' who for his 'court' chooses men dressed as women in clothing 'borrowed for the moste parte of their pretie Mopsies' (Stubbes, *op. cit.*, p. 92).
51 Stubbes, *op. cit.*, p. 37.
52 Barclay, *op. cit.*, p. 245.
53 Castiglione in his *Book of the Courtier* was agreeable to women using cosmetics provided they were skilfully applied, and in *Raffaella* we read of many face washes and unguents for hands and breast.
54 See C. Camden, *The Elizabethan Woman*, London 1952, p. 178 *et seq.*, for details of cosmetics and references to their use throughout the sixteenth and early seventeenth centuries.
55 Hazlitt, *op. cit.*, III, p. 252.
56 W. Averell, *A Mervailous combat of contrarities*, London 1588 (no pagination).

5

1 A. L., *A Relation of Some Abuses which are Committed against the Commonwealth*, 1629, ed. F. Madden, London 1854, p. 26. As the work is dedicated to the Dean of Durham, and as there are a number of references to the Church, the author may have been a clergyman himself.

A constant theme in such contemporary tracts is that money which was spent on finery would have been better spent on Christian charity. Such 'charitie', says Barnaby Rich in *The Honestie of this Age*, of 1614, 'is transubstantiated into brave apparell'; moreover, the man of fashion who buys such items as 'a Hat-band, a scarfe, a payre of Garters, and ... Roses for his shoe-strings, will bestowe more money then would have bought his great grandfather a whole suite of apparell' (p. 8 and p. 48).
2 Sir A. Weldon, *The Court and Character of King James*, 1651, quoted in *The Secret History of the Court of James I*, London 1811, II, p. 1.
3 *Letters from George, Lord Carew to Sir Thomas Roe, Ambassador to the court of the Great Mogul 1615–1617*, ed. J. Maclean, London 1860, p. 77.

This letter is dated 1617, the year after the king issued a proclamation forbidding, except on Sundays and holy-days, the wearing of 'any cloth of gold, silver, velvet, satin, taffeta'.
4 F. Moryson, *An Itinerary*, London 1617, p. 178. Like many of his contemporaries, recalling the days of a revered Queen, he lamented the demise in dress of 'darke colours ... plaine blacke stuffes' for they were replaced by light

NOTES

colours and fantastical fashions under the present king; it was perhaps inevitable that, contemplating James I, men should look back at the past with rose-coloured spectacles.

5 T. Dekker, *The seven deadly Sinnes of London,* London 1606, p. 32.

6 T. Dekker, *The Gull's Horn Book 1609,* reprinted London 1812, no pagination, but see Chapters II–IV for details of dress, and Chapter VI for 'How a gallant should behave himself in a playhouse'.

7 S. Purchas, *Purchas his Pilgrim: Microcosmus or The Historie of Man,* London 1619, p. 255.

8 The quotation is from Thomas Middleton's prologue to his play *The Black Book* of 1604. Much of the 'glistening' was achieved by the copious use of jewellery, and by gold and silver lace. Spangles were also used to decorate embroidered costume, and the huge puff-ball shoe roses, made of silk; both Webster and Jonson in their plays (*The White Devil,* 1608 and *The Devil is an Ass,* 1616 respectively) talk of such shoe roses as being large enough to hide a cloven foot, i.e. the foot of the Devil.

9 Collars of such lace, according to Henry Peacham in *The Truth of our Times* (1638) could cost as much as £3 or £4.

10 Purchas, *op. cit.,* p. 265.

11 After being divorced from the Earl of Essex, whom she was accused of poisoning with the aid of Mrs Turner, Frances Howard married her lover Robert Carr, Earl of Somerset in 1613; after the trial in 1616 the Somersets were imprisoned in the Tower.

12 B. Rich, *The Honestie of this Age,* London 1614, p. 35.

13 W. Prynne, *The Unlovelinesse of Love-Lockes,* London 1628, p. 7 and p. 37.

14 *Ibid.,* Introduction (no pagination). Like many Puritans, Prynne was deeply concerned with the biblical injunction that men and women should not wear any part of the dress of the opposite sex. After the publication in 1633 of his book *Histriomastix,* which denounced in over a thousand words, theatrical performances as 'the Pompes of Satan', especially as men usually took women's roles, he had both his ears removed. This was a punishment for his attack on women who occasionally acted. thought to be a reference to Henrietta Maria who had taken a speaking part in court masques.

15 J. Hall, *The Righteous Mammon,* 1618, in *Works,* 1634, p. 670.

16 T. Tomkis, *Lingua or The Combat of the Tongue,* London 1607, Act V Sc. VI.

17 *Calendar of State Papers Venetian* XV, ed. A. B. Hinds, London, 1909, p. 80 and p. 270.

18 T. Tuke, *A Treatise against Painting and Tincturing of Men and Women,* London 1616, p. 58.

19 Act IV, Sc. II. The cosmetics continued to be the same as used in the Elizabethan period and just as bad for the skin, being composed mainly of lead or mercury mixtures. They were attacked on the grounds of deceit, though some critics like John Bulwer in his *Anthropometamorphosis* (1650) advised women that they were also bad for the skin, 'there being a venemous quality in the paint which wrinkleth the Face before its time' (p. 159).

20 F. Quarles, *Epigrammes,* London 1695, p. 152. His epigrams were composed in the reign of Charles I.

21 J. Swetnam, *The Arraignment of Lewd, Idle, Froward, and unconstant women . . .,* London 1615, p. 15 and p. 30.

22 See, for example, *The Worming of a mad Dogge* by 'Constantia Munda' which was published in 1615. There was also, some years later, in 1619, a play *Swetnam, the Woman-hater, arraigned by women* which was apparently acted at the Red Bull in 1620. In this Swetnam was tried, convicted and punished; he was compelled to wear a muzzle 'to express his barking humour against womenkind', and eventually sent 'to live amongst the Infidels'.

23 J. Chamberlain, *Letters,* ed. N. E. McClure, Philadelphia 1939, II, p. 286.

24 Prynne, *op. cit.,* p. 43.

25 *Hic-Mulier: Or, The Man-Woman,* London 1620 (no pagination). The theme of the 'masculine' woman and the 'effeminate' man is explored in much contemporary literature. As a riposte to the above, a few days later was published *Haec-Vir: Or, The Womanish-Man, Being an Answere to a late Booke intituled Hic-Mulier;* the argument of this was that women had adopted male fashions because men had stolen theirs – their curled hair, jewellery and cosmetics etc. On the subject of these and similar publications, see B. Baines (ed.), *Three Pamphlets on the Jacobean Antifeminist Controversy,* New York, 1978.

26 R. Brathwait, *The English Gentlewoman,* London 1631, p. 93. It is difficult to know if these loose sack-like gowns – for they are described in this way by the Venetian ambassador who saw them at a masque in 1618 – are identical with the mysterious garment called the 'nightgown' which appears to be, at this time, an informal or semi-formal gown.

27 Sir W. Brereton, *Travels in Holland, the United Provinces, England, Scotland and Ireland,* ed. E. Hawkins, London 1844, I, p. 186.

28 Brathwait, *op. cit.,* p. 3 and p. 14.

29 T. Taylor, *A Glasse for Gentlewomen to dresse themselves by,* London 1624, p. 28.

In the 1630s, when the fashion had become widespread, Dean Corbet wrote a poem called *To the Ladyes of the New Dresse,* in which he muses on the fact that women 'shew your armes instead of hands'. (Quoted in F. W. Fairholt, *Satirical Songs and Poems on Costume,* London 1849, p. 136.)

30 Brathwait, *op. cit.,* p. 8.

31 T. Hall, *Divers Reasons and Arguments Against Painting, Spots, naked Backs, Breasts, Arms &c,* London 1654, pp. 109–110.

32 *Ibid.,* p. 118.

33 F. E. Baldwin, *Sumptuary Legislation and Personal Regulation in England,* Baltimore, 1926, p. 265.

34 A. Fraser, *The Weaker Vessel. Woman's lot in seventeenth-century England,* London 1984, p. 196. There were also very isolated examples of women in the early seventeenth century wearing men's clothes, the most famous being Mary Frith, born in 1589, who was possibly a hermaphrodite; as a young girl she attracted attention by her style of dress, and was the subject of Thomas Middleton's play *The Roaring Girl,* 1611.

35 H. Peacham, *The Truth of our Times,* London 1638, p. 57.

36 *Ibid.,* p. 74. 'A.L.' (see Note 1) also attacked the slashed doublets and the 'clowne-like' long breeches which made Englishmen look like 'French Apes'.

37 E. Grimston, *The Honest Man: or, The Art to please in Court,* London 1632, p. 354.

38 A. Dent, *The Plaine Man's Path-way to Heaven,* London 1601, p. 53.

39 L. Hutchinson, *Memoirs of the Life of Colonel Hutchinson,* London 1806, p. 99.

40 W. Prynne, *A Gagge for Long-Hair'd Rattle-Heads who revile all civill Round-heads,* London 1646 (no pagination).

41 T. Hall, *The Loathsomnesse of Long Haire ...,* London 1653, p. 15 and p. 67.

42 J. Bulwer, *Anthropometamorphosis: Man Transform'd; or The Artificial Changeling,* London 1650, pp. 53–8 and pp. 259–63. This is the first real attempt to discuss dress within an anthropological framework.

43 R. Steele (ed.), *A Bibliography of Royal Proclamations of the Tudor and Stuart Sovereigns 1485–1714,* Oxford 1910, p. 293.

44 J. Evelyn, *Tyrannus or the Mode, in a Discourse of Sumptuary Lawes,* London 1661, p. 11.

The only odd remnant of protective sumptuary legislation was an attempt made in 1678 to encourage the English wool trade by ordering burials in 'shirt, shift or sheet' of wool; only those who had died of the plague were to be buried in linen. Otherwise, those who wished to be buried in linen or any non-wool stuff, had to pay £5, the money going to the parish poor. This was more or less obeyed (although ridiculed), until 1814 when it was abolished.

See N. B. Harte, *State Control of Dress and Social Change in Pre-Industrial England* (p. 152) in D. C. Coleman and A. H. John (eds.), *Trade, government and economy in pre-industrial England,* London 1976.

45 Evelyn, *op cit.,* p. 4.

46 See D. de Marly, *King Charles II's own fashion: the theatrical origins of the English vest,* in *The Journal of the Warburg and Courtauld Institutes,* vol. XXXVII, 1974. Pseudo-oriental 'vests' were worn both in the theatre and at court entertainments.

The visit of a Russian embassy to London in 1662 might also have inspired a similar costume; Randle Holme in *An Academie of Armory* (1688) illustrates a 'loose Coat' as worn by the Russian ambassador on this occasion, which 'was so taken to that it became a great fashion and wear, both in Court, City and Country'.

47 A. Wood, *The Life and Times of Anthony Wood, antiquary of Oxford 1632–1695,* ed. A. Clark, Oxford 1891–1900, I, p, 509.

48 Anon., *Englands Vanity or the Voice of God Against the Monstrous Sin of Pride in Dress and Apparel,* London 1683, p. 107. With the Restoration we see an increase in attacks on the effeminacy of men's dress. This may partly be due to the fact that the styles were perceived in this way at the time, but also to the fact that, with women on the stage, it was no longer possible or acceptable to see men dressed as women. For a further exploration of this theme, see P. Ackroyd, *Dressing Up. Transvestitism and Drag,* London 1979, p. 57.

49 J.-B. Thiers, *Histoire des Perruques,* Paris 1690, p. 240.

50 *The Ladies Dictionary,* London 1694, p. 405.

51 E. R. Bristow, *Vice and Vigilance: Purity Movements in Britain since 1700,* Dublin 1977, pp. 11–16. In the belief that religion was the key to morality, the *Society for promoting Christian Knowledge* was formed in 1698.

52 B. de Mandeville, *The Fable of the Bees,* London 1714, p. 67.

53 *Englands Vanity, op. cit.,* p. 55.

54 E. Cooke, *A Just and Seasonable Reprehension of naked Breasts and Shoulders,* London 1678, pp. 3–4, and pp. 24–33.

55 *Ladies Dictionary, op. cit.,* p. 401. This was published by John Dunton and arranged roughly alphabetically under various headings in the world of fashion. Quotations from earlier periods are not attributed, so that the reader should be wary of assuming that it is all contemporary comment.

56 *Ibid.*

57 *Ibid.,* p. 414.

58 Anon., *Satyr against Painting,* London 1697, p. 4.

59 Anon., *The Folly of Love,* London 1691, p. 7.

60 See M. Evelyn (attr.), *Mundus Muliebris: or, The Ladies Dressing-Room unlock'd,* ed. J. L. Nevinson, London 1977. Nevinson's theory is that although Mary Evelyn died in 1685, the main body of the work is hers; the preface was probably written by John Evelyn.

61 Anon., *The Parable of the Top-Knots,* London 1691, pp. 1–2. This was also included in *The Ladies Dictionary* of 1694, where all the names of the various headdresses and hairstyles are listed in detail.

62 *Ladies Dictionary, op. cit.,* p. 415.

63 J. du Bosc, *The Accomplish'd Woman,* London, 1753, I, p. 123. This was a French work of 1630, translated into English in 1639.

64 *Ladies Dictionary, op. cit.,* p. 363. The 'Rudder or Stern to the body' refers to the bustle effect created partly by the back drapery of the gown, and obviously by some kind of rigid or padded under-structure. Curiously this fashion does not seem to have evoked the attacks that had been made on the farthingale, and which were to be made on the eighteenth-century hooped skirt.

65 *Englands Vanity, op. cit.,* p. 132.

6

1 Sir W. Blackstone, *Commentaries on the Laws of England,* London 1765–70, Book IV, vol. II, p. 129.

2 N. B. Harte, *State Control of Dress and Social Change in*

NOTES

Pre-Industrial England, in *Trade, government and economy in pre-industrial England*, eds. D. C. Coleman and A. H. John, London 1976, p. 155.
3 B. de Mandeville, *The Fable of the Bees*, London 1714, pp. 105–6.
4 Quoted in A. Ribeiro, *Dress in eighteenth-century Europe 1715–1789*, London 1984, p. 15.
5 *The Spectator*, 19 July, 1712.
6 *Ibid.*, 12 July, 1712. 'Leads' were weights, about an inch in diameter which were sewn into the inside cuffs of sleeves to keep them straight and unwrinkled.
7 Baron C. L. von Pöllnitz, *Travels from Prussia thro' Germany, Italy, France, Flanders, Holland, England &c*, London 1745, III, p. 287.
8 Anon., *The Art of Dress*, London 1717, p. 2 and p. 24.
9 Anon., *Female Folly: or, The Plague of a Woman's Riding-Hood and Cloak*, London 1713, pp. 2–3. Two years later another poem on the hooded riding-cloak appeared, alluding to the occasion when the Jacobite Countess of Nithsdale smuggled her husband out of the Tower by dressing him in female dress and cloak. See F. W. Fairholt, *Satirical Songs and Poems on Costume*, London 1849, p. 209.
10 The quotation, from *La Bagatelle*, is in E. and J. de Goncourt, *The Woman of the Eighteenth Century*, trans. J. le Clerq and R. Roeder, London 1928, p. 212.
11 *The Spectator*, 26 July 1711.
12 Abbé Jean Le Blanc, *Letters on the English and French Nations*, Dublin, 1747, II, p. 6.
13 *The Female Spectator*, London 1744–5, I, p. 241.
14 A. W., *The Enormous Abomination of the Hoop-Petticoat, as The Fashion Now is, And has been For about these Two Years*, London 1745, pp. 7–8, and p. 13.
15 Anon., *The Beau's Character*, 1706, in Fairholt, *op. cit.*, p. 201.
16 Anon., *The English Theophrastus, or The Manners of the Age*, London, 2nd. ed., 1706, pp. 53–5.
17 *The Spectator*, 6 March 1712.
18 F. D. Osborn, (ed.) *Political and Social Letters of a Lady of the Eighteenth Century*, London 1890, p. 23. A similar view was expressed by *The Spactator*, 16 Aug. 1711; Richard Steele in the character of a female correspondent writes that 'the Skirt of your fashionable Coats forms as large a Circumference as our Petticoats . . .'.
19 Anon., *The Man of Taste*, London 1733, p. 16.
20 Bishop George Berkeley, *The Querist*, Dublin 1735–7, Part I, Query 80.
21 T. Smollett, *Travels through France and Italy*, London 1766, pp. 97–8.
22 I. Watts, *Works*, London 1810, I, p. 244. The sermons were first published in 1753.
23 J. Wesley, *A Sermon on Dress*, London 1817, pp. 6–9, p. 15.
24 R. W. von Archenholz, *A Picture of England*, London 1789, II, p. 89.
25 S. Richardson, *Clarissa Harlowe*, London 1768 ed., VIII, p. 51. Rather more disconcertingly, some prostitutes, according to *The Spectator* (19 June 1712) wore black mourning dress, 'at once consulting Cheapness and Modesty'. In 1758 the Magdelen Hospital in London was founded for the reformation and relief of penitent prostitutes; it was a popular society pastime to attend services in the chapel, where the ex-prostitutes, who attended, were hidden behind a green curtain.
26 Anon., *Satan's Harvest Home*, London 1749, p. 4.
27 Berkeley, *op. cit.*, Part III, Query 116.
28 *The Female Spectator, op. cit.*, I, p. 163.
29 For the general background to the eighteenth-century masquerade, and the dress worn, see A. Ribeiro, *The Exotic Diversion: the Dress worn at Masquerades in eighteenth-century London*, in *The Connoisseur*, Jan. 1978, and C. Fox and A. Ribeiro, *Masquerade*, the catalogue of an exhibition held at the Museum of London, 1983.
30 Quoted in Ribeiro, *The Exotic Diversion, op. cit.*, p. 11. Another costume noted for its immodesty was apparently that of Diana; we don't know what Madame du Pompadour wore in this role when she met Louis XV for the first time at a masked ball in 1745, but at masquerades in London, the dress was a tight-fitting jacket, and a skirt of see-through white gauze, short enough to reveal the silver tassels on the garters (see *The Covent Garden Magazine*, July 1773, p. 245).
31 J. Arbuthnot, *The Ball, Stated in a Dialogue betwixt a Prude and a Coquet*, London 1724, p. 1.
32 *The World*, London 1763, I, p. 132.
33 *The Connoisseur*, London 1755, p. 240, and E. J. Climenson (ed.), *Elizabeth Montagu, the Queen of the Blue-Stockings: Correspondence 1720–1761*, London 1906, I, p. 264.

Elizabeth Chudleigh (1720–1788) had a very racy career, which culminated in her trial for bigamy in 1776, a great society event. The same year she fled to the continent, spending the rest of her life in travel, most notably to Russia where she amassed a considerable fortune.
34 See A. Ribeiro, *A sweet rococo in the dress*, in *The Times*, 29 May 1984.
35 A. Rathbone (ed.), *Letters from Lady Jane Coke to her Friend Mrs Eyre 1747–1758*, London 1899, p. 134. The 'neck' was an eighteenth-century euphemism for the bosom. The display of too much bosom, even when tightly boned stays pushed the bust up, was thought 'an immodest Liberty' which would encourage coxcombs to make 'blunt Jests and stupid Double-Entendres' (*Dress: A Satire*, London 1754, p. 12).
36 *The Connoisseur*, London 1754, p. 5.
37 *The World*, London 1753, pp. 113–4.
38 O. Goldsmith, *The Vicar of Wakefield*, ed. and intr. A. Friedman, London 1974, pp. 25–6.

A dress worn without a hoop so that the skirts trailed on the ground was known as a trollopee; a style that was carelessly elegant in a woman of fashion, but might just be slovenly in one less fastidious about her appearance, and ignorance of the correct deportment. One can speculate on

the origins of the word 'trollop' (etym. obscure, says the dictionary). It might derive (see page 103) from the name of this dress which, as worn by prostitutes, would have a slatternly appearance.
39 M. Delany, *Autobiography and Correspondence*, ed. Lady Llanover, London 1861–2, VI, p. 189. Caricaturists and satirists claimed that women incorporated into their 'têtes' of false hair, every kind of stuffing they could find – cotton wool, horse-hair, cows tails etc.
40 Lady L. Stuart (ed. J. A. Home), *Selections from her Manuscripts*, Edinburgh, 1899, p. 186.
41 For trade cards and advertisements relating to cosmetics, see the scrapbook entitled *Perfumery and Cosmetics*, compiled by F. Gillham (Victoria and Albert Museum Library, 25. L. 3).

Older women continued to use the heavy paint of their youth; in Sheridan's play *The School for Scandal* (1777) Sir Benjamin Backbite talks of a woman who is not particularly expert at making up her face to match her neck, so that she looks like a mended statue, '... the head's modern, though the trunk's antique'.
42 Quoted in F. Gunn, *The Artificial Face*, London 1973, p. 124. I am assuming that the reference is a satirical one, as no such act appears in the Statutes of the Realm, in spite of the author's inference that it was passed.
43 *The Female Spectator, op. cit.*, I, p. 84.
44 *Satan's Harvest Home, op. cit.*, pp. 50–1. Too much lace (metal braid) on the coat was derided as a sign of a fop who set too much store by his appearance. One such man was contemptuously labelled by Richardson's Pamela as 'a tinselled toy, ... for he was laced all over'.
45 *Town and Country Magazine,* March 1772, p. 242. For further information on the macaronis, see A. Ribeiro, *The Macaronis*, in *History Today,* July 1978.

There were also what Walpole calls 'macaronesses', but these ladies seem to be only distinguishable by the towering height of their headdresses.
46 Quoted in Ribeiro, *Dress in eighteenth-century Europe, op. cit.*, p. 17.
47 See scrapbook entitled *Hairdressing* compiled by F. Gillham (Victoria and Albert Museum Library, 25. L. 4.); there is no pagination, but the newspaper cutting is dated 14 Feb. 1765, in a roughly chronological sequence.
48 J. T. Smith, *Nollekens and his Times*, London 1829, I, p. 225. Dr. Johnson, too, although sometimes spectacularly indifferent to his own appearance, liked to see women wearing linen or cotton, for it was possible to tell when it was dirty, unlike silk.
49 Sir N. Wraxall, *Memoirs of His Own Time,* London 1836, I, pp. 141–2.

In the following year, 1795, a tax was imposed on hair powder. For some years this custom had been on the wane, and only worn by the elderly and conservative, officials, the clergy, and the army; but each man in the army used about one pound of wheat flour a week on his hair, and this was more urgently needed for bread, during the wars. The 1795 tax was a guinea for those who wished to continue the custom; exempted were members of the royal family, the clergy, and officers of the army and navy.
50 J. G. Milligen, *Recollections of Republican France,* London 1848, p. 323.
51 N. M. Karamzin, *Travels from Moscow through Prussia, Germany, Switzerland, France and England,* London 1803, I, p. 217. It was fashionable to adopt a somewhat oafish demeanour as part of 'republican' manners. Dr John Moore, in France in 1792, found 'a great affectation of that plainness in dress, and simplicity of expression which are supposed to belong to Republicans' (Dr J. Moore, *A Journal during a residence in France ... 1792,* London 1793, p. 430).
52 *The Life and Times of Anthony Wood, antiquary of Oxford, 1632–1695,* ed. A. Clark, Oxford, 1891–1900, I, p. 509.
53 S. Richardson, *Letters Written to and for Particular Friends on the most Important Occasions,* London 1741, p. 124. Women wearing such riding habits were often designated Amazons; *The Female Spectator* for 1745 deplored the fashion which made those who wore it 'half-Men, half-Women'.
54 R. Blunt, *Mrs Montagu, 'Queen of the Blues': Her Letters and Friendships from 1762–1800,* London 1923, II, p. 82.
55 A. Leroy, *Recherches sur les Habillemens des Femmes et des Enfans,* Paris 1772, pp. 177, 241–2. There were as many defenders of whaleboned stays. One example is M. Reisser 'tailleur pour femme à Lyon' in his *Essai sur les Corps Baleinés,* Lyon 1770. His argument is that properly made, such stays hide deformity and help posture. These arguments for and against stays were to rage on all through the nineteenth century.
56 J.-L. Soulavie, *Mémoires Historiques et Politiques du Règne de Louis XVI,* Paris 1801, VI, p. 43. He blamed the decline of the Lyons silk industry on the French queen's taste for white muslin.
57 A. Adams, *Letters,* ed. C. F. Adams, Boston 1848, p. 193 and p. 199.
58 M. Wollstonecraft, *A Vindication of the Rights of Woman,* London 1792, pp. 26–7, p. 220.
59 *Ibid.*, p. 273 *et seq.*, p. 435.
60 S. Mercier, *New Picture of Paris,* Dublin, 1800, I, p. 181 and pp. 220–5.
61 Quoted in the *Lady's Magazine,* London 1798, p. 467. The editor of the magazine adds that the approach of winter 'has done more to banish the taste for nudity among the women of Paris than all the writings of M. Mercier or any other author'.

In England, too, the display of naked statues was frowned on, not so much that they might influence women in their dress, but that they were indecent. *The Gentleman's Magazine* of 1820 described 'young females ... even while gentlemen are present, admiring a new purchased Adonis or Hercules ...' (quoted in W. T. Whitley, *Art in England 1800–1820,* London 1928, p. 263).
62 *The Lady's Magazine,* London 1794, p. 67.

7

1 See A. Ribeiro, *'If the slogan fits, wear it'*, in *The Times* 14 Aug. 1984.

2 J. P. Malcolm, *Anecdotes of the Manners and Customs of London*, London 1808, p. 449. Beau Brummell was responsible for the invention of a strap fastening the trousers under the foot; the aim was to produce an unwrinkled line, but it also served to tighten the fit.

3 *Ibid*.

4 *The Mirror of the Graces*, London 1811, p. 93.

5 *Ibid.*, p. 96.

6 S. Sibbald, *Memoirs 1783–1812*, ed. F. P. Hett, London 1926, p. 138. There is a story, beloved of the more popular books on the history of dress, that women dampened their fine muslin chemises the better to reveal the body; I have not found any substantiated reference to this, although it is not beyond belief that some of the more outrageous ladies of the *demi-monde* might have done so.

7 Captain Gronow, *Reminiscences and Recollections . . .*, London 1892, I, p. 241. After the Napoleonic wars, the Austrian authorities in Milan made the ballet dancers at La Scala wear knee-length sky-blue pantaloons,' 'so tight that the outline of the figure was more apparent and the effect produced more indelicate, than if the usual gauze inexpressibles had been used.'

8 The quotations are from: *La Belle Assemblée*, London March 1806, Mrs R. Trench, *Selections from her Journals, Letters & other Papers*, ed. by her son, the Dean of Westminster, London 1862, p. 145 and E. Eyre, *Observations made at Paris during the Peace*, Bath 1803, p. 300.

9 J. Greig (ed.), *The Farington Diary*, London 1922–8, II, p. 20, and I, p. 344.

10 Lady Sarah Lennox, *Life and Letters*, eds. Countess of Ilchester and Lord Stavordale, London 1901, II, p. 292.

11 *Ibid*. Thackeray in his novel *Vanity Fair* (1847–8) which is set in the time of the Napoleonic wars, mocks the false decorum of 'the truly refined English or American female' who worry about words like breeches, which 'are walking the world before our faces every day, without much shocking us. If you were to blush every time they went by, what complexions you would have. It is only when their naughty names are called out that your modesty has any occasion to show alarm or sense of outrage.' (W. Thackeray, *Vanity Fair*, intr. M. R. Ridley, London 1976, p. 644).

12 Miss Dean, *An Appeal to the Consciences of Christians on the Subject of Dress*, Darlington 1815, p. 9.

13 'Honestas', *A New Book . . .*, Whitby, 1816, p. 11. One of his arguments is that if we are to condemn women for their dress, it is in any case foolish to talk of such trimmings as frills and fripperies, when there are 'exposed bosoms' which may 'inflame the passions of the male sex'.

This pamphlet by 'Honestas' called forth a number of replies in support of Miss Dean. Labelling her defenders as 'Pests to society', 'Honestas' again went into print to emphasize one of his first points, that if we were to listen to such people, 'we could not possibly enter the heavenly Jerusalem'.

14 F. Place, *Manners and Morals*, in the *Place Collections*, British Museum, *Add. MS. 27827*, pp. 50–52, and *Add MS. 27828*, p. 118.

15 *The Whole Art of Dress, or The Road to Elegance and Fashion, By a cavalry officer*, London 1830, pp. 17–18. Tight-lacing was not just *un vice anglais*, but was practised by the French also. The *Journal de Paris* (16 Sept. 1808) noted that some men 'un peu gros, se faisaient faire des corsets comme les femmes pour se rendre minces'. (Quoted in A. Aulard, *Paris sous le Premier Empire*, Paris 1912–23, III, p. 724.)

16 Anon., *The Ton*, London 1819, p. 111.

17 Anon., *Indispensable Requisites for Dandies*, Dublin, N. D., no pagination.

This curious book is a collection of pop-up engravings accompanied by verses, caricaturing the fashions of the dandies.

18 Anon., *Neckclothitania or Tietania*, London 1818, p. 8 and p. 36.

19 W. Connely, *Count D'Orsay, The Dandy of Dandies*, London 1952, p. 166.

See also the novel by John Mills, *D'Horsay or The Follies of the Day*, 1844, a satirical account of this leader of fashion and his circle in London.

20 Q. Bell, *On Human Finery*, revised ed. London 1976, p. 143.

21 A. Smith, *The Natural History of the Gent*, London 1847, p. 6 *et seq*.

We are also told that the 'Gents' love slang; they speak of 'their get-up as the ticket – the term possibly being used in allusion to the badge which distinguished their various articles of dress when exposed for sale' (p. 17). In short, they buy their clothes in cheap shops, whereas a true gentleman would, of course, have his clothes made by his own tailor.

See also *Punch* on the subject of the Gents (1843).

22 Anon., *The Habits of Good Society*, London 1859, p. 141.

23 A. Walker, *Beauty*, London 1852, pp. 226–7.

24 W. H. Henslowe, *Beard-Shaving . . .*, London 1847, pp. 5–6. The author's hopes for the restoration of beards came true in the mid 1850s, when the Crimean War popularized their use. However they did not attract universal praise, *The Habits of Good Society* (1859) finding certain types such as the 'Italian Conspirator' to be rather suspect and radical. It was also important to avoid the 'foppery' of the needle-pointed type as worn by Napoleon III, 'decidedly a proof of vanity' (p. 115).

25 C. Nicoullard (ed.), *Memoirs of the Comtesse de Boigne*, London 1907–8, II, p. 39.

26 Mrs A. J. Graves, *Women in America; being an Examination into the Moral and Intellectual Condition of American Female Society*, New York, 1843, p. 38, p. 55, and pp. 104–8.

27 *Ibid.*, p. 110.

28 Anon., *Pride in Dress,* London c. 1830, p. 3.
29 Anon., *The Female Instructor or Young Woman's Companion, and Guide to Domestic Happiness,* London 1824, pp. 9–10.
30 *The Habits of Good Society, op. cit.,* p. 42 and p. 162.
31 E. Farrar, *The Young Lady's Friend,* New York, 1845, p. 368. The book is full of tips on how, for example, the modest young lady can walk in the streets without showing too much of her ankle, yet at the same time keeping her skirts free of mud.
32 M Merrifield, *Dress as a Fine Art,* London 1854, pp. 2–3.
33 *Ibid.,* p. 63.
34 Quoted in A. Adburgham, *A Punch History of Manners and Modes 1841–1940,* London 1961, p. 73.
35 H.-A. Taine, *Notes on England,* trans. W. F. Rae, London 1872, pp. 68–9. He also finds a total lack of colour sense in contemporary British art, a comment which strikes a sympathetic chord when we think, for example, of some of the Pre-Raphaelite artists of the time.
36 C. Baudelaire, *The Painter of Modern Life, and Other Essays,* trans. and ed. J. Mayne, London 1964, pp. 30–3. The title essay appeared in *Le Figaro* in 1863 although it was written some few years earlier.
37 The quotation about the prostitutes comes from an American visitor to London in 1835; it is mentioned in G. Rattray Taylor's *The Angel-Makers. A Study in the Psychological Origins of Historical Change 1750–1850,* 1958, pp. 72–3. It is this historian who makes the claim about the immorality of the working classes; he couples this with a growth in the production of pornography which is one of the characteristics of the second half of the nineteenth century.
38 Taine, *op. cit.,* p. 39.
39 A. Wynter, *Our Social Bees,* 2nd Series, London 1866, p. 271. Wynter says that old clothes dealers soothe the worries of those who sell them clothes (fear of them being recognized by friends on the backs of strangers) by saying that they were sent to Australia; this is not, in fact, the case, for 'gold-diggers and sheep-farmers are far too well off to require such leavings' (pp. 272–3).
40 Anon., *Nothing to Wear: An Episode of Fashionable Life,* London 1857, p. 13. This was first published in America, supposedly written by an American lawyer.
41 *Nothing to You; or, Mind Your Own Business,* by 'Knot-Rab', New York, New York, 1857, pp. 10–11, p. 22.
42 F. P. Cobbe, *Essays on the Pursuits of Women,* London 1863, p. 226.
43 The Ton, *op. cit.,* p. 46. In the same year, 1819, the third edition of *Dress and Address* attacked women for the 'masculine and disgusting' fashion of wearing trousers beneath their dress (p. 51).
44 Dr. E. J. Tilt, *Elements of Health and Principles of Female Hygiene,* London 1852, p. 193.
45 Merrifield, *op. cit.,* p. 83.
46 *The Family Herald,* London, vol. IX, 8 Nov., 1851, p. 445. However even Mrs Bloomer stopped wearing the costume c. 1858, after she had moved to the American west where she found the high winds tended to turn the short skirt of her tunic over her head and shoulders. See Anne Wood Murray, *The Bloomer Costume and Excercise Suits,* in *Waffen-und Kostümkunde,* 1982, vol. 2, p. 110.
47 The Family Herald, *op. cit.,* 25 Oct., p. 413.
48 *Ibid.,* 13 Sept., p. 318.
49 The costume of these girls, while predominantly masculine – they wore a shirt, cloth waistcost, trousers and boots – retained a symbol of femininity in the striped petticoat which was sometimes bundled round their waist. They were still wearing trousers in the 1880s, but by that time the criticism had died down.
50 W. F. Taylor, *Suitable Bathing Dresses as used in Biarritz,* London c. 1860, p. 11. A loose-trousered bathing dress was worn by both sexes on French beaches, a custom which resulted in 'complete decency' enabling the sexes to bathe together, and avoiding 'the mixture of leering and mock modesty' which was the rule in England.
51 F. Wey (adapted by V. Pirie), *A Frenchman sees the English in the 'Fifties,* London 1935, p. 299.
52 *The Observer,* London 1856, p. 263.
53 Until that time, men could often bathe naked, although by the late 1890s a number of local authorities had begun to put up notices enjoining the wearing of drawers. Gwen Raveret remembered in her Cambridge childhood (she was born in 1885) that ladies being rowed on the river when passing men's bathing sites, unfurled their parasols and gazed into them 'until the crisis was past, and the river was decent again'. (G. Raveret, *Period Piece. A Cambridge Childhood,* London 1952, p. 108).
54 *The Queen,* London 1868, 12 Dec., p. 345. A similar style (though apparently free from any taint of aristocratic vice) was the Dolly Varden in England, named after the heroine of Dickens's novel *Barnaby Rudge* (1841) which was set in 1780. In contemporary illustrations she is shown as a coquettish figure in a kilted-up flowered overgown, a plain petticoat, and a ribbon-trimmed straw hat.
55 C. Blanc, *Art in Ornament and Dress,* London 1877, p. 154.
56 W. B. Lord, *The Freaks of Fashion,* London 1870, p. 174. William Barry Lord was the fetishist author of this apologia for corsets. He claims the support of medical opinion in his defence of tight-lacing, and also the great contribution which the corset industry makes to employment – over thirty thousand people worked in the trade in London and the provinces, to supply national and colonial demands.
57 Quoted in C. W. Cunnington, *The Perfect Lady 1815–1914,* London 1948, p. 42.

The subject of tight-lacing is one that has attracted a considerable amount of attention. The most thorough survey is that of David Kunzle, *Fashion and Fetishism,* Totowa New Jersey 1982. He tries, not very convincingly, to link tight-lacing with emancipated views, e.g. 'the young girl of the late Victorian era tight-laced in protest against the stereotyped social role awaiting her and in hopes of

attracting a man for whom companionship and erotic pleasures weighed more than parenthood and family'! (p. 45). A much more balanced, though briefer, account is contained in Valerie Steele's *Fashion and Eroticism. Ideals of Feminine Beauty from the Victorian Era to the Jazz Age*, New York 1985.
58 E. Lynn Linton, *The Girl of the Period*, London, 1868, p. 4.
59 Wynter, *op. cit.*, pp. 377–82. He alleges that most false hair came from France. At the time of writing (1866) he finds that gold is the most popular colour for false hair. Women add a few tresses of gold hair to give a shine to their own duller locks, 'just as your fraudulent sherry manufacturer flavours his made-up wines with a little of the true growth of Cadiz'.
60 V. Steele. *op. cit.*, pp. 125–7.
61 E. Lynn Linton, *The Girl of the Period*, London 1883 ed., I, p. 313.
62 E. Lynn Linton, *Ourselves. A Series of Essays on Women*, London 1870, p. 32 and pp. 42–4.
63 C. M. Yonge, *Womankind*, London 1876, pp. 110–11.
64 Quoted in Cunnington, *op. cit.*, p. 189.
65 Mrs H. R. Haweis, *The Art of Beauty*, London 1878, p. 268.
66 *Ibid.*, pp. 23–31. See also John Leighton's *Madre Natura* (1874) in which modern dress is described as 'libels upon Nature' in its artificial constraints and irrationality. 'The English lady suffers in her corset and tight bottines in the tropical heat of Calcutta, as the Duchess shivers in her tres-décolletée costume de bal in the northern capitals' (p. 26). It was his hope that 'a New Moral Power' i.e. educated public opinion, might bring common sense to bear on this problem.
67 *The Lady's Newspaper*, London 1863, 14 Nov., p. 322, and 5 Dec., p. 375.
68 Steele *op. cit.*, p. 152.
69 Quoted in M. von Boehn, *Modes and Manners of the Nineteenth Century*, trans. M. Edwardes, London 1927, publ. in facsimile, New York 1970, II, p. 169.
70 Cunnington, *op. cit.*, p. 288; The quotation is from a magazine of 1890, which is not identified.
71 M. Beerbohm, *A Defence of Cosmetics*, New York 1922, p. 2 *et seq*.
72 M. Safford-Blake, in *Dress Reform*, ed. A. Goold Woolson, Boston 1874, p. 27 and pp. 37–8. It goes without saying that all the dress reformers wished to ban corsets, as well as radically reducing the number of hampering petticoats that women wore.
73 Quoted in A. Ballin, *The Science of Dress*, London 1885, p. 181.
74 The *Daily Mail* for 11 May 1898, reported that a Mrs Arnold of Chelsea, a long-time wearer of bloomers, had been refused admittance wearing a blue cycling jacket and trousers, at the White Horse Hotel in Dorking. This provoked a letter from a male writer one week later who claimed to be delighted at having found a hotel 'to which I can safely take my wife and sisters without any fear of seeing women dressed in the revolting dress which is called rational'.
75 Quoted in J. Laver, *The Age of Optimism: Manners and Morals 1848–1914*, London 1966, p. 185.

8

1 'Rita' (Eliza Humphreys), *The Sin and Scandal of the Smart Set*, London 1904, p. 67 and p. 70. On the subject of the fashionable sport of motoring, *The Tatler* (25 Nov. 1903), reporting on the craze from America for tattooing, noted that 'ladies who like to keep pace with the times may be adorned with illustrations of motor cars'. A Mr Alfred South of Cockspur Street was claimed to have tattooed about 900 women, but it is not clear how many chose to be decorated with cars.
2 Father Bernard Vaughan, *The Sins of Society*, London 1906, p. 174.
3 A. Adburgham, *A Punch History of Manners and Modes 1841–1940*, London 1961, p. 181.
4 Lady Duff Gordon, *Discretions and Indiscretions*, London 1932, p. 73.
5 Mrs E. Pritchard, *The Cult of Chiffon*, London 1902, p. 117.
6 *Ibid.*, p. 16 and p. 21.
7 G. Raveret, *Period Piece. A Cambridge Childhood*, London 1952, pp. 266–7.
8 F. Latham, *Is the British Empire . . .*, London 1911, p. 24. The thesis of this rather heavy-handed pamphlet is that women are totally indebted to men; even their fashions, he claims, are 'man-designed'.
9 F. Winterburn, *Principles of Correct Dress*, New York 1914, p. 79.
10 Quoted in V. Steele, *Fashion and Eroticism. Ideals of Feminine Beauty from the Vicotorian Era to the Jazz Age*, New York, 1985, p. 229. Another undergarment which made for easier movement was the girdle, which Poiret claimed to have invented c. 1906. By the First World War most young women were wearing two support items, a bra and a girdle; older women retained the all-in-one corset.
11 M. von Boehn, *Modes and Manners of the Nineteenth Century*, trans. M. Edwardes, London 1927, publ. in facsimile, New York 1970, II, pp. 119–21.
12 *Ibid.*, p. 126.
13 A. Huxley, *Point Counter Point*, London 1928, p. 368.
14 B. Nichols, *The Sweet and Twenties*, London 1958, p. 126.
15 M. Lawrence, *The School of Femininity*, New York 1936, p. 163.
16 Quoted in Nichols, *op. cit.*, p. 137.
17 *Ibid.*, p. 134. To give 'body' to the short haircuts, many women with straight hair had it permed. Permanent waving had been introduced before the war but it was a cumbersome and lengthy business; it was not really perfected until the 1920s.
18 V. Margueritte, *The Bachelor Girl*, London 1923, p. 64. In 1922, the year of the first publication of this novel,

Punch came out with a skit on the 'advanced' modern 'girl' (aged 49); Glorinda, 'diaphanously clad' and 'plastered with carmine on her cheeks and lips',

Drinks with thirst insatiate at the springs,
Of new, bizarre, sophisticated things.

19 R. Mortimer, *Modern Nymphs*, London 1930, p. 7. Chanel designed bathing costumes and beach pyjamas as part of her campaign to help women to lead more relaxed and comfortable lives; working costumes such as dungarees and sailors' bell-bottomed trousers inspired some of her resort clothes. Poiret sarcastically called it 'poverty de luxe', but Mortimer claimed that she had done more than Mrs Pankhurst for female emancipation.

20 Quoted in C. W. Cunnington, *English Women's Clothing in the Present Century*, London 1952, p. 200.

21 'T.I.W.', *Modest Apparel. An Earnest Word to Christian Women*, London 1931, p. 3 *et seq*. Nearly every page is full of the most splendid denunciation of women's dress, hair and habits, especially cigarette smoking.

22 G. F. Curtis, *Clothes and the Man*, London 1926, p. 96.

23 Nichols, *op. cit.*, p. 138.

24 D. Langley Moore, *Pandora's Letter Box*, London 1929, p. 92.

25 Report of the Dress Reform Dinner Debate, 24 June 1932, p. 3. This is included in a collection of material relating to the Men's Dress Reform Party, British Library, 1929–36. Commenting on this debate, *The Tailor and Cutter* (8 July) declared that the dress reforms proposed by the MDRP would lead to 'social anarchy', for traditional clothes were the symbols of civilization.

26 E. Schiaparelli, *Shocking Life*, London 1954, p. 96. Elsa Schiaparelli claimed to have popularized such 'falsies'.

27 *Picture Post*, London, 5 Nov., 1938.

28 *Daily Mail*, London, 18 Oct., 1945.

29 See the *Daily Mail*, London 30 Sept., 1947. On 25 Sept. Jill Craigie wrote to *The Times*, describing the New Look as anti-social.

The Liddell-Hart Collection at Liverpool Polytechnic contains a large number of newspaper cuttings relating to the New Look and its attendant wasp-waisted corset.

30 *Daily Herald*, London 2 March, 1948. The same newspaper in the following month reported that a Mrs Lily Wilson of Nelson in Lancashire had led a strike against the New Look, urging 'shorter frocks, shorter hours'.

31 *Daily Express*, London 15 Oct., 1949.

32 *American Catholic Weekly*, New York, vol. 93, 2 July, 1955.

33 P. Binder, *The Peacock's Tail*, London 1958, p. 343.

34 *Life*, New York, 11 Dec., 1944.

35 N. Cohn, *Today there are no Gentlemen*, London 1971, p. 32. It is not true, as this author says, that in the past all young men had wished to look like their fathers; ever since at least the mid eighteenth century, young men had demonstrated their rebelliousness through their dress, even by adopting some elements of working class dress.

36 *Ibid.*, p. 89.

37 P. York, *Style Wars*, London 1980, p. 142.

38 P. Binder, *The English Inside Out*, London 1961, p. 142 and p. 116. By the early 1960s men too, were wearing shoes with pointed toes, called 'winkle-pickers', which they wore with very tight trousers. *Hansard* for 25 Jan. 1962, reported that a youth wearing such shoes with Teddy-boy trousers had been refused a job at the Public Health Laboratory in Preston. The director of the laboratory stated that it was his belief that such clothes 'indicate an attitude of mind which militates against a good social atmosphere in the laboratory', and were evidence of 'certain inherent character defects'. 'Winkle-picker' shoes and pointed stiletto heels were often equated with delinquency in schools.

39 The *Sunday Express*, London 20 April, 1969.

40 'Rita', *op. cit.*, p. 68. Hugh Stutfield in *The Sovranty of Society*, London 1909, hinted darkly at the 'male butterfly' whose waistline suggests 'the corset's artful aid', and who adopted 'various other articles of women's wear' (p. 100) – he does not, disappointingly, state what these might be.

41 *Daily Express*, London 27 Sept., 1984. The council was Rugby; it was, not surprisingly perhaps, Conservative.

42 *Evening Standard*, London 13 June, 1978. The reader went on to complain about the use of the word 'blusher' for rouge; 'in these days of so much crudity and vulgarity, I'm surprised that people still know what blushing means'.

43 *Daily Mail*, London 22 June, 1985.

44 *The London Standard*, London 12 Aug., 1985.

45 *Ibid.*, 26 June, 1985.

46 R. W. Emmerson, *Letters and Social Aims*, London 1876, p. 78.

47 *Ibid.*, p. 79.

Select Bibliography

Note

In the main, only general, secondary sources are listed here along with books useful for background reading. Readers should refer to the relevant chapters for more detailed and specific references.

Adburgham, A., *A Punch History of Manners and Modes 1841–1940*, London, 1961.
Baldwin, F. E., *Sumptuary Legislation and Personal Regulation in England*, Johns Hopkins University Studies in Historical and Political Science, vol. 44, Baltimore 1926.
de Beauvoir, S., *The Second Sex*, London 1953.
Bell, Q., *On Human Finery*, revised ed., London, 1976.
Bristow, E. J., *Vice and Vigilance. Purity Movements in Britain since 1700*, Dublin 1977.
Carlyle, T., *Sartor Resartus*, London 1838.
Cunnington, C. W., *Feminine Fig leaves*, London 1938.
Cunnington, C. W., *Why Women wear Clothes*, London 1941
Ellis, H., *Studies in the Psychology of Sex vol. 1: The Evolution of Modesty*, 3rd. ed., London 1910.
Fairholt, F. W., *Satirical Songs and Poems on Costume*, London 1849.
Flügel, J. C., *The Psychology of Clothes*, London 1930.
Flügel, J. C., *Man, Morals and Society*, London 1945.
Gill, E., *Clothes*, London 1931.
Hall, C. A., *From Hoopskirts to Nudity. A Review of the Follies and Foibles of Fashion 1866–1936*, Caldwell, Idaho 1938.
Heard, G., *Narcissus. An Anatomy of Clothes*, London 1924.
Hentsch, A. A., *De la Littérature Didactique du moyen age s'addressant spécialement aux femmes*, Cahors 1903.
König, R., *The Restless Image: A Sociology of Fashion*, London 1973.

Kunzle, D., *Fashion and Fetishism*, Totowa, New Jersey, 1982.
Langdon-Davies, J., *Lady Godiva: The Future of Nakedness*, London 1928.
Langlois, C-V., *La Vie en France au Moyen Age de la fin du XIIe au milieu de XIVe siècle d'après des moralistes du temps*, 2 vols, Paris, 1926.
Laver, J., *Modesty in Dress*, London 1969.
Lecky, W. E. H., *History of European Morals from Augustus to Charlemagne*, London 1877.
Lillie, W., *An Introduction to Ethics*, London 1961.
Newton, S. M., *Health, Art and Reason*, London 1974.
Owst, G. R., *Literature and Pulpit in Medieval England*, London 1933.
Planché, J. R., *History of British Costume from the earliest period to the close of the eighteenth century*, 3rd. ed., London 1900.
Roach, M. E. (ed.), *Dress, Adornment and the Social Order*, New York 1965.
Rudofsky, B., *The unfashionable human body*, London 1972.
Sekora, J., *Luxury*, Baltimore 1977.
Squire, G., *Dress, Art and Society 1560–1970*, London 1974.
Steele, V., *Fashion and Eroticism. Ideals of Feminine Beauty from the Victorian Era to the Jazz Age*, New York 1985.
Strutt, J. (revised ed. by J. R. Planché), *A Complete View of the Dress and Habits of the People of England from the Establishment of the Saxons in Britain to the present time*, London 1842.
Taylor, G. R., *The Angel-Makers. A Study in the Psychological Origins of Historical Change 1750–1850*, London 1958.
Veblen, T., *The Theory of the Leisure Class*, New York 1899.
Wright, T., *Womankind in Western Europe*, London 1869.

Index

Note: Figures in italic type refer to pages on which illustrations appear.

Adam and Eve 19, 26–7
Adams, Abigail 116
Addison, Joseph 97
aesthetic, artistic dress 12, 96, 115, 125, 139, *141*
Aglaia 141
aglets 72
Alcuin 32
Alexander the Great 22
America
  20th century fashions 146, 157, 161, 162 *163*, 164, 168
Amish dress 13
'amour courtois' 38
Andover, Dorothy, Viscountess 82, *83*
Anglican church 164
Anglican divines 78
Anglo-Saxon dress 31–2, 34
Anne of Bohemia 45
Anne, Queen of Denmark 79, 80
Anselm, Archbishop of Canterbury 34–5
Aquinas, Thomas
  Summa Theologica 41
Aristotle 27
Arlen, Michael
  Green Hat, The 156
armour 32
Art Nouveau 149
Art of the Dress, The 96
asceticism 14, 25, 29
Augustus, Emperor 22, *23*
Averell, William
  Mervailous combat of contrarities, A 73

back
  sexual attraction of 16
Bacon, Francis 80
Bailey, David *170*
Ball, John 42
Ballets Russes 149
Bansley, Charles 70
barbarian dress 29, 31
Barclay, Alexander
  Shyp of Folys of the Worlde, The 59, 60, 62, 72–3
Baretti, Joseph 96
Baroque 90
'bath wrap' *160*
bathing costume 134, 152, 157
  bikini 163–4
  topless *168*, 170
  trunks 158
Baudelaire, Charles Piérre
  Painter of Modern Life, The 131, 132
Bayeux Tapestry 34
Beard-shaving 126

beards 22, 28–9, 31, 32, 67, 86
  pointed *34–5*
Beatles, the 165
'Beatnik Flower Power' *166*
Beau's Character, The 97, 99
Beauvoir, Simone de 26–7
Beerbohm, Max 126, 154, *155*
  Defence of Cosmetics 142
Bell, Quentin 12, 14, 125
belts 39, 43, *45*, 46, 52, 55, *58*, 124
Beowulf 32
Berkeley, George, Bishop 103
  Querist, The 100
bezants 46, 49
biblical references to dress 25, *26*, 28, *38*, 120
bifurcated garments 121, 133, 134, 144, 148
billiments 62, 63
birds, plumage 14, 68, 139, *144*, 149
  see also feathers
Black Death, the 42
Black Prince, The 46
Blackstone, Sir William 95
Blanc, Charles
  Art and Ornament in Dress 119, 135, 139
Blason des Basquines et Vertugalles 70–1
Blason des Couleurs en Armes, Livrées et Devises, Le 56
Bloomer, Amelia Jenks 132, 139, 145
Bloomer dress 17, 132, *133*, 134, 143
blouses 134, 143, 150, *151*, 152, 158, 170
bodice (of woman's gown) 70, 72, 78, 81, 89, 92, 96, 105
  see also stomacher
bodkins 67
Boethius
  De Consolatione 31
Boileau, Abbé
  De L'Abus des nuditez de gorge 92
Bokassa, 'Emperor' 15
bombast 66, 67, 68
boots (men), 59, 75, 84, 113, 125, 157
  barbarian 29, 32
  'bovver' 166
  military 22
boots (women) 39, *167*
  top-boots 126
Boswell, James, 113
Boudoir Boys 169
Braddock, Bessie 161
braid 70, 75, 89, 100
Brathwait, Richard
  English Gentlewoman, The 77, 81–2
breasts, bosom, bust 16, 39, *48*, 49, *54*, 65, 73, 77, 78, 80, 82, 92, 114, *116*, 117, 118, 120, *121*, *128*, 129, 133, 134, *135*, 143, 154, 159, 162

bust improvers *137*
  see also necklines
breeches 17, 68, 69, 72, 75, 84, *86*, 87, 110, 111, 113, 114, 122, *141*, 158
Brereton, Sir William 82
Brooke, Rupert 149
Brummell, Beau 122, 124
buckles 39, 46, 52, 100
buckram 70, 75, 89
Bulwer, John
  Anthropometamorphosis 86, 87
'bum roll' *71*, *116*
Bunyan, John
  Pilgrim's Progress, The 101, 102
Burgundian fashions 55, 57, 59
Burne-Jones, Sir Edward 141
Burton, Robert
  Anatomy of Melancholy, The 74
busk 70, 72, 78, 82
buskins 22
bustles 114, *128*, 129, 134, 137, 142–3
buttocks 114, *116*, *163*
buttons 13, 36, *37*, 42, 45, 46, 68, *85*–6, 100
Byzantine style 36

Caesar, Julius, Emperor 22
caleçons 134
Caligula, Emperor 22
Caplin, Madame Roxey
  Health and Beauty 129
caps (men) 55, *56*, 66, 67, *123*
caps and bonnets (women) 52, 58, 72, 103, 126, *127*, 130, 139, 168
Carew, Lord 75
caricatures 39, 71, 76, 77, *111*, *118*, 120, *137*
Carlyle, Thomas 17
Caroline, Queen of England 126
Casa, Giovanni della
  Galateo 65, 67
cast-off clothing 95–6, 103, 113, 122, 132
Castiglione
  Cortegiano, Il 65
catacomb paintings 26. 27
Catholicism 68, 150, 164
Cavaliers 85
Caxton, William 47
ceremonial dress 12
chador 13
Chamberlain, John 80, *81*
Chanel, Coco 156, 159, 160
Charles I, King of England 81, 84, 87
Charles II, King of England 90
Charles VII, King of France 54
chastity 13, 24, 38, 53, 103, 120
Chaucer, Geoffrey
  Canterbury Tales, The 43, 47, 49, 51, 52–3

187

INDEX

chemise, shift 36, 56, 82, *83*, 90, *91*, 103, *104*, 115–16, *117–18*, 120, *121*
Chesterfield, Lord 111
chiton 20, *21*, 22, *24*
chivalry, 38, 42
Christ, Temptation of, the *33*
Christian art 18
Christianity 13, 14, 17, 25, 29, 30, 38, 58, 126, 148, 171
Christians, early 26, 27, 28, 29, 33, 102
Christine de Pisan
  Book of the City of Ladies, The 42, 53, 55
Chudleigh, Elizabeth 105, *106*
Church Fathers 29, 31, 35
Churchill, Charles
  Rosciad, The 95
Ciriaci, Cardinal 164
Cistercian order 35
Clark, Kenneth 19
clean-shaven epochs 126
cleanliness
  eighteenth century 113
  nineteenth century 122, 127, 135
Clement of Alexandria
  Instructor, The 27, 28, 29
clerical dress 32–3, 35, 43, 86, 90, 164
cloaks (men)
  Anglo-Saxon 32
  barbarian 29, 31
  Roman 22, 24, 30
  17th century 75, 76, 77, 84
cloaks (women)
  Anglo-Saxon 32
  barbarian 29, 31
  Roman 22, 24, 30
  seventeenth-century 75, 76, 77, 84
cloaks (women)
  Anglo-Saxon *31*, 32
  Greek *21*
  Roman 23
  eighteenth-century 96
  see also himation; palla; pallium
Cluniac order 35
coats (men) 55, 60, 62, 84, 87, 89, *99*, 110,
coats (women)
  anorak 168
  duffle 168
  fur *170*
  trench 161
Cobbe, Frances Power 132
codpiece 55, 62, 65, 68, 74, 75, *86*, 87
coif 39
Coke, Lady Jane 105
Colette 156
collars 16, 49, 62, 68, 72, 75, 77, 85, *123–4*, 125, 143
  caped 114
  turned-back 43
  turned-down 112
  see also rebato; reticella
colours in dress 32, 33, 56, 57, 60, 64, 65, 68, 72, 75, 84, 85, 89, 100, 110, 111, 114, 124, 125, 126, 130, 131, 139, 147, 148, 149, 150, 158, 169
  mi-parti, motley 45, 62
Commodus, Emperor 22
Congreve, William
  Way of the World, The 92–3
conspicuous consumption 59, 119, 132, 144
Constantine, Emperor 25
contraceptive pill 167
Cooke, Edward
  Just and Seasonable Reprehension of naked Breasts and Shoulders 92
corsets (men) 169
corsets (women) 92, 105, 135, *136*, 137, 142, 147, 150, 160, 161, *162*, 163
  'divorce' 120
  'Grecian bend' 134–5, *137*–8
  stays 70, *71*, 82, 96, 103, 105, 109, 115, 118, 122, *123*, 124, 129, 143
cosmetics 24–5, 27–8, 33, 41, 47, 67, 71, 78, 80, 92, *93*, 99, 107, 111, *122*, 124, 127, 129, 135, 137–8, 142, 149, 152, *153*, *156*, 159, 161, 162, *166*
  beauty spots 73, 82–3
  patches 83, *84*, 86, 89, 93–4, *101*, 106, *107*, *109*
  rouge 33, 105, 109, 124, 126
  stibium (antimony) 33
cotton 55, 121, 150, 169
  corduroy 133
  fustian 133
  muslin 23, 115, 117, 118, 131
  nankeen 120
country clothing 113, 120
court dress
  England 35, 67, 74, 79, 80, 84, 97, 100, 114
  France 115
coxcombs 109, 111
cravats 90, 99–100, 113, 124, 125, 126
crinolines 129, *130*, 131, 134, 135, 139, 160
Cripps, Sir Stafford 161
Cruikshank, G. *123*
Crusades, the 36
cuffs 85, 87, 100, 111, 112
Cunnington, C.W. 17
Cuthbert, Archbishop of Canterbury 30, 33
cutwork 49, 62, 63, 68, 72, 78, 86
Cyprian, Bishop of Carthage
  De Habitu Virginum 27–8

dagging, 49, 51
dalmatica *26*, 27
dandies 17, 119, *122*, *123–4*, 125
Danse Macabre (Dance of Death) 58, *112*, *163*
Dekker, Thomas
  Gull's Hornbook, The 75, 76, 77, 100
  Seven deadly Sinnes of London, The 75
Delany, Mrs 97, 106
Derain, André 149
Deschamps, Eustache 47
Description de l'Isles des Hermaphrodites 67
déshabillé 82, 90, 97, 103
developing countries
  censorship in dress of 13–14
Devereux, Robert, Earl of Essex 78
Devil, the, Satan, Lucifer *33*, *39*, 42, *53*, 55, 58, *59*, 63, 68, 70, 73, 75, 77, 80, 82, 92, *103*, *122*, 126, 157, *163*
Devlin, Lord 13, 15
dishevelment in dress 165, 170
distortion of the body 35, 55, 59, *60–1*, 62, 73, 74, 75, 124, 129, *140*, 143, *144*
dolls (fashion) 96
Donne, John 68
D'Orsay, Count 125
doublets (men) 45, 49, 55, *60*, 62, 65, 67, 68, *69*, 72, 75, 84, 86, 87, 88, 89
doublets (women) 49, 72, 80, *81*
drapery, draping
  Greek 19, 62, 90
  Roman 26
  medieval *31*, 36, 38, 40, 139
  Baroque 93
  neo-classical 117
  eighteenth-century 96, 105
  nineteenth-century 120, 134, *138*, 139
  twentieth-century 150, 166
dress-makers 64, 96, 113, 147–8, 154
dress reformers 12, 17, 19, 132, 139, *140*, 141, 143, 144, 157, 158, 168
dresses
  cutaway sides 156
  'flapper' 154
  1930s style 158, *159–60*, 167
  'Marylyke Modest Dress' 164
  sun *163*, 164
  topless 167–8
  see also necklines; New Look; see-through clothes
drugs 156, 165, *171*
Dudley, Robert, Earl of Leicester 66, 67
Dufay, Pierre
  Pantalon Féminin, Le 148
Dyck, Sir Anthony van *81*, 82, *83*, 84

Eadmer
  Historia Novorum in Anglia 35
ecclesiastical vestments 29
Eden, Sir Frederick
  State of the Poor, The 113
Edward III, King of England 45
Edward the Confessor, King of England 33–4
Edwards, Anne 162
élégantes 118
Elizabeth I, Queen of England 67–8, 69, 74, 78
Elizabeth, Queen (Queen Mother) 160
Ellis, Havelock 16
Elyot, Thomas
  Governor, The 65
embroidery 33, 56, 59, 62, 63, 68, 70, 72, 75, 81, 100, 131, *136*, 137, *148*, 169
Emerson, Ralph Waldo 171
Emmwood *166–8*
England *see under* individual themes, e.g., Anglo-Saxon dress; court dress; masquerades, carnivals; sumptuary legislation, etc.
Englands Vanity 89, 92, 94
English Civil War 83, 85, 87
English Theophrastus, The 99
Englishwoman's Domestic Magazine, The 135
eroticism 16, 77, 159
  see also sexual display
Etherege
  Man of the Mode, The 89–90
etiquette, courtesy books 64–5, 67, 73, 75, 81, 84, 126, 127, 157
Eugénie, Empress of France 129–30
Eulogium Historiarum 45–6
Evangelicanism 122
Evelyn, John 93
  Tyrannus or the Mode 87, 89
Evelyn, Mary
  Mundus Muliebris, 93, 94
eyebrows
  painting 126
  plucking 47, *54*
eyelets 129

false hair 28, 36, 39, 41, *71*, 73, 77, 80, 86, 106, 109, 129, 134, 135, 139, 156
  chignons 135, *137*
false rubber bosoms 114, 159
fans 71, 78, *84*
Farington, Joseph 121
farthingale 70–1, 72, 76, 77, 78, 79, 80, 94
fashion magazines
  proliferation of, in eighteenth century 113, 116, 117, 118
Fauves, Les 149
Fawconer, Samuel
  Essay on Modern Luxury, An 95
feathers 60, *61*, 69, 71, 84, 105, 106–7, *117*
  peacock *108*, 109
Female Folly 93
Female Spectator, The 97, 104, 109
feminist movement 168–9
Fielding, Henry
  Amelia 105
  Tom Jones 95–6
flagellation *50*, 51
flowers 105, 111, 130, 149
Flügel, J.C. 12, 16, 17, 157
fops 89, 90, 92, 97, 99, 100, *101*, 124
  see also gallants
Fournier, Robin *53*

188

INDEX

Foxton, John
  Liber Cosmographiae 51
Frederick's of Hollywood 162, *163*
French Revolution 14–15, 112, 113, 117, 118, 119–20
Froissart 42
  Chronicles 56
'fun clothes' 167
fur, fur trimming 14, 15, 17, *28*, 32, 36, 38, 43, 46, 55, 62, 76, 77, 89, 170
  ermine 42, 46, *49*, 56
  fake 167
  genet 63
  marten 56
  miniver 46, 56
  sable 56, 63

gallants 68, 75, *76*, 77, 86, 97
garters *98*, 99
Gascoigne, George
  Droomme of Doomesday, The 59
gauze 103, 105, 114, 131
genitals, 16, 17, 45, 55, 70, 120, 171
'Gents' *125*, 126
George III, King of England 126
George IV, King of England 126
German fashions 29, 59–60, 62, 65
'Gibson Girl' 150
Gill, Eric 158
Gillray, J. *117*, 120
girdle 26, 56–7, 78
'Glorinda' 152, *153*
gloves (men) *125*, 126
gloves (women) 65, 93
gold, 15, 24, 31, *33*, 39, 46, 49, 51, 56, 59, 62, 63, 64, 68, 69, 70, 72, 87, 89, 94
Goldsmith, Oliver
  Vicar of Wakefield, The 106
Goncourt, Edmond de 141–2
Gordon, Sir Cosmo Duff 147
Gosson, Stephen 70, 71, 72, 73
Gothic 62
gowns (men) 44, *50*, 51, 52, 55, 56, 59–60, 62, 66, 67
gowns (women) 38, *39*, 40, 41, 43, 45, 46, 47, 49, 50, 51, 52, 55, 56, 57, 62, 72, 93, 95, 103, 106, 115, 117, 118, 122, 131, *147*, *148*, 154, *155*
  cross-over 115
  décolletée *135*, *143*, 144
  Indian cotton 169
  loose-bodied 81–2, *83*, 97
  mantua 93, 96, 100
  négligé 105
  nightgown 103
  over-gowns 70, 72, 78
  'Pompadour'/'Marie-Antoinette' 134
  sacque 97, *98*, 99, 105, 114
  sideless 43
  tea *142*, 147, 148
Graf, Urs 60–*1*
Graham, Billy 164
Graves, Mrs A.J.
  Woman in America 127
Greek dress 17, 19, *20*–1, 24
Greenpeace 170
Gregory, William 55–6
Grimston, Edward
  Honest Man, The 84
Gronow, Captain 121
Guys, C. *131*, *132*, *135*
Gwynn, Nell, *90*, *91*

habiliments 62
Habits of Good Society, The 119, 126, 129–30
hairstyles (men) 36, 80, 85, *86*, 111, 124, 141, 164, 165
  barbarians 29, 31
  Roman 22, *28*, 29
  Anglo-Saxon 32
  Norman *34*, 35
  'spaniel's ears' 113
  crew-cut 166
  punk 17, *169*
  see also lovelocks
hairstyles (women) 26, 73, 78, *79*, 80–1, 126, 152, *153*, 154, 159, 161, 168
  Roman 24, *25*
  Norman 36, 39
  sugar-loaf *76*, 77
  eighteenth-century towering 106–7, *108*–9
  neo-classical 117
  bobbed *156*
  'bee-hive' 162
  pony-tail *165*
  punk 17, *169*
Hall, Joseph
  Righteous Mammon, The 78
Hall, Thomas
  Loathsomnesse of Long Hair, The 86
Halle, Edward 70
  Chronicle 59
Hamnett, Katherine *171*
handkerchiefs 39, 122
Harper's Bazaar 162
Harrison, William 65
  Description of England 69
Harrods Catalogue 142
hats (men) 52, 59–60, *61*, 69, 75, 80, 84, *114*
  bowler 157
  Nivernoise 111
  sugarloaf 55, 72, 113
hats (women) 72, *81*, 103, *144*, 149, 159
Haweis, Mrs Mary Eliza
  Art of Beauty, The 139
headcoverings
  'couvrechefs' 58
  kerchiefs 114
  veils 13, 14, *31*, 32, 36, 38, 43, *44*, 52, 58, 139
headdresses (men) 111
headdresses (women) 63, 93, 139
  bourrelets 47, 52, *53*
  butterfly 57
  cauls 43, 72
  feathered 106–7, *108*–9
  horned 43, *44*, 47, 52, *53*
  nets 24, 39, 52
  Norman 38–9
  nuns 32–3
  pompons 105
  steeple 52, 58
  'top-knot' 93
health 96, 115, 120, 129, 144, 145, 160
Healthy and Artistic Dress Union 141
Helvétius 116
Henri III, King of France 67
Henrietta Maria, Queen of England *81*
Henry VIII, King of England 59, 63
heraldry 56
Herodotus 20, 21
Herrick, Robert
  Delight in Disorder 82
Hic-Mulier: or, The Man-Woman 81
Hildalid, Abbess of Barking 32
Hilliard, N. 68, *69*, 78
himation 21
'hip-showing ones' 20
'hippies' *166*, 169
hips 48–9, 67, 109, 114, 129, 134, 150, 156, 159, 163, 165
Hogarth, William *102*
Holbein, Hans *63*
Homer 20
homosexuality 22, 34, 74, 90, 104, 156, 158, 169
hoods 31, 32, 33, 45, 46, 52, 72
  English 63
  French 58, 62
hooks and eyes 13

hooliganism 170
hoops 97, *99*, 103, 105, 109, 114, 115, 129
horsehair 89, 100, *127*
hose (men) 45, 47, 49, *50*–*1*, 55, *56*, 60–*1*, 62, *141*, 158
hose (women) 38, 39
'hot-pants' 167
houppelandes 49, *50*–3
Howard, Frances, Countess of Somerset 75, 77
'Huile Antique' 124
humility in dress 14, 15–16
'Hun style' 29
Hundred Years War 46
hunting dress *81*
Hutchinson, Lucy 74, 75, 85
Huxley, Aldous
  Point Counter Point 19, 154
hygiene 12, 32, 113, 120, 129, 146
  see also cleanliness; health

ideal, idealized dress 12, 14, 135, *140*
immodesty 14, *48*, 49, 117, 121, *127*, 133, 134, 148, 157
immorality, shifting notions of 12–16, 18, 55, 72, 95, 96, 103, 118, 122, 130, 141, *142*, 144–5, 147, 150, 154, 164, *168*
Incroyables 113, *114*
individualism in dress 13, 25, 171
Interregnum 82, *84*, 90
Ionian dress 20, 21
Islam 13, 14
Italy 62, 64, 65, 67, 72, 73, 75, 100, 104, 111

jackets (men) 55, 68, *141*
  dinner 157
  'drape' 164
jackets (women) *134*, 138, *143*, 144
  duffel 161
jagging 60, *61*, 68, 75
James I, King of England 74, 78, 80
jerseys 157–8
'Jessamy' 114
jeunesse dorée 113
jewellery 24, 26, 27, *33*, 46, 64, 67, 69, 71, 93, 105, 107, 126, 129, 150, 159
  armlets (*armillae*) 32, *33*
  bracelets *31*, 32, 150
  brooches 20, *31*, 32, *33*, 46, 122
  chains 49, 63, 67, 161
  ear-rings 24, 78, 169
  headbands 32, 39
  Indian beads 166
  necklaces 32, 58, 71, 78
  rings 32, 46, 67, 126
  tie-pins 126
  see also armour; belts; *bezants*; buckles; buttons; swords
John of Reading 45
Jonson, Ben
  Devil is an Ass, The 77
  Epicene 80
Judaism 13, 17, 171
jumper 167
Justinian, Emperor 29, 104
Juvenal
  satires on Roman dress 22
  satires against women 24

Kelly, Grace 164
'kervynge' 52
kirtles 32, *54*, 56, 63, 78
knickerbockers 129, 134
Knox, John 64, 65
Koran 13, 26

Labour Party 161, *162*
lace 68, 69, 70, 74, 75, 77–8, 85, 87, 89, 93, 105, *107*, 131, *136*, 137
  Brussels 103
  Flanders 72, 100
  Italian 72

INDEX

laces 47
'harlots' 45
lacing 34, 36, *40*, 42, *54*, 65, 92, 111
  see also tight-lacing
Ladies Dictionary, The 90, 92, 94
Lady's Magazine, The 109, 116, 118
Lady's Newspaper, The 139
Lancaster, Osbert *166*
Lancet, The 145
landsknechte 17, 60–1
Last Judgement, the damned souls from *37*, *39*
Laver, James 16, 17
law and morals 13, 15
leather 14, 39, 84, 111, 113, 122, 166
  doeskin 120
  kid 126
  patent 125, 157
leg-pads ('Lovelilegs') 163
Lely, Sir Peter 90, *91*
Lenin 13
Leroy, Dr 115
lesbianism 156
Life 164
Lily, The 132
Lindsay, Sir David 62–3
linen 20, 32, 43, *44*, 46, *58*, 62, 63, 64, 68, 69, 99, 100, 113, 114, 120
  byssus *21*, 27
  Holland 72, 85
  Quaker 103
Linton, Eliza Lynn 135, 137, 138, 144–5
Llandaff, Bishop of
  Treatise upon Modes, A 100
London
  centre of prostitution in eighteenth and nineteenth centuries 103, 104, *110*, 118, 132
  centre of tailoring in eighteenth century 114
  make-up parlours 149
  see also Dekker, Thomas; Malcolm, J.P.
Louis XIV, King of France 87
lovelocks 77, *78*, 81, 84
Lucile 147–8, 149, 150
lust 33, 41, 42, *57*, 65, 74, 144, 150
Lydgate, John 52

macaronis *111*, 113, *114*, 124
Malcolm, J.P.
  Anecdotes of the Manners and Customs of London 120
Manchester, Duchess of 129
Mandeville, Bernard de
  Fable of the Bees, The 90, 92, 95
Manet, E. *136*, 137
manners and dress
  eighteenth century 96, *102*, 109, 112, 113, 117, 118
  nineteenth century 121–2, 126, 127, 129
  twentieth century 162, 171
  see also etiquette, courtesy books
mantles (men) *35*, 36, 45, 46
  barbarians 31
  Roman *28*, 29
mantles (women) 38
  Anglo-Saxon *31*, 32
  Virgins 27, 56
manuscript illumination, English School of *32*, 34
Marche, Olivier de la
  Parement et Triumphes des Dames, Le 56, *58*
Margueritte, Victor
  Garçonne, La 156
Marie-Antoinette, Queen of France 115, 116
Marlowe, Christopher
  Dr Faustus 71
marriage, married women 27, 39, 43, 109, 139, 142, 149
  see also maternity

Marston, John
  Scourge of Villainy, The 68, 72
masks 73, 82, *84*, 93, 104, 109–10
masquerades, carnivals
  England 59, 70, 72–3, 78, 104–5, *106*, *112*
maternity 115, *117*
Matisse, Henri 149
'medieval' style, revival of 139, 141, 158
Men's Dress Reform Party 158
Mercier, Louis-Sébastien 117, 121
Merrifield, Mrs 132–3
Messalina, Empress 24
Methodism, 95, 97, 101, 103
Miélot, Jean
  Miracles de Nostre Dame 55
military dress 22, 60, 85, 89, 124, 161
  poilus 156
  see also *landsknechte*; uniforms
Mill, John Stuart 139
  On Liberty 171
Milton, John
  Areopagitica 83
Miroir aux Dames, Le 52
Mirror of the Graces, The 119, 20
Mirroure of the Worlde, The 57
Mistinguett 150
Modest Apparel 146, 157
modesty 13, 16, 20, 23, 25, 27, 103, 120, 127, 139, 170
Monstrelet 52
Montague, Mrs 105, 114, *115*
Montaigne 64, 68
Moore, Doris Langley 158
morality
  meanings 12–17, 117
  moral qualities of dress 68–9, 82, 85, 139
  see also caricatures; religion; sermons
More, Sir Thomas
  Utopia 15, 64
Mortimer, Raymond 157
  Modern Nymphs 159
Moryson, Fynes
  Itineary, An 74, 75
motoring dress 146
moustaches 31
muffs 76, 77, *78*, 89, 93
Muslim women 13, 14

nakedness 17, 19, *21*, 31, 34, 46, 69, 82, *83*, 87, 92, 117, *118*, *121*, 134, 156, 170
Napoleon 15
Nature and dress 14, 19, 42, 86, 92, 115, 116, 129
Neckclothitania 125
necklines
  low 39, 47, *48*–50, 62, *63*, 79, 80, 83, 105, 120, 126, 133, 139, *147*, 152
  V-shaped 150, *151*
neo-classical style 117, *118*, 159
Nero, Emperor 22, 23
Netherlandish dress *58*
New Look 161, *162*
New Woman 143, 146, 149
Nichols, Beverley 154, 156, 157, *158*
Nietzsche 12
nipples 52, 80
Norman Conquest 37
  effect of, on dress 33, *34*, 36, 39
Nothing to Wear 132
nudity 19, 20, 68, 120, 157, 159, 160
nylon 162, 170
  see also stockings

O'Brien, Lady Susan 121–1
Occleve, Thomas
  Of Pride and wast clothing of Lordis men 51
official dress 12, *35*, 114
Oliphant, Mrs 141

Orderic Vitalis
  Ecclesiastical History 34, 35, 36
Orwell, George
  Animal Farm 15
Osborn, Sarah 100
Ovid
  Art of Love 24

'pagan' art 18
palla 30, 32
pallium 23, *26*
panes 66, 67
pantins (puppets) *101*
Paris
  centre of fashion in eighteenth century 113–14
  wearing of Directoire chemise in 116, 117, *118*
  demi-monde of Second Empire *131*, 132, 134, *135*
  post-war 156
Peacham, Henry
  Compleat Gentleman, The 84
pearls 46, *49*, 69, 94, 127
Peasants' Revolt 42
peascod-belly shape 68, *69*
penitents 15–16, *50*, 51
peplos 20, 21
Pepys, Samuel, 87, 90
perfume 68, 77, 89, 90, 93, 99, 109, 111, 124
periwigs 71, 78, 86, 89, 90, 114
permissive society 167
Persian dress 21, 22
perukes 100, 112
Petit Jehan de Saintré, Le 57
Petronius
  Satyricon, 22, 24
petticoat breeches, 87, *88*, 89
petticoats 17, 72, *93*, 95, 96, 97, 103, 116, 120, 126, *128*, 129, 131, 144, 149, 160, 162
Philip of Novara
  Four Ages of Man, The 38
Philippa of Hainault 45
Piccolimini, Alexander
  Raffaella 64–5
Picture Post 159, 160, 161
Piers Plowman 46
pinking 86
Pius VI and VII, Popes 120
Place, Francis 122
Plato
  Republic, The 20
Pliny the Elder 22
Pliny the Younger 23
points 45, 72
Poiret, Paul 149, 150, 154
Poland 45, 75
politics and dress 14–15, 51, 112, 113, 117, 118, 119–20, 161, *162*, 169, *171*
pomatum 106, 113
Pompadour, Madame de 105
Pope, Alexander
  Essay on Man 14
pourpoint see doublet
powder 89, 90, 107, 109, 111, 113, 127
Presley, Elvis 165
prisoners, prisons 15–16, 127
Pritchard, Mrs
  Cult of Chiffon, The 148, 149
Procopius
  Secret History 29
proletarian style 165, *166*, 167, 170
prostitutes 43, 71, 90, 92, *102*, 103, 104, *110*, 115, 118, 120, *121*, 149, 168
Protestantism 65, 68, 70, 164
Prynne, William
  Gagge for Long-Hair'd Rattleheads, A 85–6
  Unloveliness of Love-Lockes, The 77–8, 81
psychoanalysis 17

190

Punch 125, 130, *133*, *137*, 143, *144*–5, *147*, 150, *151*, 152, *153*, *158*, 159, *160*, 165
punk clothing 17, 166, *169*, 170
Purchas, Samuel 75, 77
Puritans, Puritanism 64, 65, 73, 74, 75, 77, 78, 82, 83, 90, 94, 95, 101, 103, 122, 162, 164
  dress 68, 85
purse 56

Quakers 85, 97, 103
Quant, Mary 167
Quarles, Francis 80
Queen, The 135, *148*
queens 49, 53
Quintilian
  Institutio Oratoria 23

Rachel, Madame 138
'Rational Costume' *145*
Rational Dress Association, The 144
rationing of clothing, World War II 161
rayon 154
rebato 72
Récamier, Madame 121
Redmayne's of Bond Street 148
religion and dress 13–14, 25, 52, 68, 157
  see also sermons; *and* under individual sects, e.g., Judaism; Methodism; etc.
religious orders, dress of 14, 27
  women 32–3
Religious Tract Society 127
Renaissance 13, 18, 41, 59, 62, 64
reticella 75, 78
ribbons 15, 52, 63, 68, 72, *84*, 86, 87, 88, 89, 93, 100, 103, 105, *127*, 130, 131
Rich, Barnaby 77
Richard I, King of England 34
Richard II, King of England 45, 51
Richard the Redeless 51
Richardson, Samuel
  'Against a Young Lady's Affecting manly Airs' 114
  Clarissa Harlowe 103
  Pamela 96, 103, *104*, 105
riding costumes 114, *115*
Robert of Brunne
  Handlyng Synne 43
Robespierre 117
rock and roll 164, 165
Rocco 105, *107*–8
Rolling Stones 165
Roman de la Rose 39, 43, *50*, 53
Roman dress 21–2, 23, 24–5, *28*, 29, 30
'roundheads' 85
Rousseau, Jean-Jacques 115
Rowlandson, T. *121*–2
ruffles 100, 113
ruffs 68, 69, 70, 72, 75, 77, 78, 85, 94
Russell, Jane 162
Russian Revolution 118
Rypon, Robert 42, 46

Safford-Blake, Mary 143–4
St Aldhelm 32–3
St Ambrose 27
St Anne *38*
St Anthony 53
St Basil 27
St Boniface 30, 33
St Catherine 43
St Jerome 27, 29, 55
St Paul 25, *28*, 75, 86
St Ursula 43
Salvation Army 103
sans-culottes 113
satin *see* silk
satires on dress 22, 24, 64, 68, 72, 78, 86, 89, 92, 93, 101, *108*, 109, 124

Satyr against Painting 92
scallop shapes 52
scarves 78, 82, *83*
scène galante 98, 99
see-through clothes 14, 17, 22, 106, 154, 167, 170
  'Peek-a-boo' style 152
Selfridges 149
Seneca 23
sequins 70
sermons on dress 37–8, 41, 42, 46, 77, 80, 96, 101–2, 103, 107, 146–7
servants and dress 67, 127
Seven Deadly Sins, the 47, 57–8, 75
  envy 15, 95, 144
  pride 15, 29, 30, *39*, 47, 49, 51, 59, 62, 63, 65, 68–9, *71*, 72, 73, 82, 89, 94, *108*, 109
  slovenliness 23, 29, *39*, 84, 85, 113, 170
sewing 40, 41
sexual ambiguity in dress 17–18, 25, 26, 39, 50, 51, 67, 72, 77, 81, 83–4, 88, 89, 105, 114, *115*, 121, 124, 125, 126, 132, *133*, 135, *138*, 143, 144, *145*, 149, 152, 154, *155*, *156*, 157, *158*, 161, 166, 168, *169*
sexual display in dress 13, 14, 17–18, 119, 131, 138–9, 147, 162, *163*, 165, 167, 168, *169*, 170, 171
Shakespeare, William
  Merchant of Venice, The 73
shape of the body 13, *21*, 27, *31*, 45, 52, 68, 70, 87, 96, 97, 105, 115, 120, 124, 126, 132, 134, *159*, *163*, 164
Shaw, George Bernard
  Man and Superman 157
shawls 131
shift *see* chemise
'shifting erogenous zones,' theory of 16
shiny fabrics 168
Shirley, James
  Lady of Pleasure, The 84
shirts (men) 16, 34, 56, 62, 63, *84*, 86, 141, 158, 166, 169
shoe-strings 113
shoes (men) 23, 87, 157
  'brothel-creepers' 164
  cracowes 45
  high-heeled 69
  pattens 89
  'pikes' 56
  pointed 35, 36, 38, 45, *50*, 55–6
  sandals 23, 158
  slippers 22, 24
  square-shaped 60
shoes (women) 22, 32, 78
  high-heeled 109, *136*, 137, *138*, 162, 165, 168
  pointed 168
  sandals 117
  slippers 24, 103
shorts 157, 158, 161
shoulder wings 72
shoulders, bare 92, *143*
Sidonius, Apollinarius 31
Sigismer 31
silk 15, *21*, 22, 23, 27, 30, *31*, 32, 36, 46, 56, 57, 60, 63, 64, 68, 69, 70, 72, 74, 75, 81, 82, *83*, 85, 87, 93, 94, 97, 100, 101, 105, 114, 120, 127, 130, 131, 141, 143, 154
  artificial 154
  chiffon 22, 142, *148*
  damask 36, 63
  sarcenet 67
  satin 32, 63, 67, 81, 125, 131, *148*, 159, 169
  taffeta 67, 81, 84
silver 39, 43, 46, 49, 51, 62, 63, 69, 72, 89, 94
Sin and Scandal of the 'Smart' Set, The 146
Sir Gwain and the Green Knight 47

Skelton, John
  Manner of the World Nowadays, The 60
'skinheads' 166
skirts
  long *151*, 162
  mini 17, *167*, 170
  overskirt *135*
  riding 114, *115*
  short 14, *138*, 139, 143, 149, 150, 154, 161, 164, *166*, 168
skirts (of gown) 43, 70, 72, 78, 126, *127*, 160
skirts (of man's suit) 89, 99
slashing 17, 34, 59, 60–1, 63, 68, 72, 84, 86
sleeves 20, 21, 22, 28, 29, 30, *31*, 32, 34, 36, 38–40, 41, 43, 45, 47, 49, 52, 59, 60–1, 62, 63, 68, 72, 78, 82, 84, 87, 89, 96, 111, 114, 117, 124, 126, *127*, *142*, 152
slops 75, 76, 77
'Smart Set', the 146, *147*
Smith, Albert
  Natural History of the Gent, The 125–6
Smith, Logan Pearsall 18
  Afterthoughts 146
smocks 72
Smollett, Tobias 100–1
  Roderick Random 110–11
snuff 89
socks 32, 164
Solon's laws on luxury 21, 43
Sorel, Agnès 54
Spain 65, 68, 69, 70, 71, 75
spangles 70, 75, 126
Spectator, The 95, 96, 97, 100
sporting dress
  men 110, 158
  women 119, 143, 144, *145*, 160
starch 69–70, 75, 77, 85, 114, *124*, 125, 131, 143
Staunton, William
  Visions of Purgatory 49, 51
Steele, Richard 95
Sterne, Laurence 101
stockinette 120
stockings
  men 62, 100, 111, 141
  women 72, 103, *136*, 137, 154
    body 117
    nylon 161, 168
stola 30
stomacher 26, 56, 70, 78
Stowe, Harriet Beecher 134, *135*
strip-tease 105
stripes 32, 33, 43, 62
Stubbes, Philip
  Anatomie of Abuses, The 68–70, 72, 73, 80
Stutfield, Hugh
  Sovranty of Society, The 149
Suetonius 22
suits (men) 17, 86, 87, 99, 100–1
  black 68, 125
  'mod' 165
  morning 157
  Quaker 85
suits (women) 161, 162
sumptuary legislation
  England 15, 43, 46–7, 55, 56, 58, 63, 64, 67, 69, 74, 83, 87, 95, 112
  Greece 21
sun-bathing 157
superstition 12
surcote
  men 36, 37
  women 43, *50*
sweaters 162, 164, *166*
  see also jerseys; jumper
Swetman, Joseph 80
Swinburne, Algernon 141
swords 32, 33
symbolism in dress 13–15, 16, 17, 22, *23*, 29, 51, 52, 56, 63, 70, 73, 103, *108*, 109, 158

INDEX

Tacitus 30
  Germania 31
tailoring, tailors 16, 21, 36, 42, 51, 64, 67, 69, 74, 100, 114, 124, 143, 150, *151*, 158
Taine, Hyppolite-Aldophe 130–1, 132
tassels 62
tattoos 31, 32
Teddy boys 164, *165–6*
tee-shirts (women) 168, 169, *171*
teen-agers 164
Tertullian
  De Culta Feminarum 27, 28
  De Pallio 23
Thimbleby, Lady Elizabeth 82, *83*
Thucydides 21
Thynne, Francis 68
ties 17, 143, 157, 164
tight-fitting clothing 14, 17, 21, *34*, 36, *38*, 40, *41*, 42, 47, *48–50*, *57*, 65, *75*, *78*, 96, 105, *111*, 113, *114*, 115, 120, *124*, 125, *134*, 139, *151*, 157, 164, *165–7*, 170
tight-lacing 36, *39*, 70, 78, 89, 92, 96, 103, 115, 124, *128*, 135, 163
tights
  fishnet 168
  flesh-coloured 121
  'gauze inexpressibles' 126
Tilt, Dr
  Elements of Health and Principles of Female Hygiene 129, 132
timeless dress 12–13
Tocqueveille, Alexis de 126
toga 22, *23*, 29, 30
Ton, The 124, 132
tonsure 32, 35
tracts, treatises on dress 47, 62, 82, *84*, 127, 165
  see also under individual names
trains *39–40*, 41, 43, *44*, 49, *55*, 62, *63*, 70, 106, 143
Trix sisters 154
troubadour poets 38
trousers (men) 122, *123*, 169
  barbarians 29, 31
  braccae 32
  check *125*, 126
  Cossacks 124
  'drain-pipe' 164
  jeans *166*
  Oxford bags, 157, 158
  pantaloons 113, 120
  Roman 28, 29, 30
trousers (women) 133, *134*, 141, 143, 145, 152, 158, 160, *167*, 169
  dungarees 168
  jeans 164

slacks 14, 161
Turkish 105, 132, 139, 144, 150
  see also Bloomer dress
trunk hose 65, *66*, 67, 68, *69*
Tuke, Thomas 80
tulle 131
tunics (men) 26, *45*, 46, 49, *59*, 158
  Anglo-Saxon 32
  barbarians 29, 31
  'hippie' *166*
  Norman 34, 36
  Roman 22, *28*, 30, 33
tunics (women) 47, 94
  Anglo-Saxon *31*, 32
  Norman 36, *38*
  Turkish 132, 139
  see also chiton; dalmatica; *kirtle*; *peplos*; *stola*; surcote
Turkish costume 105, 132, 139–41, 144, 150
underwear (men) 72, 170
  pyjamas 141–2
underwear (women) 103, 116, *136*, 137, 148, 169–70
  bras, brassières 150, 159, 162, *163*, *167*, 168
  corselette 154
  drawers 120, 121, 129, 132, 148
  girdles 159, *163*
  knickers 148–9, 170
undress 16, 93, *102*, *104*, 105, 121
uniforms 15–16, 152, 154, 161, 162
'unisex' fashion 169
university students, dress of 78
Urban V, Pope 45

vanity 23, 26, 30, 38, 41, 47, *48*, 49, 77, 80, 84, 89, 94, 99, 102, *112*, 121, *122*, *163*
Vaughan, Father Bernard
  Sins of Society, The 146, *147*, 149
Veblen, Thorstein 15, 144
velvet 42, 58, 59, 63, 67, 68, 93, 94, 100, 101, 105, 110, 131, *141*, 164, 169
'vest' 87, 94
vice 22, 43, 68, 75, 77, 80, 83, 90, 93, 121, 132
Victoria, Queen of England 130, 146
Vigée-Lebrun, Madame 116
Viking dress 32, 33
Vincent of Beauvais 39
Virgin Mary 52, *54*, 56
virginity, virgins 13–14, 27–8, 38, *41*, 43, *53*, 90, *91*
virtue 43, 51, 80, 92, 97, 129, 130

waist 16, 52, 67, 81, 87, 96, 134, 135, 163
  high *53*, *118*, 141, 149, 150
  wasp 126, 161, 162

waistcoats (men) 87, 112, 125, 164
waistcoats (women) 138
Waldeby, Friar 44
Walker, Alexander 126
Walpole, Horace 115
Walpole, Lady 154, 156
wantonness 30, 33, 72, 82
War of the Roses 64
Watts, I. 101–2
Waugh, Evelyn
  Vile Bodies 158
wedding dress, white 13–14
Wesley, John 101, 103, 113
wet-look fabrics 167
whalebone 97, 129, 139, 160
White, Antonia 159
Whole Art of Dress, The 124
Wigan pit brow girls 133, *134*
wigmakers 112
wigs (men) 86, 89, 90, 99, 100, 111
  see also periwigs; perukes
wigs (women) 24, 126, 167
Wilde, Oscar 15, *141*, 142
William of Malmesbury 32, 33, 34
William Rufus 34
Wilson, Harold 161
wizard masks 71, 72
Wollstonecraft, Mary
  Vindication of the Rights of Woman, A 116–17, 127
Wolsey, Cardinal 64
women
  education 116–17, 132, 139, 145
  emancipation 139, 143, 146, 149, 154
  place in feudal system 37–8
  protector of morals 126–7
  wartime employment 152, 161
Women's Lib 167
  see also feminist movement
Wood, Anthony 89, 114
wool 20, 21, 22, 27, 30, 32, 36, 38, 46, 55, 63, 64, 87, 100, 109, 120
  jersey 143
Woolf, Virginia 17
working-class costume 36, 113, 120, 165–7, 171
  see also proletarian style; Wigan pit brow girls
World War I 152, 154, 156, 158, 161, 169
World War II 149, 161, 167
Wraxall, Sir Nathaniel 113

Yonge, Charlotte Mary 139
youth, cult of 162, 165, *166*, 167, 168

zip 167
Zola, Émile 134, *136*, 137